PHANTOM
WARRIOR

Other Books by Forrest Bryant Johnson

PHANTOM
WARRIOR

**THE HEROIC TRUE STORY OF
PVT. JOHN McKINNEY'S ONE-MAN STAND AGAINST
THE JAPANESE IN WORLD WAR II**

Forrest Bryant Johnson

BERKLEY CALIBER, NEW YORK

THE BERKLEY PUBLISHING GROUP
Published by the Penguin Group
Penguin Group (USA) Inc.
375 Hudson Street, New York, New York 10014, USA
Penguin Group (Canada), 90 Eglinton Avenue East, Suite 700, Toronto, Ontario M4P 2Y3, Canada
(a division of Pearson Penguin Canada Inc.)
Penguin Books Ltd., 80 Strand, London WC2R 0RL, England
Penguin Group Ireland, 25 St. Stephen's Green, Dublin 2, Ireland
(a division of Penguin Books Ltd.)
Penguin Group (Australia), 250 Camberwell Road, Camberwell, Victoria 3124, Australia (a division
of Pearson Australia Group Pty. Ltd.)
Penguin Books India Pvt. Ltd., 11 Community Centre, Panchsheel Park, New Delhi—110 017, India
Penguin Group (NZ), 67 Apollo Drive, Rosedale, North Shore 0745, Auckland, New Zealand
(a division of Pearson New Zealand Ltd.)
Penguin Books (South Africa) (Pty.) Ltd., 24 Sturdee Avenue, Rosebank, Johannesburg 2196,
South Africa

Penguin Books Ltd., Registered Offices: 80 Strand, London WC2R 0RL, England

This book is an original publication of the Berkley Publishing Group.

The publisher does not have any control over and does not assume any responsibility for author or third-party websites or their content.

First edition: August 2007

Library of Congress Cataloging-in-Publication Data

Johnson, F. B.
    Phantom warrior : the heroic true story of Pvt. John McKinney's one-man stand against the Japanese in World War II / Forrest Bryant Johnson.
        p. cm.
    Includes bibliographical references and index.
    ISBN-13: 978-0-425-21566-1 (alk. paper)
    1. McKinney, John R.   2. World War, 1939–1945—Campaigns—Philippines—Luzon.
3.   United States. Army. Infantry Division, 33rd.   4. Medal of Honor—Biography.
5. Soldiers—United States—Biography.   I. Title.

    D767. 4. M37J65   2007
    940.54'25991—dc22
    [B]

                                                                              2006027405

PRINTED IN THE UNITED STATES OF AMERICA

10   9   8   7   6   5   4   3   2   1

To that generation of Americans who sacrificed during those
dark days of World War II

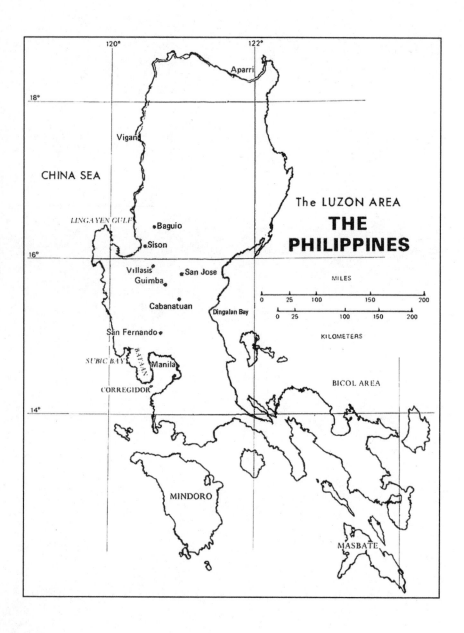

120°

122°

Aparri

18°

Vigan

CHINA SEA

The LUZON AREA

THE PHILIPPINES

LINGAYEN GULF

• Baguio

• Sison

16°

Villasis •

• San Jose

Guimba •

MILES

• Cabanatuan

Dingalan Bay

| 0 | 25 | 100 | 150 | 200 |

| 0 | 25 | 100 | 150 | 200 |

KILOMETERS

San Fernando •

SUBIC BAY

BATAAN

Manila

BICOL AREA

CORREGIDOR

14°

MINDORO

MASBATE

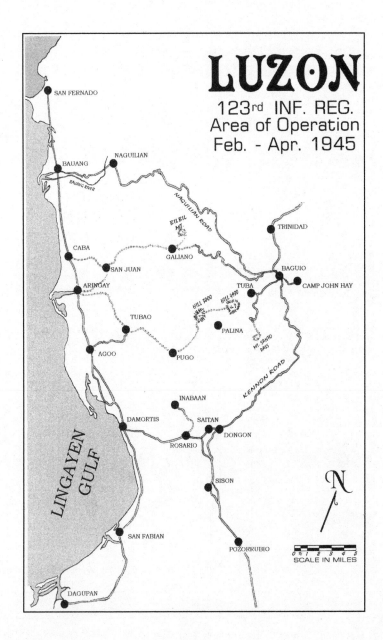

LUZON

123rd INF. REG.
Area of Operation
Feb. - Apr. 1945

SAN FERNADO

NAGUILIAN

BAUANG

BAUANG RIVER

NAGUILIAN ROAD

EILEIL MT.

TRINIDAD

CABA

GALIANO

SAN JUAN

BAGUIO

ARINGAY

TUBA

CAMP JOHN HAY

HILL 3000

HILL 4930

TUBAO

PALINA

MT. SANTO PASS

AGOO

PUGO

KENNON ROAD

INABAAN

DAMORTIS

SAITAN

DONGON

ROSARIO

LINGAYEN GULF

SISON

SAN FABIAN

POZORRUBIO

SCALE IN MILES

0 1 2 3 4 5

DAGUPAN

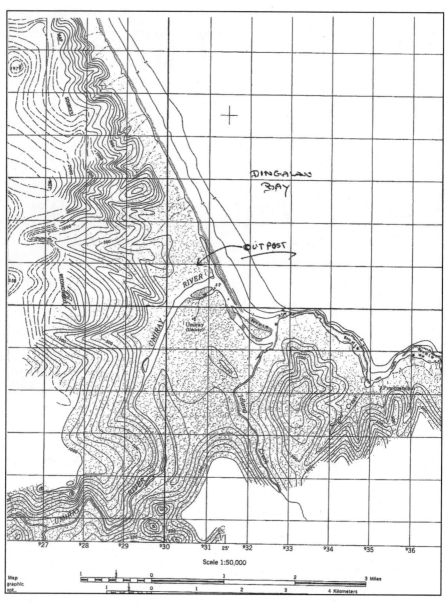

Copy of the map issued to the Connolly Task Force in May 1945. The outpost location, junction of the Umiray River and Dingalan Bay. Officially titled by the Army Map Service, "Umiray, Talabas Province, Luzon, 1:50,000. 1944"

The National Archives

**APPROXIMATE POSITIONS AT THE UMIRAY OUTPOST
MOMENTS BEFORE THE JAPANESE ATTACK.**

1. Light machine gun, .30 caliber, manned by PFC Morris Roberts and PFC Eldon Homan and Filipino guerrillas.

2. Roberts and Homan's foxhole, empty at 0530.

3. PFC Edward Colwell.

4. PFC Adolph "Red" Barrette.

5. PFC John McKinney and two Filipino guerrillas.

6. Lt. Max Ladin.

7. Tech. Sgt. Victor J. Wendling.

8. Command and supply tent.

9. Light machine guns.

10. Lt. Edwin Voss.

11. Rifleman with M1s and BARs supported by Filipino guerrillas. Inside the garrison, clumps of hyacinth appear as tree tops on aerial photos.

INTRODUCTION

So near is grandeur to our dust,
So near is God to man,
When duty whispers low,
"Thou must," the youth replies, "I can!"

Ralph Waldo Emerson

On January 23, 1946, almost six months after the end of World War II, twenty-four-year-old Sergeant John R. McKinney, a Georgia farm boy, was ordered to Washington, D.C., and stood at attention in the Oval Office in the White House.

Behind Sergeant McKinney were his family and representatives from the news media. Officers from various branches of the military quietly joined the ceremony. Two older men, also in uniform, moved in front of the others. Everyone recognized General Dwight D. Eisenhower and Admiral Chester W. Nimitz. Soft whispers floated briefly about the room.

Then silence. Harry S Truman, president of the United States of America, had entered.

Someone with a loud clear voice read an official proclamation, the citation explaining just why Sergeant McKinney, the son of a sharecropper with only a third-grade education, was invited to the White House.

The reader quoted inspirational phrases from the citation that could bring goose bumps to a patriotic American—"He fought with extreme gallantry to defend the outpost, alone with only his rifle to meet the advancing Japanese. By his indomitable spirit, extraordinary fighting ability, and unwavering courage in the face of tremendous odds, he saved his company from possible annihilation."

The president placed a blue ribbon over Sergeant John McKinney's head. From it dangled our nation's highest award for gallantry, the Congressional Medal of Honor.

"There can be no greater honor in the world," President Truman said in his short speech.

I first heard of John McKinney's deeds on Luzon in the late 1970s while gathering information for my book *Hour of Redemption.* Actually, I did not have McKinney's name then, only reports from Filipino war veterans in Cabanatuan City. They spoke of a GI rifleman who, at a place called Dingalan Bay, made an incredible one-man stand against attacking Japanese soldiers.

The Philippines suffered greatly during World War II. On my journeys in Luzon, I don't think I met a single individual who had not lost a loved one in that war. Tales of bravery, many exaggerated, were related as if they happened only yesterday and had already become legend.

My escort at Cabanatuan consisted of an interpreter, a driver/guide, and a few fellows who insisted on going along as bodyguards. We piled into a jeep, a relic of World War II, and headed into the Sierra Madre Mountains in search of Captain Juan Pajota's World War II guerrilla camp. Pajota was the hero of the battle at Cabu Bridge, where his forces held a Japanese battalion while American Rangers and Alamo Scouts liberated Allied POWs interned at Camp Cabanatuan. Often during the war, Pajota and his men eluded the Japanese by escaping into the Sierra Madres.

Armed with a good map provided by Pajota, we easily located the remains of his camp. As usual in the tropics, trees and thick brush had taken control of the area since 1945.

At the insistence of my guide, we continued up the mountain on a dirt road, the engine of the old jeep chugging and coughing as it struggled with its weight to reach a vista near the top.

There we commanded a breathtaking view of Dingalan Bay.

My guide pointed at a barren beach where a muddy river perhaps three hundred yards wide flowed into the bay.

"That is the place, sir," my guide stated. "There is where our people say a lone GI killed many Japanese!" I had journeyed to Luzon for the purpose of researching the story of the POW camp rescue. Though it was tempting, I could not permit myself to become involved in another project.

But something bothered me about that beach. It haunted me for twenty-five years, until I decided to solve the mystery of what really happened there. I remember it as a small, dark sandy area the size of two football fields with Dingalan Bay on the east, a river to its south, and dense jungle bordering the north and west. Why were American soldiers fighting in such a strange place? It seemed to have no apparent strategic importance.

In the Philippines during World War II, as in other parts of the world, thousands of Americans performed with extraordinary bravery. The veterans of that war are passing away in large numbers each day and the memories of what they accomplished are fading. Few will ever read of their individual battle experiences.

The story of a battle is more than plans made by high command or orders issued in the field as the fight begins. Battle is composed of individual sagas of men who may have once had high ideals, like love of family and country. Combat reduces all of that to one instinct—destroy and survive.

Combat is a personal thing for each warrior as his world is suddenly reduced to the small piece of land on which he must stand and fight.

In modern wars with laser-guided missiles, fast armored vehicles, stealth aircraft, and high-technology weapons, the foot soldier is still the key to victory on the field of battle. When the smoke of battle clears, it always falls on the individual rifleman to go in and finish the bloody, dirty work of war.

The struggle between American and Japanese forces on Luzon during 1945 was mostly at close quarters, often hand-to-hand. The terrain favored the Japanese Army, which lacked the mechanized equipment the Americans had depended on in other areas. On Luzon, U.S. tanks were restricted to roads or large trails. Enemy targets were often hidden in caves on the opposite sides of hills and mountains, limiting the use of our heavy artillery. And the weather often rendered aircraft cover undependable.

The Japanese would rely on their ultimate weapon, the individual warrior and the spirit within each soldier. Each Imperial soldier had received training in how to participate in futile banzai attacks or suicide bombings. The Americans would be made to pay dearly for every hundred yards gained. The Japanese mission would be to delay the Americans, inflicting as many casualties as possible, until we gave up the idea of retaking the Philippines and withdrew to Australia or Hawaii. That was a dream of Imperial Army high command in Tokyo. Their military leaders in the field knew that they, at best, could fight a delaying action, giving the main islands of Japan more time to prepare for an invasion.

With our modern weapons of armor and aircraft somewhat useless, we had to rely on our riflemen to seek out and destroy the enemy. It was as if a time machine had tossed the armies back two hundred years. Once again, war would be fought rifleman against rifleman, bayonet against bayonet, sword against trench knife. In such a conflict, many brave men became heroes. Some were officially recognized for their bravery, many were not. Most returned and never spoke of their experiences. Others perished in battle, and some died alone in unknown places in unmarked graves. The returning GIs told us that those men were the true heroes.

We have always needed heroes; we crave the knowledge of people we can respect as inspiring examples. America needs to produce great people who accomplish heroic things. We like to look at them and think that if a farm boy with no education could accomplish such a marvelous, brave feat, maybe, just maybe, so could we.

By chance, a line in a recent letter from a World War II veteran caught my attention. It mentioned a "task force sent to Dingalan Bay in 1945," and that a Private John R. McKinney had been awarded the Congressional Medal of Honor for his stand against the Japanese. Then I thought about the beach I had seen from the Sierra Madres and the stories related to me by my guide long ago. My anatomy of a battle had begun.

I learned that before the war John R. McKinney had always been a shy, gentle sort of a man living a quiet, uneventful life on a farm near Woodcliff, Georgia. Did he need to change to become a war hero?

The Army did not create John McKinney and convert him into a one-man killing machine. He was a product of his environment influenced by family, religion, personal convictions, and a love for the wilderness.

But the Army does deserve some credit. They took this young man, as they needed to do with so many others, and taught him how to fight as a soldier. He already knew how to shoot, but they issued him the best combat rifle available at the time, the .30-caliber M1 semiautomatic Garand.

In certain ways, John McKinney was not unlike other Americans who went off to war. Most of them had nothing of monetary value or power to return to; they fought because America had an enemy who threatened freedom.

John McKinney would see combat before reaching the Philippines. But he was not an aggressive leader of men. He served simply as an average soldier like most of the others.

Then in May 1945, on that beach at Dingalan Bay, fate took a hand. In one inspiring moment of courage, John McKinney proved that patriotism, bravery, and resourcefulness can come from a small simple country boy.

The battle was ferocious. Those in the fight reported that it seemed the killing would never end. John McKinney earned the Medal of Honor, and four men in his unit, fighting 150 yards away, were awarded the Silver Star. Five high awards for bravery for one battle that lasted thirty minutes.

Anyone who has survived fierce combat will tell of things happening that make no sense at all, things that defy logic and human understanding. Events unfold rapidly in a battle and seldom follow logical patterns. In reconstructing memories of combat, people often substitute details that seem logical because they simply cannot analyze or understand all that they witnessed.

How John McKinney performed his duty with such bravery while defending his buddies is almost unbelievable. Facts will produce a clear picture of the events.

But the answer to just how he survived the tremendous firepower directed at him is not easy to comprehend and falls perhaps into the mystical.

To understand the battle, it is important to know what motivated the enemy to attack that particular place at that time.

Therefore, this story includes a study of the Japanese soldier Americans fought during World War II in the Philippines. We killed so many of each other that it seems appropriate to know something about the enemy. Who were those tough little soldiers, those warriors of the sun who apparently had no fear of death? What was their training and personal character and tactics? What were they actually fighting for and with what kind of weapons? I have attempted to give the Japanese a face, a character, and in some cases, actual names.

My narrative is formulated from interviews with participants, their close relatives and friends, documents, photos, and maps from the national archives, personal observations of the battlefield and of that beautiful part of Georgia where John McKinney grew up. News media reports of the time, though often giving conflicting details, were still of value.

Quotations are taken verbatim from interviews listed in the Notes section or the bibliography of this book. To maintain continuity in the story, it was necessary from time to time to take a fictionalized approach so the events flow with ease. In some cases, logic had to be applied to connect facts or to draw conclusions when two or more individuals or documents did not agree.

Long after the war, friends noted that John McKinney, or J.R. as everyone in Screven County called him, carried a deep sadness in his eyes. Was there some horror from that battle of which he could not speak? Did he conceal secrets about his survival? Or had his mind never really released the memories of all the death and mayhem he witnessed that day?

John McKinney was never a man of many words. How could he relate his thoughts and feelings while remembering the day he fought one hundred armed men who were trying to kill him?

John R. McKinney may have been a simple country boy, an average American soldier, but when duty called, he answered with unwavering courage. This is his story.

PROLOGUE

Sergeant Yamashita Yoshi drew his sword, crawled over the small sandy ridge and onto the flatland. In his jacket pocket was his *inkan,* his personal seal with a family name carved on a clear quartz cylinder three inches long. No doubt he felt content knowing that if he was killed in battle, someone could identify his remains by the *inkan.* To a Japanese soldier, the *inkan* was as important as the GI's metal "dog tag." In his pants pocket was another personal treasure, a wristwatch, the band long since rotted away, the crystal and hands gone. Even the dial face had faded, leaving the numerals barely distinguishable. It accompanied him into combat even though it had no practical use.

Yamashita started his long crawl through the hyacinth and bushes toward the center of the outpost. Separated by only a few feet, his five men followed, silently making their way in a formation resembling a triangle with Yamashita at the point. They passed unnoticed in the darkness between the machine gun pit and PFC Edward Colwell's foxhole. Once safely inside the perimeter, they crawled faster.

Shadows faded as light of a new day began to streak the sky. Time was running out for Sergeant Yamashita and his squad.

Sergeant Morii Fukutaro, his battle flag tucked inside his shirt, crawled with one soldier to the right of the machine gun and directly toward the large foxhole where PFC John McKinney was attempting to fall asleep. As planned, two soldiers inched their way toward the machine gun, while the last two crawled to the left. Their orders were to attack the machine gun crew if their comrades failed in the attempt to take it. If this was not necessary, they were to rush the center, reinforcing Yoshi's squad.

At 5:30 AM, the machine gun, camouflaged by its green blanket, pointed silently at the spot where the long sandbar connected with the beach.

The tide was still at its high phase, but had not covered the sandbar. The southern Japanese attack group moved from land toward the bay. Even though they were behind schedule, they did have some luck. In May the tide was lower than in other months, and a "new moon" meant an even lower tide. So, at a time of the morning when the tide might normally have covered their path, the Japanese Imperial soldiers found the sandbar above water, ready for them to move easily into their attack positions.

Private John McKinney almost drifted off to sleep, but in those moments before the conscious brain surrenders, he heard a noise outside the tent. It sounded as if someone was attempting to open the canvas flaps.

"What the hell you all doing?" McKinney shouted with a smile, thinking the disturbance was one of his buddies being playful. He stood up.

No one answered. McKinney waited for another sound. Suddenly the flaps flew open.

Imperial Army Sergeant Morii Fukutaro and U.S. Army PFC John R. McKinney, two farmers the same size and age, but now enemy warriors, stood facing each other four feet apart. Sergeant Morii held his sword high, but raised it above his head, both hands firmly gripping the hilt in a classic *jodan no kamae* position. He swung the sword downward, intending to split McKinney's skull.

But in the dim light, Sergeant Morii's aim was poor. The blade missed the skull, but its razor-sharp tip sliced through part of McKinney's right ear, taking a small piece of scalp with it. The blade continued downward toward the earth, ripping McKinney's shirt as it traveled.

Dazed, McKinney managed to seize his M1 and brought it up, stock first, in a perfect vertical stroke, catching Fukutaro under his chin. The sword fell from his hand as his head snapped backward. McKinney followed through with a downward vertical stroke, smashing his ene-my's head with the butt.

Sergeant Morii's battle was over.

John McKinney's personal struggle for survival had just begun. . . .

CHAPTER 1

"Sometimes I still hear the screams!"

John R. McKinney

1995 .

Airport Marriott
Nashville, Tennessee
September 30, 1995

Time, the unconquered enemy of civilization, did to the Thirty-third Infantry Division what the Imperial Japanese Army could not.

At the end of World War II during the American occupation of Japan, the Thirty-third, with its support units, had a strength of over twelve thousand men. Returning home, the veterans formed an "association," and eventually began to publish a newsletter so those who desired could "stay in touch."

In 1995 the Thirty-third's association planned a special ceremony and reunion to be held in Nashville, Tennessee. Fifty years had passed since Japan's surrender. It would be a "golden anniversary" for the fighting men known as the Golden Cross Division.

But most of the association members were now in their mid-seventies, some over eighty, and in no physical condition to make the trip. Others, for various reasons, had severed communications with their buddies long ago, and many more had passed away.

Of the Thirty-third Division's original twelve thousand men, slightly less than two hundred would attend the September 30 reunion.[1]

Some arrived a few days early on September 25, anxious to visit with old friends and exchange war stories as best their fading memories could recall.

When they gathered in small groups before the banquet, news spread about surprises the association leaders had planned. They would be entertained on the big night by a twenty-three-piece band and three or four vocalists. The band's specialty was music popular in the late 1930s and 1940s.

Their guest speaker was unable to attend, but Colonel Larry Farnell had agreed to step in and give the address.

Then some exciting news circulated among the attendees. John R. McKinney, the Thirty-third Division's only living Medal of Honor recipient, planned to make an appearance.

Three men of the Thirty-third received the Congressional Medal of Honor for bravery during World War II. Their deeds occurred in battles on Luzon, the Philippines.

Private First Class Dexter J. Kerstetter, a cook's helper, saw his unit being cut to pieces by Japanese machine-gun fire. He seized his M1 rifle and charged into the enemy, shooting from the hip, pausing only long enough to fire rifle grenades that killed the machine gunners and scattered the remaining enemy. Kerstetter survived World War II, but died in a 1972 boating accident when he gave up his life so a family member could be saved.[2]

Another was Staff Sergeant Howard E. Woodward, who led a group of Filipino guerrillas to a hilltop position. There, they were fired upon at point-blank range by the Japanese. The guerrillas panicked, broke, and scattered, but Sergeant Woodward, suffering from poor vision since childhood, adjusted his eyeglasses and charged the enemy firing his M1 rifle and tossing grenades. Inspired by his one-man attack, the guerrillas regrouped and joined the battle. Later, the Japanese counterattacked. Wounded, the sergeant continued to return fire from a foxhole until he was eventually killed. The next morning, the attack ended. The guerrillas found thirty-seven dead enemy soldiers around Sergeant Woodward's position.[3]

No one from the Thirty-third had seen the third hero, John R. McKinney, since the war ended. He had attended none of the reunions, joined no veterans' organizations, and never wrote so much as a Christmas card to any of his military buddies. Those who knew him during the war were not surprised. McKinney had been remembered as a shy, "private sort of soldier" who was polite, uneducated, and always did what his superiors told him to do without complaining. After the war it seemed John had returned to Georgia and vanished.

But John R. McKinney had not vanished, at least not completely. Some in Screven County, Georgia, claimed to know where he could be located. But then, he usually was not where they expected him to be.

There were reports that he disappeared for days, only to be seen briefly at the country store or church. Then he was gone again.

If they really wanted to find J.R., as everyone called him, they should have inquired of his sister Betty, her daughter Sue, Sue's husband, Danny Lynn Derriso, or Danny Lynn's sons, J.R.'s grandnephews.

That is exactly what a reporter for the Thirty-third's association newsletter did in 1986, forty-one years after the war. With a bit of good journalistic investigation, he contacted Sylvania, Georgia, officials, who located J.R.'s family. The result was a phone interview and report in the Thirty-third's newsletter. The members learned that John McKinney had never married and spent most of his time farming or fishing. The reporter concluded that J.R. was still trying to bury the memories of the war.[4]

Then in 1995, a Sylvania community program expanded into a statewide effort that would eventually involve the Georgia highway commissioner, the lieutenant governor, and the state's governor. It was spearheaded by J.R.'s nephew, State Trooper Danny Lynn Derriso, who, along with others, believed John McKinney should attend the Thirty-third Division's fiftieth reunion. Everyone, especially the state government, thought this was a great idea—everyone except John McKinney.

Sol Rocke, J.R.'s squad leader during most of World War II and now mayor of a small town near Chicago, along with a few veterans became involved. Finally, a reluctant J.R. agreed to make the journey to Tennessee. The state of Georgia furnished an official car to be driven by Officer Derriso. Officer Derriso's youngest son, Dent, would be permitted to travel with them.

For this occasion, John McKinney was given a new two-piece suit, complete with a white shirt and paisley tie. The family speculated that the tie was J.R.'s first since his Army discharge in 1946 (except for an appearance before President Truman at the White House).

During the reunion, some noticed a very stiff and uncomfortable John R. McKinney. Lynn Derriso remembered that J.R. "was very uncomfortable about the whole Nashville trip."[5]

The party made a stop in Athens, Georgia, where Lynn bought his uncle a Western-style gray felt hat at the Franklin Sporting Goods store. Although it was intended as a dress hat, J.R. later wore it for good luck when hunting and fishing. In fact, it became a prized possession used the year round in all kinds of weather.

J.R. said little on the journey, but no one expected him to carry on a conversation. He watched the scenery quietly until they passed a large lake at the edge of Nashville. His head turned and he stared at the water while the car continued. "Bet there's some good fishing in that there lake, Lynn," he said.

They arrived at the Marriott before the banquet. Cameras flashed as J.R. entered the reception room. He posed for photographs with Sol Rocke and a number of other veterans who approached with an extended hand and a warm comment: "Hi, Mac. Remember me?"

Finally the banquet. Again J.R. was in front of the cameras, sitting briefly with different dignitaries, including the Thirty-third association's president, at the speaker's table. He then returned to his table and a chair between Lynn and Dent. That table was to the right front of the speakers.

The band began, thrilling the audience with old favorites. Applause followed a Glen Miller tune, then a jumpy patriotic march, ending as a spotlight beam focused on the association president, J.B. Faulconer, who introduced the speaker, Colonel Farnell.

After a short talk, the band began to play "Stars and Stripes Forever" and the spotlight came alive again, dancing about the audience, pausing at tables so each had a second or two in the glow. It swept to the ceiling and floor, finally resting on President Faulconer.

John R. McKinney placed his knife and fork across his plate, turned to Lynn, and said softly, "I'm ready to go."

It is possible that Lynn did not hear J.R. because the music smothered practically all other sounds. Or maybe, in that brief moment, while all eyes were on Mr. Faulconer, the words simply did not register quickly.[6]

"And now," the dignified Mr. Faulconer announced, "I have the honor to present a very special guest." His left arm moved in a sweeping motion, hand pointing into the semidarkness. "A great American hero, a member of our own Thirty-third Infantry Division . . . a soldier awarded the Congressional Medal of Honor for bravery, Sergeant John . . . R. . . . . McKinney!"

Applause blended with the music as the audience rose to their feet. The spotlight swept the room, coming to rest on J.R.'s table. John McKinney's chair was empty.

.   Heads turned; murmurs and whispers sifted through the crowd. Where *was* the guest of honor?

Lynn Derriso's large muscular frame lifted slowly from the table, followed by Dent. They left the banquet room through double doors and moved swiftly down a hall to the bathroom. No J.R. Then out a glass door to a patio lined with pine trees.

There they found their uncle standing in the shadows next to one of the trees staring into the darkness.

Lynn spoke first. "Uncle J.R., you okay?"

"Yep. You all go on and finish your dinner. I'm not an inside kind of person. I got nervous in there with all them people. I was uncomfortable," J.R. responded slowly.[7]

"I know. I understand," replied Lynn. "They're calling your name. Maybe you could return and wave at 'em just once?"

A pause of several seconds followed. Then J.R. answered, "I'm speaking my mind now. I'm here 'cause people wanted me to be here. I've posed for picture-taking and sure 'nuf shook a lot of hands. Them's all good people. They're real nice to remember me. But . . . it's time for me to go."

Lynn nodded, "Yes."

But J.R. hesitated. His attention seemed fixed on something in the darkness. He finally spoke.

"I moved about. Maybe that's what helped save me. I think about that a lot."

"Moved about?" Lynn asked, looking down at his son as if expecting a look of understanding.

Dent stood silent with no change of expression. He remained close to his father's side. As a well-mannered, disciplined young man, he knew he had to be silent when adults were talking.

"Sometimes, I still hear the screams," J.R. added.

"Screams? Who's screaming?"

"Them Jap boys. When they were a-coming at me!"

"A daydream?"

"Yep, I still hear 'em once in a while. And shooting. Like firecrackers echoing in the woods far away. Seeing them fellows today kind of reminded me."

Lynn swallowed hard before replying, "You want to be alone a while, Uncle J.R.?"

"Nope," came the fast answer. Then he continued. "The Lord saved me, Lynn. We know that. Least that's what everyone tells me. But I keep a-wondering. Why so many boys had to die? Moving about saved me. Now I'm certain of it."[8]

J.R. turned, and in the dim light, Lynn noticed his eyes had flooded.

Then J.R. added with a sniffle, "I sure would like to test the fishing in that there lake we saw this morning. Maybe, before we leave." He started toward the door.

"Of course," Lynn assured, taking his uncle by the arm. "Now, what's this *moving about,* something you learned on Luzon, or you taught yourself?"

"Nope," J.R. replied with a grin. "Learned from a friend in the swamp a long time ago." He looked down at his grandnephew. "When I was about your age, Dent."[9]

Sixty-three years earlier
Along South Fork Creek
Screven County, Georgia
1932

A boy crossed the cotton field in darkness only minutes before the sun peeked over wooded hills behind him. He moved swiftly, his calloused bare feet making no sound in the soft earth as he maneuvered between cotton plants, heavy with open pods of white fluffy balls ready for a fall harvest.

He reached the edge of the woods and crouched low as he moved, cradling a single-shot, bolt-action Winchester .22 rifle. Then he paused a moment as he entered the line of trees and breathed deep, slow breaths as if he had been trained to do so. He exhaled under his arm to hide the vapor of warm breath as it mixed with cool air.

There he waited motionless for two or three minutes. Had the guards spotted him? He saw them move in the faint light of dawn. They were awake, but there was no alarm.

It was time to prepare for the hunt. Carefully he opened the rifle bolt, inserted one .22-long rifle cartridge into the chamber, then closed the bolt slowly. With thumb and index finger, he pulled the firing pin straight back, cocking the weapon. The slight *click* sound it made could not be avoided.

He waited another five minutes. The noise did not attract attention. Still no alarm from the guards.

Confident he had successfully slipped past the sentries, he began to move slowly along a pig path into the dark shadows.[10]

If one of the large black crows on guard high in the trees had spotted him, he would have warned others with his fast cawing and instantly each would have repeated the call, warning all creatures. Man had entered the woods.

Now the boy knew he was safe to continue. He had come for squirrels, not crows. Dawn brought light slowly to the woods. But then, bright-colored leaves of maple, hickory, dogwood, and sweet gum decorated the trail with a colorful canopy as he moved cautiously, paused, then continued.

The sun began to warm the air and pull apart the thin morning fog. A slight breeze cooled his face. Both he and the animals were alert for any motion. But now, with a wind, no matter how slight, he had learned long ago that he must travel into it, else his scent might be detected.

Even at age twelve, John R. McKinney was no stranger in the wilderness.

With each step calculated, he moved slowly through the woods toward the swamp and South Fork Creek. There in hardwood trees he expected to find the family dinner, fat gray squirrels.

Soon he was beneath towering oak trees, their dark limbs holding draping curtains of Spanish moss, which moved in a gentle motion with the breeze.

Here the sunlight had begun to break through with soft beams, scattering more pale morning fog.

He paused, listening for squirrels chattering as they played near the creek. But all was oddly still.

Suddenly, to his right, something moved in the fog. At least, he thought he saw a movement. He crouched lower and froze. Minutes passed. Then something made a sound behind him. Not a twig breaking, but a slight noise like a bush rustling. Was it a gust of wind? He turned, rifle ready.

Again, something moved—this time on the opposite side of the trail. It had traveled completely around him, remaining invisible in the fog.

J.R. knew there were no deer or wild pigs in the swamp because he traveled that area almost every day. And those animals, like wild dogs, were noisy and easy to see.

His mind searched for a logical explanation, applying everything he had learned during six years of hunting. What could cover that distance so quickly without being seen?

Ghosts! Old Jenk, the African American who owned a small country store three miles away, once told him there were ghosts along South Fork River. Jenk thought they might be wandering spirits of dead slaves who had tried to escape to Black Island during the 1850s. Supposedly, they perished in the swamp before reaching freedom.[11]

J.R. did not believe in ghosts. Jenk said the ghosts came out at night and disappeared at dawn. It was now past dawn. J.R. had explored the swamp many times at night, never seeing a ghost.

J.R. crept a few feet forward. Then, to his front, another movement. A frightening thought raced through his mind. He might be totally surrounded and no longer the hunter, but the *hunted*! But *what* was hunting him?[12]

He stared at the patch of fog. The mist began to break apart into streamlike clouds, still hugging the ground. There, between two bushes, sat a large bobcat. His eyes, holding a lazy stare, were fixed on J.R., large round-topped ears pointed forward directly at the boy.

The two hunters remained statuelike, staring silently at one another. Then J.R. remembered another conversation with old Jenk only a month before.

"I've been hunting these parts years before you was born, boy," Jenk had said. "You shore is a good hunter, but you have lots to learn. You ever seen Burr Bobcat in them swamps? Now, that's a hunter!"

J.R. replied that he had never seen the cat, but did notice his tracks at the riverbank from time to time. He concluded the cat must be a big one, because the track marks were as deep as those "a hound dog makes."

Jenk guessed the cat weighed about thirty pounds based on J.R.'s information.

"That's thirty pounds of muscle," Jenk went on. "One of da Lord's most perfect creatures. He gave that cat everything he needs to live in da swamp. He don't hunt for sport. No, sur! Like you, he hunts to stay alive. He kills only what he and his family needs, nuttin' more."

Jenk's knowledge about the cat and many animals in the county seemed to be unlimited. "Burr Bobcat can teach you a trick or two. He's got patience no folks, black or white, got. He can run like the wind, swim or climb whenever he wants. And he's smart. He lets the game come to him when he can. You remember that and study what the cat do in the swamp. Only thing . . ."

"What?" asked J.R.

"You ain't never gonna see the cat unless he wants to be seen!"

J.R. admitted years later that he had not thought much about Jenk's conversation at the time. Something young boys learned to accept is the fact that elders are constantly giving advice about hunting.[13]

That morning Jenk's words came back to him: ". . . unless he wants to be seen."

Now J.R. wondered why. *Why* would the cat allow himself to be seen? Was he playing a game? That would not be likely for an animal who had a reputation of avoiding man.

J.R. decided to turn to his left, moving back about thirty degrees. The cool fall air had given him a chill and he knew he must exercise his limbs or cramps might set in. The moment he turned, he looked over his shoulder. The cat had disappeared.

The boy traveled about thirty feet, his thoughts returning to the squirrels. His mother was expecting five of the animals to roast for the evening meal. He had only seven or eight .22 cartridges, none to waste on the cat or anything else. His eyes shifted from earth to front, from side to side, as he cautiously moved on. A trip over a fallen branch or a tumble into a bush would announce his presence as much as a crow's call. Then he froze with a look of disbelief. The bobcat was once again sitting to his front, only twelve feet away, as if he had been waiting at that position. And once again their eyes locked.

Now J.R.'s youthful mind was even more confused. How did the cat change positions and move that distance so swiftly without being seen?

The boy shifted direction, returning to the original path, which led to the river. His heart pounded and he tried to resist the temptation to speed his pace to put yardage between himself and the cat. He maintained, instead, his low creeping profile, placing each foot carefully in front of the other.

He heard a splash from a fish jumping and knew he was near the river.

Then, another shock. There, in the path blocking his way, the bobcat sat waiting. Like a phantom, the cat had changed positions three times without a movement being noticed.

But J.R. knew this was no ghost. He decided to challenge the cat by proceeding directly toward him.

As he took his first step, the cat made a strange noise, not a purr, hiss, or screech, but a "whirring sound." Then he turned and bounced toward the river where a smaller cat waited.[14]

J.R. confessed he had not seen the other cat until the big one ran to her. Its dark brown fur mixed with gray presented perfect camouflage with the autumn colors in the swamp.

The boy sat down on the sandy trail with his rifle across his lap and watched the two cats lightly touch noses, then disappear into the brush.

Jenk was right. J.R. had learned something new from a wild creature. That was a wonderful thing about nature. Everyday the wilderness shared some new experience.

Now J.R. understood. The bobcat had avoided a direct confrontation by changing positions, then permitting himself to be seen for a reason. He had confused the boy and succeeded in distracting him from the original destination so another cat could retreat from possible danger.

J.R. got his quota of squirrels later in the morning, never thinking that what he learned from the cat would help save his life someday.[15]

CHAPTER 2

"Georgia must be next to paradise."
John R. McKinney

John R. McKinney had been hunting and fishing since he was six years old. At least that is what he reported to his sister, Betty.

When he was very small, his father, Dewey, escorted him along trails in the woods to build confidence and make sure he knew how to find his way home.

Combined with those adventures, J.R. accompanied Dewey to a number of small ponds and muddy streams that were within easy walking distance from their cabin. Father shared knowledge with son in the basic skills of fishing, emphasizing the discipline of patience. "You'll learn patience from fishing," he told the boy, "that will be important when you start hunting."[1]

But Mr. McKinney was a farmer, not a true fisherman or hunter. Of course, he had those skills, as did all farm boys, but different responsibilities as he grew older and married took priority.

Dewey, a tall slender man accustomed to sweating in rows of cotton, explained to John that only rich people thought of hunting and fishing as sport. With the McKinneys, it would be a job to gather food for the family, and it fell upon the younger men until they were strong enough to work the fields. For the impoverished McKinney family, the arts that Dewey was teaching his son were for family survival. The faster young John could produce food from his new education, the faster Dewey could return to the fields and be productive as a sharecropper.

The people in the "big house" who owned all the land in that part of the county naturally expected production from their sharecroppers.

Land had always been related to power in Georgia. But land alone, without men working it and making it productive, was far less valuable.

After the slaves were freed, who would work the land still owned by plantation families? Even after the plantations were broken into smaller acreage, a plan was desperately needed to make the land productive once more and help rebuild the South. A system evolved that was relatively fair, known as sharecropping.

The term described exactly what the farmers did. They worked the fields, cultivating and harvesting crops for the landowners, who, of course, could not do all the work themselves. For their labor, the "croppers" were loaned a cabin to live in and a small piece of land on which they could raise chickens, even a few pigs, and vegetables and fruits for their families' existence. Once the crop, be it cotton, corn, or whatever the property owner dictated, was harvested, the worker retained a percentage of the sales for himself.

Dewey McKinney had a "one-horse farm"; that is, he was responsible for twenty-five acres, but he did not have a horse. He had been furnished a strong, friendly mule who pulled the plow or, when necessary, a four-wheel wooden wagon, or did a number of chores when Dewey needed his assistance.[2]

Their home, the cabin in which John McKinney was born, was near the little village of Woodcliff, a few miles from Sylvania, Georgia.

Dewey McKinney, like all sharecroppers, was poor, and as his family grew, the Great Depression that swept America made poor people even more destitute. But the McKinneys had one advantage over starving people in the metropolitan areas standing in soup lines. Dewey's family could live off the land, which provided the basic food they needed, that is, if one was a vegetarian. Meat was in short supply and expensive, too costly for the average sharecropper. But the rivers had an abundance of fish, and the woods and swamps were packed with quail, rabbit, wild turkey, squirrel, and in some places deer and wild pig. Yet, very few had time to fish or hunt. The first obligation was always to the "boss man's" farm.

Dewey McKinney had a plan. To be successful and survive when he became too old to work his one-horse farm, he needed sons: men not only to help with twenty-five acres, but to do labor throughout the county and bring home a small income to improve the family's standard of living.

Dewey's wife, Nattie, would provide him five sons, delivering Ralph when she was sixteen, John R. two years later, Dewey Jr. three years after John. In three more years, Jack would follow, and finally Hamp as Nattie turned twenty-six.[3]

With all those sons, Dewey relaxed with the thought that survival had been practically guaranteed. But some time had to pass before each would be strong enough to chop firewood or walk behind a mule and plow the fields.

Nattie prayed for a girl, even though they knew the problems of feeding another small child. Nattie's prayers were answered in 1932 when, at age twenty-eight, she gave birth to Betty.

Dewey had reached age forty, an old age then for a man who had spent most of his life working in the elements.

A serious problem struck the family shortly after Dewey Jr. was born. John R., then eight, suddenly became ill and had to remain home from school.[4]

Nattie, like all farm mothers, knew hard labor and the additional chore of bearing and raising children. Now she had a sick boy at home, in a cabin heated by a fireplace and wood-burning stove, and a two-month-old Dewey to worry about.

John R's condition took a turn for the worse. The boy's breathing became labored and he developed pneumonia.

Dewey managed to find a doctor who arrived in time to save John's life. There were no antibiotics then, and no medical facilities within miles of the cabin. But country doctors were known to perform amazing feats in their profession. This one, whose name unfortunately is lost to history, saved John by slicing a hole in his back near the shoulder blade and inserting a rubber tube into the lung to drain the fluid that blocked his breathing.[5]

Recovery would be slow and, of course, during those weeks, it was difficult for an eight-year-old to remain still. As John moved about, the tube also moved, causing a larger wound, which, when finally healed, produced an ugly scar.[6]

Nattie stayed by his side when she wasn't caring for Dewey Jr. and doing the usual chores expected of a farmer's wife.

During the months that followed, she shared with John every bit of knowledge she could remember from her grade school days. She began to notice that his power of concentration had become very limited. During writing practice, a single sentence often required a minute or two to create. No matter how hard she worked with John, his grammar and spelling remained poor. A single word written on a piece of paper was like a work of art as he struggled to perform correctly.

During that long recovery time, John's parents began to call him J.R., a nickname so familiar in the county in later years that many never knew his true name.

When J.R. finally returned to school, he was far behind the other children and lacked the ability to catch up. He finished the third grade and left public school forever.[7]

For many farm children during the Depression, school was a luxury that could not be afforded. They were needed to work on the farm for family survival.

As J.R. became stronger, he helped his mother with work about the cabin and caring for his younger brothers, and eventually his baby sister, Betty.

One evening Dewey came home with some special gifts and a good idea to help his son strengthen his damaged and weak muscles. He presented J.R. with a pocketknife and a slingshot he had made from the Y fork of a maple tree branch. Rubber straps were cut from the discarded inner tube of a tire and fastened to the wood with fishing line, wrapped and tied to hold the rubber in place. The pouch was made from a small piece of soft leather.[8]

Using small stones as missiles, the first targets were empty tin cans placed on a fence post. J.R. immediately became fascinated with the sport, and proficient at hitting the cans at different distances and angles. His father noticed that the boy had an unusual amount of patience and concentration while using the sling. Soon his accuracy became a legend among nearby sharecroppers.

The family was rewarded one evening a few weeks later when J.R. returned home with a rabbit he had killed with his sling.

With family praise and pride in his first accomplishment since his illness, J.R. constructed a new slingshot. Although the design was similar to the original (the classic, familiar to all boys), now wider strips of rubber were used, requiring a stronger pull and delivering the missile with increased striking power.[9]

Soon J.R. was spending every spare moment in the wilderness. After completing his chores, he would be off fishing somewhere or hunting with his sling in the woods. And the wilderness and his skills soon provided the McKinneys with an ample supply of squirrel, rabbit, and even an occasional wild turkey or quail.

Apparently, this is when J.R.'s life became more isolated and when father and son drifted apart. Perhaps Dewey believed he had completed J.R.'s basic education and the farm demanded his complete attention. Whatever the reason, by age nine, J.R. developed a reputation of being a "wanderer" and a "loner." Only, his wanderings were in the woods and swamps, and he never returned to the cabin without meat for dinner.[10]

Around the cabin, J.R. carried on lengthy conversations with his mother, and soon his younger brothers and sister, but had little to say to visitors and relatives (mostly cousins that visited) or others he met at church on Sundays. Like most Georgia boys, he was polite, respectful, and obedient but not very talkative.[11]

By age ten, J.R. was noticed more frequently around the Malcum Parker Country Store. As usual, he said little, but studied everyone carefully. It seemed to the quiet, shy J.R. that people had so many interesting things to say, and J.R. was a good listener. Part of his education would come from paying careful attention to people who had traveled to far-away places. (Some had come from Sylvania and even Savannah.)[12]

He also enjoyed hearing local gossip from other sharecroppers.

The store of old Jenk Newton, the African American, was a fascinating place to visit, but it catered mostly to "colored folks." Of course, that made it all the more fun for J.R. There he heard about the bobcat and other wild animals and a variety of trivial things "white folks" did not bother to discuss, including how to clean a river carp and make the ugly fish safe and tasty to eat.

Electricity reached the area in the late 1930s—not for the sharecroppers' cabins, but Parker's store became "electrified." And with this new convenience came some modern changes. The Coke icebox became a "Coke machine." A case was installed for fresh meat and an ice cream cooler decorated the rear wall. The big block of ice lasted longer and the battery-powered radio was replaced with an electric one, complete with a large speaker to ensure that everyone in the store could hear the news or enjoy music and religious sermons delivered by some preacher far away.

And perhaps equally important was wiring for electric lights. With artificial lighting, sales increased. Now customers could shop late into the night after their work in the fields.

Both Mr. and Mrs. Parker operated the store, sometimes together, but usually separately, for the family had many enterprises, including a very large spread of land farmed by twelve different sharecroppers. Some of the croppers, like Dewey McKinney, operated one-horse farms; others two-horse farms (fifty acres).

To all of these families, Malcum Parker was, indeed, the "boss man," tightly controlling everything himself, dealing out orders strictly but fairly.[13]

Malcum was a huge man with big shoulders and a stern disposition. Savannah salesmen knew him to drive a tough bargain but as someone who was always fair in final decisions. Those close to him, his family and croppers, knew he also had a jolly side to his personality seldom seen by outsiders.

But mostly Malcum was a businessman, and a very good one.

John McKinney was, of course, not the only shy, wide-eyed farm boy frequenting the Parker Store. The Parkers knew the boy as one who caught a lot of fish and could knock a squirrel out of a tree with a rock from his handmade slingshot.

And it wasn't just from stories told by J.R. People actually saw the evidence as he passed the store with a string of fish and two or more squirrels tied to his rope belt almost every day.

An interesting relationship developed between businessman Malcum Parker and the quiet, young hunter J.R. Mr. Parker recognized the possibility that J.R. could kill more game than the McKinney family needed if the boy had improved hunting capabilities. The storeowner handed J.R. a cloth bag containing old ball bearings one day. The shiny, heavy steel balls proved to be a great improvement in killing power. Malcum was rewarded with two freshly killed (and cleaned) rabbits.

But Malcum Parker had something else J.R. believed he needed as the ultimate killing weapon, a .22 rifle. Actually, the Parker collection of firearms, at least those known to customers, hung on the wall directly behind the checkout counter. There were two shotguns, one a double-barrel and one a pump model, and the new Winchester single-shot bolt-action .22 rifle.

J.R. spoke with his father about the gun and received a rather cool response. The family certainly appreciated J.R.'s ability to provide fish and game. What he pulled from the ponds and streams or killed with the ball bearings was both a blessing and adequate.

A disappointed J.R. approached Mr. Parker with a proposal. The hunter was sure he could increase his quota if only he could even *borrow* the .22.

The business mind of Malcum Parker sparked with a thought, a plan that would benefit both his country store and the McKinneys.

Malcum had another .22 identical to the Winchester, but previously used by a hunter who had traded it in for a shotgun.

The bluing on this rifle had faded and the varnish on the hardwood stock had a few scratches down to the grain. But the owner had taken good care of the functional parts, which were clean and well oiled.

Malcum Parker offered J.R. a deal. He would *loan* the boy the rifle for one year and provide .22-long rifle cartridges in exchange for squirrels, rabbits, and fish, the excess that the McKinney family did not need. In a year, at age twelve, the Winchester would belong to J.R. free and clear. Then he would either pay cash or continue to trade game for cartridges.[14]

In a way, the borrowed rifle became part of the sharecropper's program, and the Parker Store stocked some extra fresh fish and meat to

sell to those who had no time to hunt or fish or else lacked the necessary skills.

The day the final deal was consummated with a handshake between
Malcum and an excited J.R., one of those salesmen from Savannah visited the store.

The salesman knew of J.R.'s reputation as a woodsman, and when
he saw the boy proudly holding the rifle, he commented, "You should
do good with that model, J.R. It's famous for its accuracy. I understand
you were quite a hunter with a slingshot when you were a lad."

J.R. looked puzzled, then he frowned. "I weren't no *lad,* sir!" John
McKinney did not know the word "lad." Somehow it simply had an
unmanly sound.[15]

And so began the marriage of John R. McKinney and the rifle, the
first being only a borrowed, used .22.

Within a day of target practice, J.R. became a crack shot. By the
second day he could hit a rabbit on the run, and by the end of the week
had learned the trick of shooting a quail in flight. The bird required a
little more practice. It was necessary to allow it to reach a cruising altitude of several feet, level off, and fly straight forward. At that moment,
when the bird leveled off, J.R. knew he could fire his rifle.

The squirrels he provided Malcum Parker had all been shot through
the head, thus protecting the valuable meat. From the beginning, those
seeing the results never questioned J.R.'s ability to shoot with extreme
accuracy. And in the years to come, no one ever would.[16]

J.R. knew the importance of keeping his rifle clean and oiled as the
previous owner had. Mr. Parker told him the old Army saying, "A clean
rifle shoots straight."

At night he and the other children sat on the floor of their cabin,
and by the orange glow of kerosene lamps and a brighter light of the
fireplace the other children did their homework and read stories to one
another until time for bed.

J.R.'s time was devoted to disassembling and cleaning his rifle and
lying before the fire listening to the reading.

For years, J.R.'s education was what he learned from his brothers
and sister, heard at Parker's store or at the Baptist church, or what his

mother told him of the world as he helped her with the chores about the cabin.[17]

All twelve sharecroppers' cabins on Malcum Parker's land were identical, built to the same specifications some twenty years earlier.

The wall planking was rough-hewn, the blade marks clearly visible on the wood. Red bricks, so readily available in Georgia, laid with cement mortar, formed a foundation elevating the structure some two-and-a-half feet above the ground. This protected the home and occupants from streams of rainwater. It also allowed good ventilation and a place for children, cats, dogs, and other small animals to find shelter from the weather.

The framing was two-by-two and four-by-four boards, also rough-hewn. Each cabin came standard with a living room/kitchen combination, two bedrooms, a wood-burning stove and oven, a wooden icebox, and one fireplace. A porch ran the front length of the building. One could enter either through the main living room door or another door to the first bedroom. All the windows came with glass panes, some had screens, some did not.

In the backyard was the outhouse (toilet) and the hand-dug well (a well dug by hand), often lined with brick, and each cabin had a small garden that produced a variety of vegetables, all for the use of the family.

Although the sharecroppers were poor, existing without the luxury of indoor plumbing, electricity, central heat, or air conditioning, they did have a roof over their heads and the basics for survival.

More than five years after J.R.'s encounter with the bobcat, Nattie, taking an afternoon break from her duties, accompanied him to South Fork Creek, where he needed to check some fishing brush hooks he had set up the night before.

Brush hooks were made of fishing line with hooks and bait hung from limbs that protruded from the riverbank out a few feet over the water.

J.R. used a slip knot to tie the lines to the branches. If a fish swallowed the bait and hook, the more he pulled on the line, the tighter the knot became. The system was an old one for fishermen in the South, but J.R. had mastered a special technique for releasing the line. He'd invented a knot that he simply tapped or flipped with his finger and it became undone. He kept the knowledge of how to tie this special knot a secret for many years.[18]

Nattie had visited riverbanks many times with her son, but this day she had a special purpose. They sat near the river on a patch of packed white sand mixed with gray clay. She finally approached her favorite subject—religion.

John McKinney accompanied his family to church each Sunday, but was always reluctant to enter the old brick building. Often he asked to remain outside and wait. There, in the open air, he explained, he could "do all the praying he needed for the week."[19]

Depending on Nattie's mood, J.R. was granted his wish with only a mild scolding now and then.

J.R. and Nattie discussed their feelings that day. Now, at almost eighteen, J.R. assured his mother he believed in God, heaven and hell, and all the things any good Christian believes. But J.R. also stated that he thought he could talk with God whenever he wanted, especially in the solitude of the wilderness.

"I don't have to be in a church to pray, do I, Mom?" he asked seriously.

"Of course not," she assured him.

Because J.R. revealed his feelings so seldom, even to his family, Nattie needed to be assured. Now that her son had become a young man she did not want him straying from God.

J.R. was always on the move, working from time to time at other farms to earn a little spending money, but mostly escaping to the woods and river where his thoughts and dreams remained private.

"The preacher says paradise and heaven are the same," Nattie said. "We all think heaven is up in the sky, beyond the stars we see at night. Where do you think paradise is, J.R.?" she asked, testing her son.

"Shucks! Don't know for sure," he answered. "Things are so peaceful, so beautiful around here, I think paradise is nearby. Yes, ma'am, Georgia must be next to paradise."[20]

Those who knew J.R. believed he was truly blessed. He never complained about being poor. He was even proud when he received his first pair of slightly used working boots at sixteen and a pair of Sunday-go-to-church shoes at eighteen (his parents believed his feet had stopped growing by then). He didn't need the shoes, and boots were only useful in very cold weather.

To J.R., his entire world was the woods and his family. To him, his world was indeed paradise, or next to it. He had his rifle and fishing equipment. Actually, he had no need to go anywhere outside that world.

Dewey McKinney's idea of building a union of sons who could support them someday had been a good one. But developing international events and evils in a world they did not know would soon split the family apart and take John R. McKinney far away from his paradise.

CHAPTER 3

"Don't live in shame as a prisoner.
Die and leave no such horrible crime behind you."
General Hideki Tojo
Chief of Staff, Japanese Imperial Army
"Instructions for the Military"

There are primitive impulses within everyone, which, if not controlled, can quickly lead to barbarism. In the case of soldiers, extreme brutality is impulsive, a result of anger, fear, hatred, and frustration. Yet, with some armies, brutal acts were premeditated, calculated, and actually encouraged by leaders.

Through recorded history nations have continued to commit horrible acts of violence upon one another. But by the 1940s, the so-called civilized world had agreed on how warriors should behave on the field of battle, how prisoners of war and civilians caught in areas of conflict would be treated.

Surely, it was naïve to believe that all combatants would abide by international laws, treaties, and the "golden rule": those recorded and unwritten codes that show that participating nations are civilized.

In 1941, the guidelines for battlefield behavior or warrior conduct were followed mostly by the Western world. However, Nazi Germany soon demonstrated that a treaty was only to be followed if it fit their needs. A few years later, Russia retaliated on Germany, setting the so-called civilized world back hundreds of years by acts of brutality—payback for the behavior of Nazi troops during their invasion of the "Motherland."

To the Imperial Army, which had seized control of the Japanese government, the idea of war fought with restrictions was silly. They looked at war as something one does not begin unless there are plans to win. Victory must be the only goal, and with victory come the rewards—territory, riches, raw materials, slaves, and women. The same things conquerors had expected for thousands of years.

The world learned that Japan won battles, then tortured and destroyed those who surrendered, including civilians, women, and children. To Japan, the conquered were captives, not prisoners.

Later, GIs found evidence of horrible acts committed by Japanese soldiers on noncombatants that could not be comprehended. The Americans soon learned that the Japanese soldier preferred death rather than surrender. The Imperial warrior resorted to suicide attacks (the banzai charge) when there was no chance to survive. Many committed suicide by knife, shot themselves, or held a grenade to their chest and pulled the pin.[1]

Allied leaders concluded that the enemy soldiers were crazy, illogical fanatics.

But Japan, a culture understood by very few Americans at the time, knew full well the purpose of these acts. The Japanese leaders had a plan of conquest and occupation and a well-organized, disciplined strategy to accomplish their goals.

Much of that became implemented in the 1930s as the military convinced the Japanese masses that Asia belonged to Japan. It was impossible for them to be defeated, the leaders assured them.

To secure the future of their island nation, everyone must be prepared to sacrifice for the emperor and country. Many may die, but Japan, they believed, would always survive because it was protected by their gods.

What factors in history, culture, and national conditions permitted the Imperial military to be successful in leading an ancient people into modern aggression?

For more than two hundred years prior to 1900, Japan had isolated its archipelago to prevent the influence of outside people with non-Japanese ideas. Trade with other countries during that time was almost nonexistent.

For two thousand years, the Japanese had believed themselves pure of race. Once their doors were forced open in the late 1800s, Westerners found them to be arrogant, belligerent, and constantly expressing an attitude of superiority.

Forced into the twentieth century, though, the Japanese quickly realized there was a lot of catching up to do with the rest of the world. Industrially and scientifically they were truly a hundred years behind the West.

Japan then developed war equipment desperately needed to defend itself. It was not about to be colonized, as England had accomplished in Hong Kong and Singapore, the Dutch in the Indies, and the Spanish in the Philippines.

Japan began to develop a Navy modeled on the British and an Army following German and American ideas and tactics.

When the U.S. seized the Philippines and other islands from the Spanish at the end of the 1800s, the Japanese knew that if they did not become a strong power, the same thing might happen to them.

The Japanese purchased more modern war equipment from Western powers, then modified each item to fit their needs.

By the early 1900s, Japan had defeated a world power—Russia; impressive for a country that thirty years earlier still followed a feudal system and was armed mostly with swords, the bow, and primitive firearms.

The Japanese bloodline connected them indirectly to the sun goddess, Amatherasu. This belief came from their Bible, the Kojiki. People of Japan could trace themselves to Amatherasu's first earthly emperor, Jimmu.[2]

Emperor Hirohito, direct descendent of the sun god and ruler of Japan during World War II, granted complete power to the military, instructing them to protect Japan as the samurai had for hundreds of years. Japan's schools began to emphasize a curriculum of emperor worship, self-sacrifice, and militarism. To die for the emperor, people were told, would be the most honorable sacrifice one could offer.[3]

As historian and Imperial Navy veteran Kunio Yahiro recalled many years after the war, "I survived the war and have carried heavy guilt, guilt that I did not die for the emperor. Now, at last, Hirohito is dead and my guilt can die with him."[4]

It was, and perhaps remains, difficult for Westerners to completely understand the thinking of the average Imperial Japanese soldier. Actually, with the exception of a few fanatics (which many nations have at one time or another), the Japanese soldiers wanted to live and return home to loved ones as much as any GI. But their culture and conditioning were totally different.

The Imperial soldier had been drilled to believe that surrender was not only a dishonorable act, but a crime against the emperor and Japan. The fundamental rule would be to die in combat rather than withdraw to fight another day (though some units did withdraw). If a soldier could not die in face-to-face combat, then killing himself rather than surrendering remained the acceptable course of action.[5]

With all the differences between Japanese and American culture, one similarity did exist at the beginning of World War II. The majority of men drafted into service were from rural areas, small towns and farms. Many were poor, had little or no education, and both Japanese and Americans had experienced difficulties brought on by a "great depression."

The average Imperial soldier was five feet three inches tall, wore a uniform that seldom fit, carried very few supplies or rations, and had marching stamina that mystified Western observers.

But what really motivated those small Japanese "soldiers of the sun"? What made them charge into battle waving swords, screaming, and using bayonets like some medieval lance when they still had not fired all the bullets in the rifles?

Japanese men were raised in a male-dominated society, spoiled and pampered, developing a superego early in life that was continually fed by first their mothers, then every female they encountered. The "golden rule," "ladies first," and compassion were not in the Japanese male's vocabulary. Except for parents and ancestors, he knew *he* came first.

As expected from a spoiled individual, most Japanese men inherited a temper, but in their crowded land saturated with tradition, social procedures, and formalities, they learned they had to control that trait. During stress, a man was expected to lose his temper, releasing anger and frustration in any way he desired. Combat certainly provided opportunities to express anger.

For over one thousand years, the masses in Japan had served some sort of lord. People were basically fatalistic, expecting a destiny that, at the least, was frustrating, but most likely unpleasant. Born in a family of farmers, for example, meant one could be nothing but a farmer. Individual ideas on how one might change his destiny certainly existed, but traditions and culture discouraged "free thinking."

Individualism, except for an artist or craftsman, was not appreciated or rewarded. Working within the group and thinking of the group as one became the appreciated practice. For the lords, it was much easier to control the group than individual free thinkers moving about the country and possibly causing trouble.

The Japanese became a self-critical people. Perfection had always been stressed and punishment for a mistake was harsh. They feared being accused of committing even the smallest error. Nothing in their mind could be worse than humiliation before one's peers.

When Japan encountered the Western world in the 1850s, an inner conflict developed. It was one thing to be pure of race, but quite another to acknowledge the scientific achievements of the "barbarians," or outsiders. This produced a split in thinking: One felt superior in some ways, but vastly inferior in others—which produced more frustration and anger in one who, before, believed himself and his country to be superior.

Historically in Japan, human life had been cheap. Compassion and sentimentality or caring for one another was basically limited to family and friends. Feelings, other than sadness, were seldom expressed openly. Hugs and handshakes were exhibitions of feelings, affection, or trust among Westerners. The "no touch" society of the Japanese believed that the different degrees of a bow showed respect. Callousness developed among the Japanese over their long history, partially the result of the basic influence of their culture.

Robert Lapham, an American guerrilla leader who fought the Japanese on Luzon for four years, recorded his observation: "Japanese are habitually blind and deaf to the feelings of others."[6]

Ray C. Hunt, another guerrilla leader, described the Japanese he observed during the war as "unpredictable with changing psychology and abrupt changes of mood, vastly differing from Occidentals: one moment calm, smiling, reasonable, even generous, the next, storming in some inexplicable rage and acting like savages."[7]

Juan Pajota had worked with Japanese on his home island of Leyte prior to the war, then fought them as a guerrilla leader serving under Lapham on Luzon. He reported, "Often, Japanese would behave as if angry with themselves for showing concern for a stranger. Maybe they exploded because they revealed feelings they were supposed to keep hidden or were afraid someone in the group may laugh at them."[8]

Some have tried to blame the sudden shifts in mood of the Japanese on a lack of a fixed religious faith. Confucianism and Buddhism, adopted by the Japanese from the Chinese, are philosophies or attitudes toward existence. Shintuism, which the Imperial military declared the national religion, is not a true religion by Western standards, but ancestor worship with no moral code except self-criticism and self-sacrifice. This analysis is interesting, but does not provide a solution to the perplexing question of just why some Japanese behave with a constantly flipping personality or mood.[9]

Young Japanese males entering the military were in for a rude awakening. Their days of being pampered were over. The training would be extremely difficult. Of course, in combat the soldier could expect to die while fulfilling his duty. But in boot camp and through advanced training, brutality and cruelty were standard procedure. The recruit could be slapped, kicked, and beaten daily for no reason except to toughen the spirit. And when the cadre became tired of dealing out physical abuse, troops were lined up so they could slap and beat one another.[10]

The structure of the Imperial Army loosely resembled the ancient feudal system the masses had been accustomed to for generations. Now officers were the "lords," acting directly for the emperor, or so the recruits were to believe.

Average soldiers had no human or legal rights. Loyalty to the emperor and absolute obedience to superiors (who spoke for the emperor) were expected.

GIs entering boot camp in America, by comparison, were aware they had certain rights as individuals (though they may have doubted this from time to time). They knew they must disobey an illegal order, and they received a brief introduction to international law in regards to war. If punishment became too harsh during basic training or at any time, the soldier reserved the right to complain to his commanding officer, the Inspector General (the IG), or even send a message to his senator.

American soldiers received education on behavior expected of them in combat and how civilians and prisoners should be treated. Infractions of these rules were isolated, and not the standard practice of the United States military.

The average Japanese soldier was totally ignorant of things like international law and moral codes of compassion. No one told him there were rules of war written in Geneva. He knew only about obedience, sacrifice, and that war most likely would be a struggle to his death. He did not expect to return home unless with honor. Since surrender was prohibited, he had to be victorious or dead.

With harsh treatment in boot camp, the Imperial soldier feared his officers and NCOs more than the enemy. The enemy kills, but the cadre could humiliate, stripping a man of all honor. It is no wonder that there were a high number of suicides amongst Japanese recruits.[11]

Once the Army was given full power, they implemented a strange form of Bushido, "the way of the warrior," emphasizing dying as much as serving.[12]

For generations, until 1900, the Japanese class of samurai lived by Bushido and a code of honor, serving lords and masters much the same as medieval knights in Europe.

The samurai class had the power of life and death over the masses. They needed no court to hear a case. Basically, in the field, they possessed the power of *kirisute gomen,* the privilege to strike down any subject of lesser rank, according to the samurai's judgment or mood.

In the old days, a samurai did not sacrifice his life needlessly. He had been drilled and educated to be much cleverer than that. By surviving, he continued to serve and fight again. But if he brought dishonor upon himself or his master, ritual suicide was the accepted fate.

With the Imperial Army's new form of Bushido, the forfeiting of one's life for the emperor became the standard philosophy taken to an extreme.[13]

For his blind obedience to commanders, the Japanese soldier experienced two rewards, pride and the right to carry special weapons. Prior to 1930, the people of Japan were accustomed to being unarmed. Many had only a knife, the *tonto,* and trained to defend themselves with martial arts without weapons.[14]

These included forms of what later became known as judo and kung fu borrowed from the Chinese, and tae kwon do from the Koreans. They also developed their own art, karate or "empty hand" (without weapons).

During medieval times only royalty and the samurai carried weapons, first swords, the bow, and a variety of blades. Later, firearms introduced by Dutch, Portuguese, and a few English traders were added to the arsenal.

By the end of the 1800s, the samurai were ordered by the government to disarm and put away their swords. It was time for a modern army.

As a new form of government emerged, molded after European countries, the military struggled for control. And then, as the new Imperial Army emerged, each foot soldier began to receive a special gift from the emperor: a rifle.

The average soldier could not be a true samurai because those days were gone and he had not been born of that class. Regardless, the emperor declared that he would have a blade similar to the spear the ancient warriors once carried into battle, only now his blade was a bayonet. The emperor's seal, the chrysanthemum, had even been stamped upon the rifle. The simple, obedient soldier believed he possessed a gift from a god.

Even though officers may not have been of samurai heritage (though some were), they and noncommissioned officers, including the rank of corporal, were granted permission to carry a saber. They could use their family's samurai sword, if one existed, or a government-issue, mass-produced blade, less magnificent perhaps, but still effective. (Some labeled the samurai sword a "saber" due to the slight curve in the blade.)

As a result of the brutal, intensive training, the cultural traits, the blind obedience, the group mentality, and the strong sense of pride and honor, a major problem existed with the Japanese soldier. Conditioned to work with the "group," he simply lacked the ability to think or reason as an individual. This produced soldiers who were at a complete loss when their leaders were killed.[15]

Without leaders, the Imperial soldiers' tactics or behavior became spastic, hysterical, and usually suicidal. Attacks on Allied positions sometimes lacked good creative planning. Or, when a successful plan was once devised, they continued to use it over and over again. Alert GIs never fell victim to the same tactic or trick a second time. Japanese infantry often launched wave after wave of attacks when no other plan could be formulated.

American soldiers were conditioned to be imaginative and to think on their feet. The GI knew that he must be prepared to assume command if a superior was killed or incapacitated. Yankee ingenuity as well as bravery saved many individuals and units in World War II.

In the 1930s, Japan unleashed its highly trained armies on Manchuria and China. With ample news coverage, the world soon learned of Japan's brutality against the conquered people. Officers and NCOs strengthened their spirit, they claimed, by beheading thousands of Chinese civilians. Soldiers were permitted, even encouraged, to rape and murder at random. Civilians were used for bayonet practice. Many were tortured or burned to death for amusement.[16]

To those who knew Japanese history, the behavior of their military in China came as no surprise. Through centuries of civil war, the Japanese had shown their own people little or no mercy after a battle.

But to most Americans, the war in China was between Asians, and far away. Wrapped in the spirit of isolationism, they closed their minds to atrocities in China.

Europe had problems with Nazi Germany, and that is where the American focus remained. The discussions centered on how much help should be sent to Great Britain and Russia to stop Hitler while remaining neutral.

In 1940, world affairs began to take a turn for the worse. Japan's aggression in China brought an American embargo of raw materials, which the empire desperately needed.

Japan had succeeded in building a strong military including aircraft and carriers to deliver them. But most everything about the Japanese and their military was superficial. Regardless of progress in technology, their thinking and psychology was still feudal. The worship of an emperor as a god was not in itself their problem. The methods and desires of the Imperial Army, though, was about to lead millions to their death.

The people of Japan had become hypnotized with their military's early success in Manchuria and China. Fascinated and excited by Imperial Army propaganda, they naïvely believed what their military government told them. Asia, they were convinced, did indeed belong to the Asians, not the colonial-minded Americans, French, and British.

At that time, few Japanese knew anything of world affairs, and most were unaware of the atrocities their Army was committing in conquered lands.

By early 1941, the Imperial Army felt invincible, but somehow their plan of total war in Asia just wasn't working to perfection. The military draft of fighting men was mishandled. Skilled technicians, those needed to build and run manufacturing plants, were drawn into the Army as regular soldiers. Few farmers were left to plant and harvest crops. Soon people in the big cities found food in short supply.[17]

The military even had problems with organization. Every nation has experienced interservice rivalry, but by mid-1941 Japan's Army and Navy were behaving like *enemies*. The practice of withholding secrets, plans, and strategies from one another had gone beyond competition between armed forces. Partly, this was due to the fact that their Army and Navy were created and developed in different traditions.

The Army followed the code of the samurai warriors, while the Navy modeled itself on modern fleets of the Western world, especially

Great Britain. The Japanese Navy considered itself superior to the Army, more modern in thinking and technology.

This feuding only added to Japan's other problems. Raw materials needed to wage war, such as iron, oil, rubber, copper, aluminum, etc., were not only in short supply (thanks in part to the U.S. embargo), they had not been stockpiled to prepare for a lengthy war.

As World War II began, the Japanese also suffered from a shortage of manpower, spreading themselves thin throughout the Pacific. Even though their initial plans for attack were brilliant, it soon became obvious that everything lacked depth. Food, medicines, and munitions were in short supply as their armies occupied so many places far from home.

Not all Japanese were "warmongers." Many politicians and businessmen continued to push for a peaceful solution through 1941. Even a few top military leaders expressed serious concern about entering a war with America.

They warned that America had always followed a tradition of "fair play," and if her friends or territories were harmed, revenge could be severe. The emperor suggested his politicians pursue peace through every possible avenue. But all this would be pushed aside by the wave of action planned by the military.

The United States had not only cut off exports of so many things needed in Japan, especially oil, it also demanded the Empire withdraw from conquered territories from which raw materials could be extracted. To Tokyo, America was engaged in economic blackmail.

To control the Pacific, the Japanese knew they must prevent the powerful U.S. Navy based at Pearl Harbor from coming to the rescue of any of her island bases. In addition, the British Army and Navy in the Pacific had to be destroyed in order to assure successful conquest of Southeast Asia.

Most Japanese leaders expected the U.S. to fight a limited war after an attack on Hawaii, then negotiate a peace in order to concentrate all its efforts against Hitler in Europe. Imperial officers assured their government that America would seek peace after fighting a limited offensive to ensure their West Coast remained safe from invasion. The U.S.

would surely grant all captured territories to Japan, avoiding fighting a war on two fronts (the Pacific and Europe).

The great Japanese miscalculation was based on observing the strong support for isolation and neutrality in America. This they incorrectly analyzed. The United States must eventually help its British friends, but would turn its back on people in the Pacific, so they thought. Asia, the Japanese calculated, would soon be under their rule, once that American fleet was neutralized at Pearl Harbor.

CHAPTER 4

*"There is no such thing as impregnable
defense against powerful aggressors who sneak
up in the night and strike without warning.
We have learned that our ocean-gate
hemisphere is not immune from severe
attack—that we cannot measure our safety
in terms of miles on any map anymore."*

President Franklin D. Roosevelt

Radio Fireside Chat

December 9, 1941

**Screven County, Georgia
December 1941**

Ten-year-old Betty McKinney pulled back slowly on the reins commanding the mule to halt. Then she gave the leather strap a little tug, guiding the wagon to the edge of Stoopto Road. The dirt was still soft from yesterday's cold December rain. As the wagon creaked to a stop, she leaned over to see if the steel-clad wooden wheels had sunk into the mud.

Then she stood up on the bench seat and stared at a line of trees about a hundred yards away. With a small hand, she shielded her eyes from the winter sun, which sat low on the horizon.

There was J.R., walking slowly through the field, cradling his old .22 single-shot rifle in his arms, followed by twelve-year-old Hamp.

When Betty was born, their father gave J.R. the assignment of guarding and teaching her the basics of fishing and hunting. The same assignment continued when Hamp came into the world.

Later, Betty believed that their father recognized that "Jake," as she affectionately called J.R. during her youth, was physically weaker than the other boys due to his childhood illness. Dewey also had difficulty understanding J.R.'s independent thinking and his persistence of doing things "his own way."[1]

With J.R.'s hunting skills, it seemed logical to let him continue as the family's "meat gatherer" while the other boys sought more physically demanding jobs at nearby farms. Although J.R. did occasional "odd jobs" for neighbors, and lent a hand with the farming, he never considered himself a serious farmer.[2]

Betty had developed a bubbly personality like her mother Nattie and, even at ten, her face suggested she might develop into an attractive young lady. Though she already knew a little about tracking animals and fishing and could chop wood (all thanks to J.R.'s guidance), Betty was no tomboy. Nattie would see to her daughter becoming a lady, a farm girl, of course, but also a lady.

That afternoon along Stoopto Road, Betty was on a special assignment to bring her two hunting brothers home earlier than usual.

"Jake, Jake!" she yelled, stretching on tiptoes to get J.R.'s attention.

He waved, but then turned and started toward the trees.

"Jake! Wait!"

She jumped from the wagon, her bare feet sinking into the soft earth.

"Jake! Hamp! You all wait up for me, ya hear!"

Betty began a dash through the field, her light brown hair bouncing at her shoulders, an unbuttoned dark wool sweater flowing behind her.

The boys halted and Hamp, holding a slingshot J.R. had made for him, faced his sister, who was rapidly closing the distance between them.

J.R.'s .22 rifle was the same one that he'd gotten from Mr. Parker eight years before. It remained the only gun in the McKinney family.

"Here's your best gal!" said Hamp to J.R.

"Hi, Hamp. What did you shoot, Jake?" she asked, panting for breath.

"Four squirrels," he replied, turning to show the game tied to his belt. "Got a rabbit spotted up by the trees."

"Them's nice ones. May I come along, please, please," she begged, still trying to calm her breathing.

J.R. laughed. "Sure. The rabbit is in the brush up yonder." He pointed with his rifle. "Reckon he's laying low, hoping we'll forget about him. Move up ahead real slow like I taught you, and flush him out for me."

Betty reported years later that the thrill of joining their hunt caused her to momentarily forget the purpose of her trip.

"Oh!" she exclaimed, placing both hands to her cheeks. "I almost forgot."

"What?" asked Hamp.

"Mama said you all gotta get on home now."

J.R. often remained in the woods alone after dark, but their mother knew that with young Hamp along, they would return by dusk.

"Is something wrong?" J.R. inquired.

Betty's eyes were wide as she reported, "The president's gonna talk on the radio tonight, about eight o'clock!"

"The president! What for?"

"Don't know. Pa says we can all go to Mr. Parker's store and listen to the radio. Everybody from all around gonna be there, Ma says, including me. I get to stay up late. The president's gonna tell us about the war!"

"What war?" asked J.R.

She shrugged her shoulders. "Don't know what war. I'm just a girl. Daddy gonna see you boys when we get home."

The Parker Store remained the community center for sharecroppers in that part of the country and for anyone who happened by. None of the local cabins had electricity, and battery-powered radios were too expensive, a luxury one could only dream of owning! The Parker Store had more than one radio, and when there was a broadcast of anything of interest, a boxing prize fight, a ball game, or the Kentucky Derby, people were invited to stay and listen as long as they desired. That night the radio would bring the president of the United States to the nation, including twenty-five farmers and their families at the Parker Store.

The hunting party crossed the field and reached the wagon. J.R. announced that he would drive. The waiting mule was turned and they began to roll up Stoopto Road. Back at the tree line, one lucky rabbit survived another day.

Betty remembered that J.R. seemed locked in deep thought, quieter than usual during the ride home.

The wagon turned onto a smaller dirt trail that led up a gradual sloping hill to their cabin.

Betty, sitting as usual next to J.R. on the driver's bench, broke the silence.

"Remember!" she said tugging at J.R.'s shirtsleeve and pointing to the edge of the trail. "Right here, wasn't it, Jake?"

"Yes," he acknowledged, "but forget about it, Betty. That was last spring."

Somehow children have a way of remembering an incident, resurrecting the memory, oblivious to the discomfort the thought might bring to others.

"A good thing you tried to do, Jake," she said.

"Sure enough," added Hamp.

Betty was referring to the previous spring. With their father Dewey driving the wagon, the family was returning from Sunday church service.

Before World War II separated the McKinneys, they traveled together to their Baptist church every Sunday. J.R. is not remembered as a churchgoer, but that doesn't mean he never attended. That day, as usual, he requested permission to remain outside during the service with his customary excuse: "Jesus can hear my prayers out here, can't he?"

Nattie knew her son's discomfort in crowds and, as before, assured him, "The Lord can hear you wherever you are."[3]

Now, on a chilly December afternoon, Betty thought back several months to that particular Sunday. Their wagon wheel had run over a quail's nest at the spot she pointed to. Only J.R. and Betty noticed the accident. He instantly leaped to the ground from the rear of the wagon.

Dropping to his knees, he attempted to repair the nest. The wagon continued on another thirty yards to the cabin's front porch and the family went inside to prepare for Sunday dinner.

Some minutes later, as food bowls passed from hand to hand, Dewey finally asked, "Where's J.R.? Not like him to miss dinner, or any food for that matter!" There were a few chuckles around the table. Everyone knew J.R.'s fondness for any kind of food.

"He had no particulars for any special thing, except the fish he caught," Betty said later. "He just liked food, and he would eat anything you gave him."

"The wagon wheel ran over a nest of baby quail," Betty answered. "Jake's trying to fix it."

"Where?" puzzled Dewey.

"Down the trail a bit."

Everyone paused. The room was quiet. J.R.'s behavior was sometimes "different" and his reasoning difficult to understand.

"You all eat!" their mother ordered. "I'll see to J.R."

Nattie removed her apron and kicked off her high-heeled Sunday shoes as she started out the door, followed closely by Betty.

They found J.R., still on his knees gently replacing twigs, rebuilding the nest around four young chicks. Nattie kneeled down beside him.

"Aren't you hungry, J.R.?" she said softly. "Dinner's served."

"Tell 'em to eat," he replied. "I'm almost done. I'll be there soon."

"I did," she said. Then Nattie noticed her son had been crying. "You understand," she added, "if you touch the chicks, the mother may not return to feed them."

"I know. I'm not touching them. It don't seem fair. Everything deserves a chance to grow up. When it comes time for them to die later, then that's nature."

Nattie hugged her son and pulled him to his feet, almost forgetting that he was now five feet eight inches tall.

"Come on, dear," she said. "You've done all you can. Let 'em be now, and nature will do the rest."

Betty had stood behind her mother, remembering the times J.R.

took her fishing and insisted that small fish be returned to the waters, not only because there were laws governing the size one may keep, but because he knew it gave them a chance to grow up. The same was true of animals. He never killed anything young, even if passing up game meant he had to hunt longer to get his quota for a meal.

At first, no one spoke when J.R. sat down at the table. All were busy eating "like they were starving," Betty related later.

Then the oldest brother, Ralph, stated in a mocking voice, "J.R. was saving them chicks just so he can shoot 'em out of the sky someday!"

J.R. glared at Ralph and replied, "We were taught in church to protect helpless things and care for the suffering. That's what Jesus told us to do."

"Jesus been talking to you out in the swamp, J.R.?" Ralph continued in his tease.

Betty came to J.R.'s defense. "Just maybe he did, Ralph!"

"Yep. Maybe," J.R. injected, his glare turning to a smile.

"You all hush!" Nattie scolded. "Eat your dinner and be thankful to the Lord for all this food."[4]

Eight months had passed since the quail incident. Now, the December darkness conquered the farm quickly as they reached the cabin. Gray smoke rising from the brick chimney assured them that a warm fire awaited.

Inside, the main room had its familiar orange glow from kerosene lamplight and the wonderful aroma of baking bread.

"Soon as you clean those squirrels, J.R., I'll fry 'em up and dinner will be ready," said Nattie. "You all who have homework, try to get it done before we eat. We have to be at Mr. Parker's before eight."

Betty remembers sprawling on the floor in front of the fireplace, using its light to begin her school assignments. She admitted that her eyes may have been on the book pages, but her total attention remained on what their father was explaining to the boys at the kitchen table.[5]

Dewey told them that since Sunday afternoon he had spent most of his time at the Parker Store with other farmers listening to radio broadcasts about the Japanese attack on Pearl Harbor. He reported the details and how the other men seemed in shock, refusing to believe the news. "Why would a tiny country like Japan attack America?" they asked one another.

Dewey McKinney went on to tell of President Franklin D. Roosevelt's official announcement to Congress and the American people the day before. With a pencil, Dewey had written down the president's words on the back of a page from a 1940 calendar so he could repeat the information to his family. He began to read the president's words, "Yesterday, December 7, 1941—a date which will live in infamy—the United States of America was suddenly and deliberately attacked. . . ."

"What's infamy?" Hamp interrupted.

"Means forever."

Then their father concluded with the last of the speech: "With confidence in our armed forces—with the unbounding determination of our people—we will gain the inevitable triumph, so help us God!"[6]

They discussed the little knowledge they had on the world's situation during dinner. Mostly what they learned about Japan's war in China and Germany's conquests in Europe came from others visiting the Parker Store. The best information seemed to be brought in by the more educated traveling salesmen who visited from Savannah, Sylvania, and Atlanta.

There was the smell of rain in the cool night air on December 9, 1941, as the McKinney family left their cabin about 7:30 P.M. and walked the three-quarter-mile path to the Parker Store.

They were joined there by other farm families who drifted in from several directions. All stood about in a sober atmosphere waiting for the president to tell them what events had developed during the past twenty-four hours. Some even expressed hope that Mr. Roosevelt would assure them that everything had already been resolved. Perhaps there had been a mistake and there would be no war. Conversations were in muffled voices "like we all were attending a funeral."[7]

At 8:00 P.M. a hush fell on the store as the voice of President Roosevelt came from the radio speakers. He began his "Fireside Chat #140":

The sudden criminal attacks perpetrated by the Japanese in the Pacific provide the climax of a decline in international immorality. Powerful and resourceful gangsters have bonded together to make war on the whole human race. . . . The Japanese have treacherously cut the long-standing peace between us. Many American soldiers and sailors have been killed by enemy actions. American ships have been sunk. American airplanes have been destroyed.[8]

Those who held hopes that there would be good news could feel their disappointment drape over them. But J.R. told Betty that he suddenly felt a strong sense of patriotism, "stronger than ever before."

The president outlined the history and past relationship between the U.S. and Japan, and stated that the course the Japanese Imperial Government followed paralleled that of "Hitler and Mussolini in Europe and Africa."

Then he had more depressing information about places most of the farmers knew existed, but little more than that.

"So far," he continued, "the news has been all bad. We have suffered a serious setback in Hawaii. Our forces in the Philippines, which include the brave people of that commonwealth, are taking punishment, but are defending themselves vigorously. The reports from Guam and Wake and Midway Islands are still pending, but we must be prepared for the announcement that those three outposts have been seized. The casualty lists for these first few days will undoubtedly be large."

Roosevelt cautioned about repeating rumors before information was confirmed and instructed everyone, especially the news media, "It must be remembered by each and every one of us that our free and rapid communication these days must be greatly restricted in wartime. It is not possible to receive full, speedy, accurate reports from areas of combat. To all newspapers and radio stations—all those who reach the eyes and ears of the American people, I say this: You have a most grave responsibility to the nation now and for the duration of the war . . . . You have no right to deal out unconfirmed reports in such a way as to make people believe that they are gospel truths."

He assured his listeners that America had been in the process of gearing up for a war. Some National Guard units had been activated months earlier in anticipation of conflict. There was enough food for all of us, he said, and raw material supplies were sufficient. Yet, each citizen must be prepared to make sacrifices. Then he stated, "It is not a sacrifice for any man to be in the Army or Navy of the United States. Consider it a privilege. . . . The true goal we seek is far beyond the ugly field of battle. When we resort to force, as we must, we are determined that this force shall be directed toward ultimate good as well as against evil. We Americans are not destroyers—we are builders! We are going to win the war, and we are going to win the peace that follows."[9]

No debates followed the president's speech on the radio and nothing was said "along party lines." The president of the United States had spoken and the people, including the news media, supported him. A time of national crisis drew Americans together, and the voices of those who had preached a doctrine of "neutrality" were smothered. How could one be neutral or critical of the president at a time when Americans were being killed by Japanese in the Pacific and by German submarines on the waters of the Atlantic?

There was no cheering or applause in the Malcum Parker Store as the president finished his talk. A few eyes were dry, many were not. It was a solemn time, leaving most people perplexed and fearful of what lay ahead. If the men left for war, who would work the fields? How would those at home survive?

Each night through the Christmas season and into January, the McKinney family sat before the fireplace for over an hour and discussed the news from the war front as relayed by radio at the Parker Store and newspapers brought there by those traveling salesmen.

The older boys talked of joining the Army, but Dewey insisted that J.R. wait as long as possible.

"Let the draft come for you, son," he said. "The family needs to survive, and you and I are the providers."

Dewey had turned forty-five. At that age, it was unlikely the military would need him. But alone, he could not successfully work even a one-horse farm. There were discussions regarding the possibility of Dewey seeking employment at a factory in Sylvania, eight miles away.

As the family made plans for the future, one night the subject of girlfriends and the best way to say good-bye came up. Ralph, Dewey

Jr., and Jack all admitted that they had dated, but none had a serious relationship. Saying good-bye to those girls would not be pleasant; neither would it be disastrous.

The shy J.R. confessed he once took a girl for a ride in their wagon, and even walked with another girl in the moonlight. Everyone laughed. J.R. had no serious romantic involvements to be concerned with.

Ralph, never missing an opportunity to tease J.R., suggested, "Maybe if J.R. goes in the Army, he's gonna meet some city girl and she'll kiss him!" More laughs.

J.R.'s face flushed, noticeable in the glow from the fire. "Ahh, I don't need no girlfriend," he answered. "If a girl kisses me, I'm just gonna have something to worry about. What I need a new girl for? I got Ma and Betty, the best two gals in the world, a-waiting for me!"[10]

CHAPTER 5

"The reconquest of the Philippines was different
from any other Pacific campaign. It
was the only one in which large organized
guerrilla forces backed by loyal civilians
made an important contribution to the
defeat of the Japanese."

Major Robert Lapham

Lapham's Raiders

Simultaneous to the Japanese air attack on the U.S. fleet at Pearl Harbor, American bases in the Philippines suffered devastating assaults.

The Philippines, a chain of some 7,107 beautiful islands, had been moving toward independence from their occupier, the United States, who seized their country from Spain in the late 1800s.

In 1935 the first president of this American commonwealth, Manual L. Quezon, invited General Douglas MacArthur, then Chief of Staff in Washington, to come to the islands and build a defense force, modeled on the Swiss "citizen soldier" concept. MacArthur was given the rank of Field Marshal by the Filipinos and ten years to build their army. By that time, the details for Philippine independence should have been resolved.

MacArthur's task would not be an easy one. Washington had little money to spend on the Philippines. As a result, MacArthur's army would be mostly equipped with obsolete weapons.

In the U.S., a few National Guard units were activated and sent to the islands. With these men, MacArthur had over thirteen thousand U.S. troops to train twenty thousand Filipino regulars and 100,000 raw reservists.

But eighty-seven different dialects are spoken throughout the islands, producing a tangled mess of misunderstandings. By late 1941, none of the units had actually trained together.

With most of the Philippine army concentrated on the main island of Luzon, plans for defense seemed adequate and simple: fight a delaying action while withdrawing to an area difficult for the enemy to penetrate, and prevent access to the valuable harbors at Manila Bay, Cavite, and Subic Bay, then wait for help from the massive U.S. fleet at Pearl Harbor.

Unfortunately for the Philippines, their mere geography and the presence of those American bases would be detrimental to their future. Their islands were situated between Japan and the oil- and rubber-rich areas of Southeast Asia.

At dawn on December 8, 1941 (December 7 in Hawaii), over 750 Japanese bombers and fighters hit American air and naval bases on Luzon, catching most U.S. aircraft on the ground. The Japanese land invasion began two days later.

As planned, MacArthur initiated the strategic withdrawal into the mountainous peninsula of Bataan, establishing his headquarters on the tiny island of Corregidor, which blocked the entrance to Manila harbor, and waited. But the U.S. fleet had been crippled at Pearl Harbor and Washington's focus was on the war in Europe. There would be no help coming to the Americans on the Philippines. They were written off as expendable.

General MacArthur departed Corregidor by PT boat. He arrived in Australia on March 17, 1942. There, he faced a press conference and announced, "The president of the United States ordered me to break through the Japanese lines and proceed from Corregidor to Australia for the purpose, as I understand it, of organizing the American offensive against Japan, a primary objective of which is the relief of the Philippines. I came through and *I shall return!*"

On April 9, 1942, American defenses in the Philippines collapsed.

The Filipino-American army on Bataan, more than eighty thousand men, surrendered and the famous "Death March" began as they were moved from the battlefields north eighty miles to Camp O'Donnell.

During the march, Americans experienced firsthand the brutality of the Imperial Army. Over 2,200 U.S. servicemen and twelve thousand Filipino soldiers were beaten, hacked, or shot to death along the route. Since the Japanese followed the medieval warrior code of Bushido (and not Geneva Convention Articles of War), they believed surrender a dishonorable act. The Allies were not prisoners, but "captives."

A month later, Corregidor surrendered. Their defenders joined their comrades at O'Donnell and other prisons scattered about the islands.

At O'Donnell, disease, starvation, torture, and beatings killed American and Filipino soldiers in staggering numbers. In May and June 1942, the death toll reached more than five hundred men a day.

Late June brought a change at Camp O'Donnell. A new Japanese commandant was assigned with plans to begin a phase of pacification with Filipino soldiers, but no particular orders regarding the disposition of Americans.

Over the next several weeks, the Filipinos were released after they agreed to sign a statement of allegiance to Japan and promise never to take up arms against the Empire again. It was a promise very few Filipinos planned to keep. They were sworn members of the United States Army and that was where their loyalties remained.

The American captives were eventually transferred to a variety of work camps. About 6,500 were sent to Cabanatuan, a former army training post just outside the city of the same name. A few hundred were shipped to Davao Penal Colony on the island of Mendanao. With the Americans now in slave-labor camps, the Japanese were ready to grant independence to the Philippines. But it didn't take long for the islanders to realize that their independence was simply freedom from American dominance. They were now under control of the Japanese, who offered no definite plan for freedom.

Before World War II, the Japanese had never expressed any hatred for the Filipinos. Of course, they did believe they were racially and culturally superior to all non-Japanese Asians. The government of the

Philippines was to be modeled after the so-called puppet government established in Manchuria a few years earlier. So the Empire moved ahead with such plans, believing everyone was satisfied.

But the Japanese proved to be bad administrators, and the affection most Filipinos still held for the Americans soon became obvious to the conquerors. Once again, as in Manchuria and China, the Imperial Army seemed preoccupied with demonstrating their racial arrogance and superiority while diplomats attempted to phase in the new government.

All things considered, it is still difficult to explain why the Imperial Army turned their inhuman cruelty on the people of the Philippines. To some degree, it may have been resentment that the Filipinos desired to remain with America, and not be under Japanese control.

In some situations, the Japanese Army might justify their actions as necessary to teach the rebellious Filipinos how to behave. The frustrated Army attempted to seek and destroy pockets of people believed to be supporting guerrillas, and villages supporting guerrillas were destroyed. Those thought to be members of a guerrilla band were tortured for information and executed.

But otherwise, the brutality against the general population defies explanation.

The Filipinos had a long-standing reputation of being a fun-loving, peaceful people, but they were not to be intimidated for long. The Americans had seen another side of the Filipino personality during the insurrection in the early 1900s. U.S. troops learned that the islanders could easily become emotional, enrage quickly, and drift into becoming the most vindictive people our Army had ever encountered.

After the insurrection, a healthy relationship developed between the people of the Philippines and Americans. Schools, roads, libraries, and factories were built and trade was established to help the islands prepare for independence. Many in the Philippines came to regard the U.S. as "big brother," which Filipinos called a "colonial mentality." Mostly, they respected America and counted on the U.S. for protection.

Now that the Americans were beaten and MacArthur had seemingly deserted, Filipinos still refused to show affection toward the Japanese.

By mid-1942, the angry Imperial Army initiated a system of barbarism, torture, and terrorism directed toward civilians. The Army roamed Luzon, ignoring local laws and customs, beat, slapped, and raped women at random, and forced their "subjects" to bow to the lowest-ranking soldier.[1]

For artillery practice, entire villages were leveled, the surviving inhabitants rounded up and either beheaded or bayoneted to death. "Village rape" was common, often organized by officers who usually participated in the crime. Women as young as twelve and as old as fifty were repeatedly raped by platoons of infantry while families were forced to stand by helplessly and watch.[2]

The Filipinos had never really had a country. Spain dominated the islands for over four hundred years; then the Americans came, promising independence. After thirty-five years, there was still no freedom, only occupation. Now, Japan was proving to be the worst of all masters. The Japanese had no one to blame but themselves for what followed. Unfortunately for the Imperial Army, they failed to capture all American soldiers during Bataan's surrender. On Luzon, about one hundred GIs from various branches of service managed to elude enemy patrols and escape through the lines into the mountains and the agricultural area known as the Central Plains. On other islands, a few resourceful soldiers and some civilians joined guerrilla bands and began attacks on the Japanese.

The Filipinos may never have had a country, but they did have their families and town mates, which they treated like relatives because most usually were distant kin.

General MacArthur knew the Filipinos, and he was certain they would fight ferociously to protect their families and barrios. He counted on that to keep the enemy off balance, perhaps preoccupied, until he could form an army and return. But he also knew that the Filipinos needed leadership. There are, of course, a few "born" leaders in every culture, but most Filipinos had never been given the opportunity to lead anyone.

Leaders had to materialize, men the Filipinos could admire, experienced men they would respect and follow into combat.

Then, at a time it was most needed, fate produced something beyond MacArthur's wildest expectations. The American soldiers who had survived Bataan began to link with small guerrilla bands. As news spread of Americans joining the guerrilla movement, small "bands" quickly grew into sophisticated military units.

But the Americans had to first prove themselves not only worthy of trust, but sincere in their desire to fight the Japanese. They could have hidden in the mountains and waited for MacArthur to return someday. The Filipinos would have fed them and most would have survived. But as it was, they organized the guerrilla units and led them into battle. Naturally, the American guerrillas encouraged their men (and civilians) to continue to support the old concept of government, assuring them that the United States would return to rescue them.

Affection for the Americans and the freedom they promised was not the only motivation for Filipino allegiance. The vicious and inhumane treatment of these people by the Japanese sparked a flame that, in a short time, developed into one of the most violent guerrilla wars ever experienced by any nation.

Second Lieutenant Robert Lapham joined a loose group of freedom fighters in Central Luzon and promoted himself to major. With a civilian mining engineer, Harry McKenzie, and a number of Filipino officers who'd also avoided the Death March, they began to organize what became known as the Luzon Guerrilla Armed Forces (LGAF). Two lieutenants, Juan Pajota and Edwardo Joson, were promoted to the rank of captain by Lapham and assigned as commanders of their areas. By the end of the war, the LGAF numbered over thirteen thousand highly disciplined, well-trained soldiers. Joson and Pajota were then promoted to the rank of major in the United States Army.

Ray Hunt, one of the few Americans to actually escape the Death March slaughter, recovered from tropical illness with the help of villagers and began to organize a fighting force.

Other men, like Captain Joe Barker, Colonel Gyles Merrell, Captain Jack Spies, Private Leon Beck, and Colonel Claude Thorp, remained mostly in Central Luzon with their guerrilla armies.

Captain R.W. Volkman, an Eleventh Division intelligence officer on

Bataan, and his signal officer, Donald D. Blackburn, made their way to the northern provinces. There they organized and trained troops and waited.

Throughout 1942, Filipinos flocked to Americans in magnetic fashion, and in some cases, begged them to lead the resistance.[3]

To the islanders, the Americans were brave and, indeed, intelligent.

Actually, the American survivors of Bataan may have been brave, but they had no idea how to conduct a guerrilla war. None of them ever attended a military school on the subject because none existed. No books or even Hollywood movies were available to provide guidance in unconventional warfare. None were born great, though many would achieve fame later for their military accomplishments. In the beginning, they simply wanted to survive. Leadership was something dumped upon them, but they polished and perfected skills as the dangerous war "in the shadows" wore on.

The American leaders maintained contact when possible, often launching coordinated attacks on the Japanese, but generally operated independently of one another. By September 1942, they had already gathered vital intelligence data, attacked patrols and convoys, destroyed enemy outposts, and begun to wreck lines of communication.

As Robert Lapham reported later, "It was always a mean, dirty struggle to the death."[4]

The guerrillas appreciated that their movement could only flourish in an environment where they had the support of the majority of civilians with the courage to endure the continued threat of destruction of everything they loved.

Yet, even with that support, more than half of those one hundred Americans who escaped Bataan would die before MacArthur returned. Many died of wounds and disease. Some were killed in gunfights with the Japanese. Still others were captured or simply gave up the fight and surrendered. Those who did were either shot, beheaded, or tortured to death.[5]

With all their brutality and military training, the Japanese were never completely successful in stamping out the resistance. They had no schooling in counterinsurgency. The only tactic they knew was to deal out more brutality. Then, before the end of 1942, they had another enemy to contend with among the Filipinos.

Luis Taruc broke from the American concept of government in the mid-1930s and began a movement that he hoped would result in a separate political party by the time Philippine independence was granted. Taruc's vision for this new party, socialism, was a little different from socialism in other parts of the world.[6]

Basically, he wanted large land holdings broken up and rights given to the peasants.

He was convinced that pure socialism and communism would never be successful in a nation whose people had been Christian for hundreds of years (eighty-five percent were Catholic in 1941), and partly he became frustrated because he could not rid himself of his own belief in Christ.

Throughout Central Luzon, thousands of peasants came to Taruc for guidance and to listen to his ideas about what he called a Christian-democratic-socialist party.

The leaders of the communist party were a different breed. Their cold, hard ideas and lack of acceptance of God could not be tolerated by Taruc. Unfortunately for Taruc, his followers would be labeled by the rest of the world as communists.

Disagreements between the socialists and communists would, by necessity, be put aside when the Japanese invaded Luzon. Taruc, at age twenty-eight, was appointed commander in chief of the combined socialists-communists.

Commander Taruc formed his men into well-disciplined squads and called his army Hukbo ng Bayan Laban sa mga Hapon, or "The People's Army to Fight the Japanese." By mid-1942, they had become known as the Hukbalahap, and finally, the Huks.[7]

At least in the beginning, the Huks and the Luzon Guerrilla Armed Forces had one thing in common, the elimination of their mutual enemy, the Japanese. In early 1942, the Huks won some hard-earned victories in a number of skirmishes with Japanese patrols. But it soon became evident that their accomplishments might be ignored by the Americans once MacArthur returned.

As the war continued, supplies arrived by U.S. submarines for the

LGAF, but not for the Huks. In fact, civilians and members of the LGAF were instructed by American commanders to ignore the Huks.

Once radio communication was established between LGAF units and MacArthur's headquarters, orders were issued to consider the Huks communists and, therefore, enemies of the U.S.[8]

Taruc's dream of a separate political party once freedom was granted lay in jeopardy unless the Americans recognized the Huks as a popular movement among the people of the Philippines. Friction between the strong communist members of the Huks and the somewhat middle-of-the-road socialists reached a flash point. Skirmishes developed in various provinces as Filipinos began to kill one another in a struggle for control.

The communists insisted that their party's survival depended on impressing the Americans with victories. For that, they believed, they needed the new weapons delivered by submarine to the LGAF. The Huk logic, distorted as it may have been, was simple: Destroy other Filipino guerrilla units, take their weapons, then use them to fight the Japanese. The American leaders and their guerrilla units now faced two dangerous enemies.

When Robert Lapham and the other American Army personnel safely avoided the Bataan surrender, a United States Air Corps lieutenant also escaped. Bernard Anderson, with the help of Filipinos along the way, made it safely to the Sierra Madre mountain range along the east coast of Luzon. There he found men, former members of the Filipino-American army, who needed someone in Tayabas Province (now Aurora) to lead their resistance group.

Lieutenant Anderson promoted himself to colonel and organized a guerrilla force that, like Lapham's, would number in the thousands by 1945. His area of influence eventually extended south through Bulacan Province and the very edge of Manila.[9]

Bob Lapham's force operated mostly west of Tayabas Province in Nueva Ecija, but he and Anderson communicated when practical, and often discussed plans for special missions.

One of the men serving as a bridge for this liaison was Major Lapham's most respected Filipino commander, Captain Juan Pajota.

Pajota had established a headquarters near Barrio Macatbong on the eastern slope of the Sierra Madre Mountains high above the flatlands of Nueva Ecija and the central plains.[10]

Before the guerrillas enjoyed the luxury of radio, messages were sent by the "bamboo telegraph," which was the most reliable means of communicating.

Bamboo telegraph was the slang name given to an ancient means of sharing information. Many Americans never really understood how it functioned. In fact, some 1940-era Hollywood films depicted Filipinos sending messages by beating on drums and calling it bamboo telegraph. On Luzon, the Filipinos never used drums to communicate.

The bamboo telegraph was simply a method of supplying information using runners traveling between barrios, moving in something like a relay race. Most of the time, the information was reliable. If a runner was captured by the Japanese, no written message existed. True, a few were caught and tortured. Most of those died rather than revealing anything critical.

The Filipinos had long had a reputation of being fond of gossip. Details on just about everything had been passed from place to place and back again. Yet, during the guerrilla war, information sent by bamboo telegraph remained surprisingly accurate.

Colonel Anderson's area of Tayabas included not only the Sierra Madre Mountains, but the coastline with Baler and Dingalan Bay. The Japanese had taken over a sawmill at the north end of Dingalan Bay. From there they sent freshly cut timber to various areas where barracks were being repaired. Anderson's men maintained a constant surveillance of the sawmill activities, and reported that the Japanese showed little interest in the rest of the coastline south of Dingalan Bay during the early war years.

Bob Lapham remembered Bernard Anderson. "He was not ruthless or reckless, but extremely calculating and cautious."[11]

Cautious, yes, but with Anderson's area of responsibility, it became difficult for him to adequately train and inspect each unit or squadron (the designation used by the guerrillas to confuse the Japanese). The enemy knew the size of they American Army's company, battalion, and division, but the title "squadron" was not listed in any Imperial Army manual indicating how many men were assigned.

The Huks were also in Nueva Ecija and Bulacan. Because of the internal fighting between socialists and communists, some became disenchanted and joined up with the LGAF, including Anderson's units. A few, unhappy with that decision, returned to the Huks. Still other Huks refused to commit themselves to either the LGAF or the communists until MacArthur returned and the final victor in the war became obvious.

Whatever the reasons, Colonel Anderson apparently had difficulty completely controlling all his men in the Sierra Madre and Dingalan Bay area. As a result, the loyalties of many guerrilla warriors, especially around Dingalan Bay, seemed to be in question in both Pajota's and Anderson's headquarters.[12]

CHAPTER 6

Refrain your voice from weeping and
your eyes from tears, for your faith
shall be rewarded and they shall come back
from the land of the enemy.

Jeremiah 31:16

Screven County, Georgia
Early Autumn 1942

John R. McKinney was not a man wrapped in complexities, nor had his shy, gentle personality changed since childhood.

With the world at war, it was not long until J.R. received his draft notice. The family was, of course, concerned. They'd expected that summons to come someday. How would someone like this quiet man survive in the Army?

But John McKinney was far more flexible than they realized. The family knew hardship from growing up poor and long hours in the fields that yielded few rewards. And J.R. had the advantage of not only understanding nature, it was as if he and the wilderness were one.

Like his older brothers, he picked cotton, planted peanuts, and had walked hours barefooted behind a mule-drawn plow. He never complained to anyone about anything, except perhaps when the fish "weren't bitin'" on a particular morning.

No doubt the peace and solitude J.R. found in the Georgia wilderness near Woodcliff formed some of the basic structure of his personality.

That and hours of plowing fields in rows of cotton alone can produce a man who is accustomed to saying little. He had always been happier hunting and walking the trails through the woods and swamps or fishing in the muddy streams that crisscross Screven County, cutting her into something that, on a map, looked more like a jigsaw puzzle.

Alone and comfortable with his thoughts, he created questions in his mind without criticism or argument from anyone. His curiosity centered mostly on the mysteries of the wilderness. The answers he would seek alone.

The mule did not need to strain as he pulled the McKinneys' faded, old wood wagon along the tightly packed dirt of Stoopto Road that morning. And he would complete the eight-mile journey to Woodcliff before there would be a reward of water and oats.

Dewey McKinney, Sr., sitting on the driver's bench seat, held the reins loosely and muttered a casual comment to his wife, Nattie, from time to time.

The youngest brother, Hamp, now almost thirteen, sat between them, staring at the mule, and said nothing. His thoughts, he later told his sister Betty, were focused on searching for an explanation. Why were his brothers being taken from him to go fight in a war? He felt both proud and angry that they were leaving.[1]

First the oldest, twenty-two-year-old Ralph, joined the Seabees. Then Dewey Jr., or "Tink" as they called him, volunteered for the Army, not waiting for the draft to pull him in.

Nattie McKinney, like so many mothers, prayed the draft would not call John R. For reasons she believed sound, she would not permit him to volunteer. She strongly felt her son was a very special young man. His hunting and fishing had always provided food for the family. If he had to leave, it would surely cause more hardship for those who remained. But she also thought of J.R.'s physical handicap, the lung damage when he was a child, still evident in the deep, ugly scar next to his left shoulder blade, his shyness, the soft, gentle manner, his simple, uneducated mind.

Every Sunday since it all started in December, she talked to God about J.R. He was not an "Army-type man." Maybe he could be spared from the war. Must she give up all her sons, including this special boy?

But the draft of the Selective Service had the names of all age-qualified men in the country. The draft would reach into every city and farm and sharecropper's cabin. The military would decide who was physically fit for service. The military would feed and take good care of the men until it became their time to die.

Nattie McKinney once told her daughter, as she remembered the trip that day in the squeaky wagon, that somewhere along the road things became clear to her.

"The Lord knew the Army was gonna need J.R. The country needed him! How could I have been so selfish to think I could keep him home a moment longer?[2]

"Then, slowly, as if someone was lifting a terrible weight of sadness from my shoulders, I began to realize that J.R. will do fine. Perhaps a simple mind will be more open to learning new things, especially since much of it is similar to his experiences. How to hike and shoot a rifle and follow orders without question."[3]

J.R. McKinney, wearing his "Sunday" shoes (his *only* shoes), denim trousers, and a wash-faded shirt with his draft notice and instructions folded in the pocket, sat next to his sister, Betty, on the smooth wooden bed of the wagon.

Betty held J.R.'s hand, squeezing it now and then, and would not release her grasp until they reached Woodcliff.

Sitting across the bed from the two, fifteen-year-old brother Jack continued to stare at J.R. as if waiting for the brother he idolized to speak. Jack had announced proudly the day before that he would enlist in the Navy on his seventeenth birthday if the war wasn't over by then.

And J.R. finally did speak to his brother. "A long time ago Dad told me I gotta protect Betty. Learn her all the stuff I know about hunting and so forth, case she ever got lost. I've been a-showin' you and little Hamp all the tricks I've learned. Both you all done real good. Now it's your job to take care of her, Jack, till you leave. Then you show Hamp so he can take over. You all take care of her till I come home!"

Jack's eyes squinted for several moments, then he replied while nodding yes. "You come home, J.R.!"

" 'Course," John McKinney assured him.

Betty suddenly reached up and affectionately touched the dimple in J.R.'s chin.

"Sugar bowl!" she teased with a giggle.

"Ahh, hush!" J.R. pushed her hand away, his blue eyes flashing with a smile.

With loose-hanging sandy brown hair already bleached from working in the sun and a small frame of five feet, eight inches, and 145 pounds, John R. McKinney resembled hundreds of other skinny country boys in America leaving for the Army that week.

It never occurred to him that someone else might tease him about his dimple. That was a special privilege he allowed Betty to enjoy. The brothers mentioned it from time to time, and the result was usually a wrestling match.

The wagon moved onto Rocky Ford Road. Again, the dirt was hard-packed, free of ruts, and with only a few holes.

Dewey McKinney, Sr., turned his head and called out over his shoulder, "J.R., did you go and say good-bye to Uncle Russ?"

"Yes, sir."

"How's business?"

J.R. grinned. "Uncle Russ complained about competition, but the government ration of sugar ain't gonna hurt him none."

Uncle Russ had operated a moonshine still for years on a remote strip of land in the Ogeechee River known as Black Island.

Russ met J.R. at the bank of the Ogeechee nearest the little village of Rocky Ford and rowed him across the waters in a leaky, flat-bottom boat. When it was tied to the shore, no one would believe it was still in use because of its terrible condition. That was exactly what Uncle Russ wanted.

"Government agents from the big cities a-lookin' for my still will be scared to even step into this here boat," he once told his nephew.

J.R. spent an entire day with Russ the week before the trip to Woodcliff, and was offered the usual dented metal cup containing a sample of the latest batch of "white lightning." J.R. politely took a sip and handed the cup back to his uncle.

"That boy never were much a drinker," Russ reported to Betty McKinney. "But he sure was curious about stills and what makes 'em work. I taught him all I know. Not certain he's ever gonna try the business, though. He's always busy huntin' something."

Uncle Russ spent most of that day with J.R. They lay out on the warm sand that stretched from the tree line on Black Island and disappeared into the dark waters of the Ogeechee. They watched fish jump for a while, then talked about "revenuers," the draft, and who the Japanese were and why they would be so foolish as to bomb Americans. A serenade of crickets announced the coming evening before Russ rowed J.R. back to shore.[4]

The wagon slowed to a halt at the "crossroads" in the center of Woodcliff. A hand-painted sign stating "Bus Stop" had been nailed to a light pole.

It seemed to Betty McKinney that the journey was much too short. Soon, a bus would take her favorite brother and friend away, and she began to cry when she thought she might never see him again. Comfort came when J.R. gave her a long hug.

J.R. had always been a stranger to his father. They never argued; J.R. was too respectful for that. Yet, everyone recognized a distance existed between them.

Now, Mr. McKinney felt compelled to speak as all fathers must at a crucial time.

"Son," he began, trying to catch the eye of J.R.. But the young man stared down at the sandy ground. "You have some good things to give to your country while you're in the Army," his father continued. "You are small, but strong, hard work has made you strong, and you can walk farther than any city boy. Remember to always be polite and respectful and obey the orders of your superiors. Learn from the older fellas. You are good at shootin'. Maybe you can teach your new friends a thing or two about that. And, Lord, you have patience, more than your brothers. Reckon you learned it from all that time in the woods, and us being poor. And you are plenty brave!"

John R. McKinney, who usually had difficulty looking into his father's face, suddenly glanced up. Father and son's eyes finally locked.

"Yes, you're brave," Mr. McKinney continued. "No more than knee-high to a grasshopper and you was off into them swamps, all by yourself. Shucks! I've known some grown men who wouldn't be going into them swamps alone! You are plenty brave, son. You be proud who you are. And remember, we are all plenty proud of you."

And then for the first time that Betty could remember, J.R. and his father embraced. "Not a cool how-do-you-do hug, but one of them both . . . we all could feel."[5]

John McKinney at age twenty had never been on a bus because he never had anywhere to go that walking couldn't take him to.

Now he was on board that huge vehicle with only one person he knew, another county resident, Junior Brown. They would not meet again for a long time.

The hardworking people of Screven County knew the pain of giving up their sons to fight for freedom.

The first call to arms had been in 1779 when the British marched through the central Georgia countryside. During World War I, they lost thirty men killed in Europe. In 1942, the county had a population of about twenty thousand men, women, and children. By the end of 1945, fifty-seven men from Screven County had died fighting in World War II.

CHAPTER 7

*"In my opinion, the M1 rifle is the
greatest battle implement ever devised."*
General George S. Patton

In early 1941, America, watching war developing in two parts of the globe, began to awaken from its isolation slumber.

Congress appropriated funds to expand airpower and the Navy. Sixteen million Americans registered for the first peacetime draft.

President Roosevelt activated National Guard units, including the historic "Golden Cross," the Thirty-third Division.

To the people of Illinois, it seemed the Thirty-third and the United States grew up together. Its troops played a key role in the early "Indian" campaigns, helped suppress the 1898 Philippine insurrection, and won praise for its performance during World War I. Although the Thirty-third was in combat for only a few months, nine of her soldiers received the Congressional Medal of Honor for bravery.

The shoulder patch of the Thirty-third is circular with a gold Greek cross of equal arms on a field of black. Reportedly, one of the division's regiments painted a yellow cross on its equipment during the Moro campaign in the Philippines. Yellow was a forbidden color to the Muslims. The practice carried over into World War I, and this led to the shoulder patch.

After activation in March 1941, members of the Thirty-third moved to their first training site, a military reservation crudely chopped out of thick woods in Tennessee known as Camp Forrest. Ironically, a Northern unit would be training, not in Illinois or Wisconsin, but at a post named for a Civil War enemy, Confederate General Nathan Bedford Forrest.

When they arrived, Camp Forrest was nothing more than a conglomeration of wooden buildings, streets of mud, and a parade field pocked with pools of stagnant water. The troops set about improving conditions, and began training in a serious effort to bring themselves to a state of combat efficiency.

Officers and cadre were mostly from Illinois, though a few called neighboring Michigan home.

When the Japanese struck Pearl Harbor on December 7, 1941, all furloughs were canceled and the men of the Thirty-third were ordered to prepare to "move out" on short notice. At first, only a few were sent to industrial areas of Tennessee and Alabama for antisabotage guard duty.

By January 1942, America's situation in the Pacific was rapidly deteriorating and infantry units were desperately needed to stop the fast-moving Japanese military. The 132nd Regimental Combat Team was sent to New Caledonia, where it was incorporated into the Americal Division. By the end of 1942, they would see combat on Guadalcanal and in the Solomons.

Infantry divisions back in the States reorganized for faster mobility and greater striking power. The Thirty-third soon became little more than a skeleton division, but continued to train in the hot, sticky Tennessee climate. They did not realize at the time how that Tennessee weather was preparing them for future tactical situations.

In September 1942, fortunes of the Thirty-third took a turn for the better when they received orders to proceed to Fort Lewis, Washington. There, troops found a modern Army installation waiting. Barracks, kitchens, and dayrooms were in immaculate condition. The beauty of Mount Rainier, fifty miles to the south, was enjoyed, along with the crisp invigorating weather, unlike the exhausting climate of Camp Forrest.

For a while, the Thirty-third shared Fort Lewis with the Forty-fourth Infantry Division and the Eighty-seventh Mountain Infantry Regiment.[1]

On September 25, 1942, almost a year into the war, Fort Lewis received a special visitor. President Franklin D. Roosevelt arrived to inspect the post, and promised the troops that they would soon have the very best in modern weapons and equipment.[2]

While infantry divisions in the States continued to reorganize and train during 1942, the early months of that year saw numerous victories for the Japanese military in the Pacific. It seemed as if nothing could halt the arrogant Imperial Army.

In January, the Japanese occupied Manila as American and Filipino forces under General Douglas MacArthur completed a strategic, preplanned withdrawal into the mountains and jungles of Bataan and the island fortress of Corregidor.

Allied forces holding on in the Philippines and delaying the Japanese advance were promised help: more troops, planes, and ships. But Washington had written off MacArthur's men as expendable. No help arrived.

The British surrendered Singapore, Malaysia, Hong Kong, and were driven out of Burma. The Japanese invaded Borneo and the Dutch East Indies as American forces on Wake Island and Guam surrendered.

By the end of April 1942, Allied forces were forced to surrender in the Philippines. The Japanese, now holding most of Southeast Asia, landed on the northern end of New Guinea, threatening Australia.

The first Japanese attack on the United States mainland came on February 23, 1942. An enemy submarine off the coast of Southern California fired shells into an oil refinery, starting fires and setting off a major panic among West Coast citizens, who feared a Japanese landing.

With all the fear and frustration in the United States, President Roosevelt signed Order #9066, authorizing the relocation of more than 100,000 Japanese Americans from their homes to remote internment camps around the country. The government had no way of determining who among them could be trusted or who might be involved in espionage or even resort to sabotage.

In retaliation, Japanese forces in the Philippines rounded up American civilians and dependents of military personnel and imprisoned them inside the walls of the old University of Santo Tomas.

A mood of depression became the major enemy among civilians in the U.S. Factories ceased production of Chevrolets, DeSotos, Plymouths, and Studebakers. Ford Motors also stopped production of automobiles, and joined Willy's Truck Company in producing a small, strange new vehicle for the military called the jeep.

But soon American superiority in science and industry became obvious to even those Japanese who still ignored their own economic and raw-material inadequacies.

In the U.S., the propaganda mill was successful in convincing civilians that U.S. military might depended on Americans' ability to outproduce the enemy.

Americans had long thrived on taking the initiative. They were no longer lost in depression. The mood shifted. Now everyone looked to the military to take every chance to strike back at the Japanese.

In February 1942, Navy fighter pilot Edward O'Hare became America's first World War II ace by downing five Japanese bombers in four minutes as the enemy formation approached the U.S. carrier *Lexington* off the Solomons. Awarded the Medal of Honor, O'Hare later disappeared on another mission. But only two months into the war, he had proven that the U.S. also produced good aircraft and pilots. Later, grateful Chicago citizens changed the name of Orchard Airfield to O'Hare Field.

Unknown to the Japanese, U.S. intelligence personnel had broken most of their codes, giving our military a tremendous advantage in battles to come. At the Coral Sea, a Japanese invasion force heading for Port Moresby, New Guinea, was intercepted by the U.S. Navy. Suffering heavy losses, the Imperial Navy turned back.

Lieutenant Colonel James Doolittle led sixteen bombers off the carrier *Hornet* (something the Japanese believed impossible) for an attack on several cities in Japan. This surprise air raid pushed an arrogant and angry Japan into trying to prove their superiority by attacking the U.S. island of Midway.

Knowledge of the Japanese code again paid off. The Americans were waiting to trap the enemy fleet near the tiny islands.

The battle at Midway quickly became a disaster for the Imperial Navy, which never again had the superiority they enjoyed during the first four months of the war.

The bloody battle for Guadalcanal proved that American land forces were determined to go on the offensive. By December 1942, the U.S. marines who led the initial attack on the island were reinforced by Army troops.

On New Guinea, the Imperial Army had been halted by the Australians. With Americans entering the battle, the Imperial Army was forced on the defensive.

Back at Fort Lewis, three days after the presidential visit in September, the Thirty-third Division created a new infantry regiment; the 123rd. The existing 130th and 136th regiments were tapped for commissioned and noncommissioned cadre to help form the 123rd.[3]

The 123rd would soon become the home of John R. McKinney.

From October through December, "filler replacements," draftees and volunteers, poured into Fort Lewis. These raw recruits came from practically every state in the Union. The Thirty-third would no longer be an Illinois or "Yankee" division. These new men brought with them their religions, dialects, personalities, and diversified talents; the basic fibers that made up America now connected them as members of the Golden Cross Division.

* * *

Since the development of gunpowder, armies have continued to invent new firearms to more effectively kill one another.

In the late 1800s, the U.S. Army received lever-action rifles and pistols with revolving cylinders, replacing earlier single-shot weapons. By 1905, the .45-caliber automatic pistol had replaced the revolvers.

In the 1930s, militaries around the world, including Japan and the U.S. Army, still employed bolt-action rifles in a variety of calibers as "the standard foot soldier's weapon."

What the American military needed was a new type of rifle that could give her soldiers an edge in future conflicts.

By the late 1930s, with war escalating in Manchuria, China, and Europe, the U.S. Army tested a rifle invented by John C. Garand, and approved it to be the standard weapon for the infantry.

What was so special about Garand's invention was the fact that it functioned as a "semiautomatic"; a cartridge was fired and ejected and another entered the firing chamber automatically each time the shooter pulled the trigger. It was not necessary to crank a bolt back and forth to eject a cartridge and inject a new one.

It was officially called the U.S. rifle, caliber .30 M1 Garand, but GIs quickly shortened the name. Mr. Garand's invention became simply the M1.

His rifle would serve the U.S. military through World War II, the Korean War, a host of "police actions," and into the early days of the Vietnam War.

The men who most needed the M1, the combat infantry, received them slowly until after Pearl Harbor. Many GIs, trying to repel Japanese advances throughout the Pacific, were still fighting with the reliable but slow-firing bolt-action rifles.

The M1 fired a .30-caliber, full-metal-jacket ("ball") bullet from an eight-round clip, which was automatically ejected after the last round fired, producing as it left the rifle a distinctive high-pitched metallic "ping." This sound brought criticism of the weapon. At close quarters, the enemy would know the GI's rifle was empty, and a few precious seconds would be required to insert another clip of ammunition.

For combat, the rifleman would be issued one or more cotton cloth bandoliers with ten packets, each a little larger than a pack of cigarettes. Each packet held one eight-round clip, giving the soldier eighty rounds per bandolier.

Usually in battle, the forty-four-inch long M1 had its ten- or sixteen-inch bayonet attached, producing a formidable weapon, even without ammunition. It seemed to most GIs that some accuracy was lost when the bayonet was affixed.

The American rifleman was trained, and practiced for countless hours, with the M1 and bayonet to prepare for hand-to-hand combat.

The rifle was strong, constructed of forged steel, with a tough but beautiful walnut stock, and weighed about ten pounds. In training the GI learned that even a small man, swinging it as a club, could smash muscle and crush an enemy's skull.

J.R. McKinney, like so many other GIs enduring the hours of bayonet training, did not realize at the time that the skills developed would eventually save his life.

As always, the military had precise and prescribed movements for the most effective way to kill an enemy with an empty rifle. These were called "butt-strokes," shortened by the men to "strokes." The butt, or end, of the rifle stock was capped with a heavy steel plate to protect the wood and add a little balance weight. The butt could be forced upward (vertically) or horizontally to strike the opponent. Movements, or "follow through," were completed by either plunging the bayonet into the enemy or striking his head with the butt. This was also accomplished by holding the rifle straight, braced by extending the forearm, hand closed around the stock near the front sight. The other hand grasped the pistol-grip area of the stock just behind the trigger guard.

All men in an infantry unit—cooks, mechanics, typists, drivers, and foot soldiers—were trained first as riflemen, qualifying with the M1 before completing basic training (boot camp) and moving on to their specialty training.

Many soldiers, because of early experience hunting, had a natural aptitude for shooting. Private John McKinney easily qualified with the M1 as an "expert," and became fascinated with the weapon's capabilities. Compared to his .22 single-shot, bolt-action rifle at home, the M1 was technology beyond his wildest dreams. The rifle's fully adjustable rear sight, complete with a recently developed locking bar, permitted the sight to be tightened once it was set.[4]

His .22 had only "open" or fixed sights and required physically moving the rifle up and down or left and right to compensate for conditions. The M1 could be adjusted for "windage" (the force of the wind) and for elevation or distance. To McKinney, President Roosevelt had kept his promise by delivering a wonderful new weapon.

"Sure wish I had one of these good old rifles back home," J.R. wrote his sister Betty. "Would make deer huntin' mighty easy."[5]

Another new weapon arrived for the foot soldier. The Army had long recognized the need for a small, lightweight weapon to fill the gap between pistol and rifle. An idea would come from an average American in an unusual situation.

David Williams, serving time in prison for moonshining, convinced authorities he had an idea for a new, small rifle unlike any produced. Naturally, prison officials were reluctant to give an inmate access to all the tools necessary to build a gun. But over time, Williams was convincing and successful. Authorities were impressed, and arranged for him to work with engineers at Winchester Arms Company.

By June 1942, six months into the war, the final version of Williams's invention was delivered to the Army. The little rifle, only thirty-five inches long, was officially the U.S. M1 carbine, a .30-caliber semiautomatic (some models had a "selector" switch, permitting full-automatic firing). Affectionately nicknamed the "war baby," to every GI during World War II, Korea, and Vietnam, it was simply the carbine.

The carbine was a shoulder weapon about one-half the weight of the M1 and, of course, much shorter. It fired its .30-caliber, full-metal-jacket cartridge from a fifteen-round detachable (reusable) box magazine. Thirty-round magazines were available, but many GIs believed them unreliable. Some reportedly caused cartridges to jam; others fell out of the weapon while the soldier was crossing rough terrain.

Carbines were welcomed by men carrying cumbersome equipment such as mortars, bazookas, and radios. Officers and NCOs found it valuable in addition to their .45-caliber automatic pistols.

The carbine had less range and hitting power than the M1 rifle, but its ease of handling, especially in jungles, made it perfect in the Pacific, where longer-barreled rifles often became entangled in the brush.

Except for some World War II–era modifications, there was nothing new about the powerful Browning automatic rifle. It had seen limited use in World War I, and remained the Army's standard full-automatic weapon for a rifle squad. It also fired a .30-caliber cartridge, but at a capability of 550 rounds per minute from a detachable twenty-round box magazine.

The "BAR," as this rifle was called, combined the portability of a rifle with the firepower of a machine gun (which usually required two men to operate effectively).

The A2 version of the BAR had a collapsible bipod for resting the front of the barrel on a hard surface. But the bipod added more than two pounds to the already heavy (twenty-pound) rifle, so some GIs simply removed it.

In World War II, the Army infantry squad of nine men was tactically organized around a single BAR. Thus, a four-squad platoon had firepower available from four BARs.

The Thompson submachine gun, or "tommy gun," was the only American submachine gun in production at the beginning of the war. It fired a .45-caliber cartridge (the same as the Army pistol), originally from a fifty-round drum. But the drums were heavy, noisy, and bulky. They were replaced by twenty- and thirty-round magazines. Despite its heavy weight of eleven pounds, the Thompson was popular with NCOs and many officers for its firepower and reliability.

Even though the tommy gun was effective, its cost of manufacture became a problem. A new lightweight (eight-pound) submachine gun was introduced in December 1942. Modeled after the British Sten gun, the U.S. version was made of stamped sheet metal welded together into an ugly but reliable fast-firing weapon. It also fired a .45-cartridge, the same as the pistol and tommy gun, from a detachable magazine at a rate of four hundred rounds per minute.

It was officially labeled the U.S. submachine gun, caliber-.45 M3, but the GIs dubbed it the "grease gun" due to its resemblance to the automotive tool of the same name.

Not only was the grease gun effective and useful, especially for paratroopers and tank crews (because of its small size), its cost to produce in the 1940s was under twenty dollars each.

As with all infantry divisions, the riflemen of the Thirty-third were not only proficient with their M1 rifles. They also cross-trained with the other small-arms weapons. In combat, it was recognized that any of the weapons, including BARs and machine guns, might become the only means of defense.

* * *

In the area of small-arms weapons, the Japanese had developed nothing much new by 1942. Many modifications to their basic infantry rifle, the bolt-action, Type 99, 6.5- and 7.7-caliber Arisaka, were mostly useless in combat. This included adjustable sights for firing at aircraft, an interesting idea but not practical.

First introduced to the Japanese infantry for their conquest of Manchuria in 1936, the Arisaka, despite its many alterations, was still in use in 1945.

For the average five-foot-three-inch soldier, this fifty-inch rifle was much too heavy and cumbersome, and it only balanced when affixed with its 15½-inch bayonet.

But the weapon, copied from early German Mausers, was easy to clean, required little maintenance, and proved reliable in combat. Opinions differed on its accuracy. The soldier learned to compensate for bullet drop or striking left or right of the target. Bullets often tumbled and broke up after being fired. But regardless of what the news media propaganda told the American public, in the hands of an experienced determined Imperial soldier, the Arisaka was a deadly weapon.

It wasn't the long, clumsy, outdated Arisaka with which Japan planned to win battles in the jungles of the Pacific. Their most valuable weapon on the ground was the fighting spirit of each warrior.

One weapon the Imperial soldier lacked was a reliable submachine gun, most needed in the jungle where the enemy is difficult to see. Japan did produce about ten thousand Type 100 submachine guns in 1942, but very few reached their infantry on Pacific islands. By comparison, that same year the U.S. manufactured over two million tommy guns.

But in the scientific field, the Japanese had made interesting progress. Their top physicist, Yoshio Nishina, had been working with molecular fusion since 1939. He successfully constructed Japan's first cyclotron in 1940, and discovered Uranium 237.

Nishina added to his team of unique scientists Shinichiro Tomonago, who would become world famous as a physicist in future years, eventually awarded the Nobel Prize for his achievements.

In 1941, Professor Nishina was chosen by the Japanese government to head a top-secret project; the goal, to create a new superweapon.

The scientists all knew that their work on splitting the atom would be applied to developing an explosive device with devastating capabilities. They were not certain just how powerful that device would be, but they agreed it might destroy a fleet of ships or even an entire city. Their job would be to develop the weapon; how it would be delivered was not their concern. First, they must prove they could build, test, and perfect the function of the weapon.[6]

The Imperial Japanese Navy had its own ideas of what to do with the device, and it had the aircraft to deliver it.

The world was aware of Yoshio Nishina's early work with the atom and fission, but as the war began, he and his team and whatever projects they were working on disappeared in a cloud of secrecy. At least in the field of science, once again Japan was shut off from the West.

From the beginning, Nishina's project, like so many others in Japan at the time, suffered from lack of raw materials. He needed uranium, about one thousand pounds of it. That would be enough to make two bombs.

By early 1943, Bunsaku Arakatsu, a former student of Albert Einstein, had been appointed liaison between the Navy and the scientists, thus assuring they, not the Army, would have control of the weapon.

Naval officers gave Nishina two years to complete his project and have the bombs ready for use. The target date, summer 1945. And they assured the scientists that they, the Navy, would provide the needed uranium in time to meet the deadline. Their friends, Nazi Germany, had already agreed to furnish the precious ore.[7]

CHAPTER 8

It was a mild winter at Fort Lewis in 1942. Training of the new "filler" troops in the Thirty-third Division continued at a steady pace. Then, in March 1943, the entire unit suddenly moved to the southern California desert. Everyone knew they were being prepared for the war in North Africa. Why else train in the desert?

The new home for the Thirty-third, known as Camp Clipper, occupied a small part of the Mojave sands about thirty-nine miles from Needles. Typical of desert climates, nights could be near or below freezing, and the days dry, almost unbearably hot. Sandstorms ripping through the camp made the routine forty-mile marches in 130 degree heat torturous, but the troops quickly became acclimated as much as any physically fit individual could.

The men were often broken into small patrols to move on forced marches with little food and only one canteen of water for the day, less than half the normal amount needed for any kind of walk in the desert.

The Mojave presented the perfect opportunity to test (and learn to depend on) the new compass and the M1 rifle, which operated perfectly in the dusty, sandy conditions.

Though gossip or rumors floated from tent to tent, as such things always have in the military, the thirteen thousand men of the Thirty-third were still certain that each day brought them closer to Africa.

John McKinney wrote to his mother almost every week. As expected, his penmanship was primitive. Spelling and grammar remained "third-grade" quality, but his mother and sister understood all the words and the feelings they conveyed. Nattie McKinney noticed that J.R.'s vocabulary began to expand almost immediately after he entered the Army. All those new words were spelled as they sounded to J.R.

"Ain't no place to fish in this here desert," J.R. wrote home in April 1943. "Just like the Bible says about the desert, not much livin' here. Ain't no ponds or creeks. No fish 'cause ain't no water. Could shoot jack rabbits. Ain't no need 'cause Army is a-feeding me good. But tell Betty them silly-lookin' rabbits is almost as big as her. Sure wanna come home."[1]

* * *

While the Thirty-third continued to tan and sweat in their desert training, encouraging developments in the North African war brought a new focus on the situation in the Pacific. The Allies had agreed at the beginning of World War II that Europe would be the first priority. But the German Army, trapped between U.S. forces and the British in Tunisia, had run out of fuel, ammunition, and food. By mid-May 1943, the Germans had surrendered more than 275,000 men to the Allies. Plans were already under way for the invasion of Sicily and Italy, and they did not include the Thirty-third Division.

Shortly after reveille on May 12, 1943, the division commander announced, "The Thirty-third Infantry Division has been alerted for a move overseas."[2]

There were many details to be worked out, but time enough for at least the large majority of men to enjoy a ten-day pass to be with loved ones before departure.

After completing the required physical examination and getting updated immunization shots, Private John R. McKinney headed for Georgia for his first visit home in almost a year.

He learned that his brothers in the service were doing well, at least according to their letters. Betty and the two younger brothers, his father and mother were all in good spirits, despite their worries about

J.R. and the news of the war that they learned mostly from the radio at Malcum Parker's store.

Excited as they were to have J.R. home for a few days, the family agreed that they should give him all the time he needed to hunt, fish, and be alone, if that was what he wanted to do. This was not easy for Betty, who became like a shadow of her brother, "following him everywhere and sometimes just simply sittin' and staring at him and waitin' for him to speak. He was my hero."[3]

Betty finally persuaded her shy brother to pose in full uniform with his dogs. The photo would be one she treasured for the rest of her life.

Oddly, J.R. showed no interest in hunting during his visit. Perhaps the Army had given him enough opportunity to shoot for a while. But fishing was another matter. He would spend some time with Nattie each morning after his father left for chores in the fields, and then seize his old fishing pole and be off to the muddy riverbanks. Naturally, Betty went along with him.

Mostly, they sat on the bank, waiting for a fish to take the bait, and talked little. J.R. had educated his little sister long before that "silence is one of the secrets to catching fish."

But on the last day before J.R. was to board a train at Rocky Ford for the West Coast, Betty could hold back her feelings no longer. The thrill of having him home now was conquered by worry and sadness.

"Jake, where they gonna send you next?" she asked, trying to hold back tears.

He turned and brushed a lock of brown hair from her face with the back of his fist.

"Don't know for certain," he finally answered. "I think the desert in Africa 'cause of the war there. Least that's what all the fellows are talking."

"Daddy says we're beatin' the Germans in Africa. Daddy says maybe you'll go to Italian!"

"Italian?" J.R. chuckled. "Is there desert there?"

"Don't know," she said.

J.R. laid his pole down on the sand and stretched. "Don't you worry, ya hear! Wherever they need me to go, I'll go. And I'll write soon's they tell me."[4]

Perhaps some long-forgotten member of the Army's medical examining team knew just how much weight John McKinney gained during that short visit home. "He never stopped eating until the day he left," Nattie remembered. "And he told us the Army had always given him plenty of food, but it just didn't always taste right!'"

Whatever the report on his weight gain during that short time, it would be his last gain for two-and-a-half years.

The different regiments began to make preparations to leave the United States. The 123rd was moved to Camp Stoneman at that time, just outside San Francisco. "We are moving one step closer to the enemy," the division commanding general announced.

Then began orientation courses to educate the men on what to expect during their journey at sea.

In late June 1943, the men of the Golden Cross Division were awakened in the middle of the night and told to assemble with all possessions, as few as they were, and their military equipment. After a few brief announcements, they shuffled with heavy "barracks" bags on their shoulders onto waiting ferries, which took them through the fog and darkness to piers at San Francisco. The men of the 123rd boarded the *Brazil*, a former South American tourist cruiser converted for use as a troop carrier, in silence.

Their destination was a guarded secret. In fact, there had been no news media announcements. There were no parades or cheering crowds to send them off. No loved ones blowing kisses or waving little flags.[5]

In two days they were far out to sea, away from the eyes and ears of America, or her enemies. Finally, the official announcement ended all the rumors. Their destination, the Hawaiian Islands.

John R. McKinney knew very little about world geography, so the announcement did not stun him as it did many others who had remained firmly convinced the Army must have had a reason for all that desert training. North Africa had remained the logical choice.

J.R. had no idea where Hawaii was, but he did know, of course, about the Japanese attack on Pearl Harbor.

At the first opportunity, J.R. approached his platoon leader, Sergeant Al Johnson, a tough Chicago native and member of the original Thirty-third cadre.

"We ain't going to Africa, Sergeant?" McKinney naïvely asked.

Sergeant Johnson smiled. "That's right, Mac. We're heading to teach them Japs a lesson!"[6]

While the Thirty-third Division had been training in the Mojave Desert, American forces were gaining some much-needed victories in the Pacific.

But the war was far from over. The Japanese Empire, despite its losses in 1943, seemed more determined than ever to hold on to those territories it had conquered in such a short period of time.

The Japanese Navy was not yet defeated, and there were millions of Imperial soldiers still scattered about the Pacific and Southeast Asia.

In February 1943, the Imperial Navy successfully evacuated eleven thousand troops from Guadalcanal, leaving behind thirty thousand dead comrades.

Tarawa fell at a cost of one thousand U.S. marines and sailors. In the four-day brutal battle, only seventeen Japanese soldiers survived of their original 4,700-man garrison.

The focus of much of the fighting in the Pacific would be on New Guinea.

Admiral William F. "Bull" Halsey led the Navy fleets, while Army General Douglas MacArthur commanded all American forces in the Southwest Pacific.

Admiral Halsey answered to Admiral Chester Nimitz. But this strange command structure worked well as the commanders agreed the majority of the time on strategies and methods of implementation.

The Japanese military, on the other hand, continued to have disagreements on practically everything, creating havoc even during crucial times.[7]

By mid-1943, the leapfrogging tactics of attacking some islands while bypassing others was successful for General MacArthur, mostly because of American dominance on the sea and in the air.

Japanese merchant shipping fell victim to American submarines.

This created even more problems for Japan. The raw materials they desperately needed were rapidly disappearing with each sinking ship.

The Japanese gave no indication of giving up the part of New Guinea they already held. With Australia sitting only one hundred miles from New Guinea's coast, the island held strategic value for both the Allies and the Imperial forces.

Australian troops returning from the war in North Africa were rushed directly into the struggle on New Guinea, and were assisted by American soldiers. They began a six-month campaign to drive out the Japanese.

It quickly became obvious to MacArthur's staff that all fresh units slated for New Guinea and other islands, which would serve as stepping-stones on his return to the Philippines, must have intensive amphibious-landing and hand-to-hand-combat training.

Practically none of the men of the Thirty-third Infantry Division had visited Hawaii, so they were not shocked when they arrived in July 1943 to see barbed wire and machine-gun emplacements on the beautiful beaches.

Martial law had existed on the islands since December 7, 1941, and had changed practically the entire way of life once enjoyed by tourists, servicemen, and the locals.

The islands continued to prepare for an invasion, but Naval vessels and air patrols ensured the Japanese would never again succeed in a surprise attack. But blackouts and strict civilian supervision by the military reminded everyone that the war had been there and could come again.

Upon their arrival, the Thirty-third was divided into different units, which were sent to small islands to strengthen defenses. John McKinney, with the 123rd Infantry Regiment, occupied the island of Kauai.[8]

There, the 123rd broke down into smaller detachments. Some were sent to beach defense areas and ammunition depots.

Each of these areas became the responsibility of junior officers, platoon sergeants, and squad leaders. The special jungle combat training they had expected would not begin for some weeks, but lessons learned in operating as small units would prove valuable later in New Guinea and the Philippines.

After weeks of "attack alerts," emphasis finally shifted to what they all had been looking forward to, squad training in the tropics.

Major General Percy W. Clarkson arrived in Hawaii on October 18th to take command of the Golden Cross Division.

A husky veteran of World War I, General Clarkson brought twenty-seven years of military experience to the Thirty-third. And his men soon learned that he possessed the aggressive air of a fighter, but often seemed relaxed and was not a stickler for formality. The general knew he had a difficult assignment to prepare the division for the long struggle back through island jungles to the Philippines.

By New Year's Day 1944, U.S. marines had successfully invaded the Marshall Islands. Once these islands were securely in U.S. hands, the tension lessened in Hawaii, for it seemed highly unlikely that the Japanese could attack. Consequently, the Thirty-third was relieved of defense duty and finally began jungle training. Their first experience would be learning to live in and off the jungle.

The men of the Thirty-third did not know it yet, but New Guinea was to become their first combat assignment. Kauai and Maui have vegetation and mountains almost identical to New Guinea. The islands had perfect locations for training.

A training center was constructed, and graduates from the Ranger school at Schofield Barracks were recruited to form the teaching staff.

The M1 and carbine functioned perfectly in the jungle despite the thick brush, humidity, sand, and dust. Most soldiers had already learned to trust their weapons, but this new test in the tropics fully convinced even the most skeptical that the two rifles were virtually indestructible. With proper care and cleaning, they never jammed or misfired.

Hours of firing from the hip suggested the importance of that technique in jungles, where an enemy might suddenly appear at close range, leaving no time to sight the weapon from the shoulder. This was, indeed, strange to "county boy" sharpshooters like John McKinney. Then there was more training with both the .30-caliber light machine gun and the heavy (water-cooled) weapon, as well as additional familiarization with the Browning automatic rifle (BAR).

Mortar men learned how to quickly and effectively fire their light (60mm) mortar without taking time to use sights.

Then came long hours of stream crossing, bayonet assault, and hand-to-hand fighting. Platoons and squads were separated into fire teams to practice the art of reducing or at least attacking pillbox fortifications. Although the men had already experienced considerable training in these tactics, new ideas and procedures were needed now that the Army had combat-experienced men returning from battle zones to explain just what it was like fighting the Japanese.

The introduction to the flamethrower weapon and to the employment of demolition charges was the grand finale, easily capturing everyone's attention. Then a "postgraduate" course in jungle warfare followed, once all division elements had finished every phase of the initial schooling.

Now training became more of a participation exercise under mock combat conditions, using live hand grenades and explosives to simulate real conditions.

By late February 1944, something new had been introduced to the Thirty-third, amphibious training. Indeed, the emphasis on small-unit landings on beaches was something new to the entire Army.

To prepare for this schooling, units were transferred to beach areas and all men, cooks, clerks, drivers, supply men, and rear-echelon personnel as well as riflemen, underwent amphibious training.

In the beginning the exercises were limited to shore-to-shore movements, so the troops became acquainted with only the LCVP (landing craft vehicle, personnel) and the larger LCM (landing craft, medium).

Everyone had to master climbing down cargo nets with their combat equipment.

Once all that was complete, the men, sectioned into "boat teams," took to the water in Navy-manned boats. After circling some four or five miles offshore, the landing craft headed back.

When the LCVP ramp dropped, the troops raced across the white sands and practiced attacking pillboxes, some made of concrete, some of logs and sandbags. And as with all military combat training, they did it over and over again.

In early March 1944, amphibious training ended and the Thirty-third returned to routine basic drills, firing small arms and gaining more familiarization with alternate weapons. By now, each man was very familiar with every small weapon in his unit's arsenal, including the .30-caliber machine gun.

Finally, the Army was convinced the Thirty-third Division was ready for combat duty with its three infantry regiments, the 123rd, the 136th, and the 130th. Each regiment had its support units ready, field artillery battalions, engineers, and medical battalions.

The Thirty-third's commander, General Clarkson, was ordered to take a quick trip to Australia to meet with General MacArthur. From there, he made a brief tour of a section of New Guinea, then returned to Hawaii. With his usual sincere and confident manner, General Clarkson spent time visiting each of his battalions, telling them to expect a "move-out" alert any day. This personal visit was a great morale booster and gave every man the opportunity to see his commander up close. The general expressed his pride in his men, assuring them that he was confident in their proficiency. In the wake of his talks, a new spirit swept over the division. They were, indeed, ready to meet the enemy.

Because of security concerns, the general could not disclose the division's destination, but everyone had guessed that New Guinea had to be the only choice. In April 1944, New Guinea represented the outer perimeter of General MacArthur's advances in the Southwest Pacific. Though the marines were slugging it out with the Japanese on a variety of Pacific islands, Army infantry divisions were engaged in fierce fighting in New Guinea.

Before the Golden Cross departed for "points unknown in the Pacific," they were given some days of rest so they could party and say good-bye in their own individual ways to Hawaii.

But many of the units, including companies in the 123rd Regiment, were far away from even the smallest town and had not seen a woman for months.

Some officers and NCOs did manage to find transportation on supply trucks and jeeps and visited "civilization." Others procured large quantities of beer for the men from their headquarters.

Those returning from towns brought a variety of interesting souvenirs.

One afternoon in mid-April 1944, J.R. McKinney was sitting on the ground outside his pup tent listening to Roy "Punchy" Phillips, a winner of thirteen pro boxing matches in the welterweight class. Punchy had also been the champion of that class at Fort Lewis while the Thirty-third was based there.

Punchy might have been a tough fighter in the ring, but outside and with his buddies, he was a very easygoing, soft-spoken young man who enjoyed relating blow-by-blow accounts of his most difficult matches.

As often happens in the military, unlikely friendships develop. Such was the case with J.R. and Punchy, who found the Georgia country boy a great listener who politely never interrupted a narration and, for that matter, did not even ask questions.

But that day Punchy was interrupted by two of their friends.

The first to speak was PFC Gerry "Ramp" Rampy, a five-ten Midwesterner who usually spent any idle moments reading paperback Western novels. With Ramp was PFC Gene Maziarz, a handsome Chicago native carrying a small "Brownie" camera.

"You fellows want to join us over at Sergeant Johnson's quarters?" Ramp asked.

J.R. said nothing as Punchy answered, "We're taking it easy. What's up with Sarge?"

"We heard they got some kind of party going on," Gene replied. "Sarge got us some beer from HQ and he may have some dames!"

"Dames?" Punchy responded as he stood up and dusted his khaki pants off with a large hand. "Come on, Mac," he said to J.R. "Let's go have some fun!"

J.R. got to his feet slowly and joined the three for a short hike down the dirt trail. As they neared Sergeant Johnson's small cabin, Ramp held out his arms, holding his friends back a moment.

"Wow!" he exclaimed. "Look at that!"

All four could easily hear loud talking, laughter, and beer bottles clanking, but that was not what shocked them. On the outside front wall of the cabin, next to the door, was a large, primitive WELCOME sign and under that, a big surprise. Nailed to the wall was a complete set of a woman's undergarments, a bra on top, a foot above a girdle attached to a pair of silk stockings, turned slightly, revealing the seam on the back.

Expecting that the display might be trophies from a recent conquest, the men quickly entered. A few more enlisted men were there along with Sergeant Al Johnson and their medical officer, Second Lieutenant "Will" Foley. The lieutenant had been an optician before the war, attended two years of ROTC at the University of Maine, and received a direct commission when hostilities began. He was a jolly officer who truly enjoyed being with the riflemen. It did not matter to him that his tough friend Sergeant Johnson was three years younger and had only completed grammar school.

At first, Johnson and Foley teased the new men that they had all "just missed the gals" who had now gone home.

Much later the truth was revealed and the mystery of whom those undergarments belonged to solved.

Sergeant Johnson and Lieutenant Foley confessed they had purchased the garments in a store in town and brought them back to the camp as a party joke. Disappointment was overcome with the help of the ample supply of beer. With it all resolved, PFC Gene Maziarz persuaded the two jokesters to step outside for a picture-taking ceremony with the girdle.[9]

Luxury liners once used for tourist cruises from San Francisco to Australia had been converted to troop transport use, and now the Thirty-third would be crammed aboard one.

On April 21, 1944, the 130th Infantry Regiment, known as the Blackhawks, boarded its transport ship. On April 25, the 123rd followed on the *Matsonia*. Then the 136th boarded the *Monterey*. By April 30, all units of the Golden Cross Division had bidden aloha to the Hawaiian Islands. The men had helped defend the territory for a while, but most important, learned valuable lessons about infantry tactics and survival in the tropics.[10]

Morale was now at an all-time high. Confident with months of jungle training, the men of the Golden Cross knew they were ready and would soon be going into combat, or so they believed.

CHAPTER 9

New Guinea

In early 1942 the Japanese had Australia in their sights when they invaded the 1,500-mile-long island of New Guinea. This largest island in the Pacific held some of the riches needed for Japan's survival—rubber, hemp, gold, silver, and in the cultivated areas rice, tea, coffee, corn, and tobacco. But important to the Imperial Army was the fact that Australia sat ready for the taking only one hundred miles from part of New Guinea's coast.

With so many fast victories in the Pacific at the beginning of the war, the Japanese were certain they were ready to take on Australia. But this could only be accomplished when their Navy was in place to lead the way.

When General MacArthur arrived in Australia in mid-March 1942, he received command of the U.S. Thirty-second and Forty-first Divisions and the Australian Sixth and Seventh, which had just been ordered back from duty in the Middle East. With these troops he planned to hold the Japanese in New Guinea and, thereby, protect Australia from an invasion.

MacArthur would rely on his imagination and skilled strategy (for which he later became so famous), but he also needed a lot of luck.

On New Guinea, the Imperial Army pushed to within thirty miles of Port Moresby, then suddenly stopped and withdrew. Some of the luck MacArthur needed began to unfold. Japanese carriers whose aircraft were to support the offensive at Port Moresby had retreated after the Battle of the Coral Sea. Planes slated to assist Imperial land troops were lost at the Battle of Midway, and their infantry on Guadalcanal faced serious defeats. Japanese convoys heading for New Guinea were attacked and virtually destroyed by Allied aircraft.

MacArthur knew the time was right to go on the offensive. He faked an attack at Salamaua on the east coast of New Guinea, but his men surprised the Japanese and seized Lae to the north. He then turned his troops on Salamaua, engaging a confused enemy. Soon MacArthur was ready to fight for sections of land farther north along the east coast employing a new type of attack—aircraft-assisted amphibious landings.

Another enemy besides the Japanese waited for the Allies on New Guinea. The entire island was hot and humid, its jungles and swamps saturated by almost year-round rains. Insects and leeches thrived in this environment, and so did the diseases they carried. Australian and American troops began to fall from scrub typhus, malaria, dengue fever, dysentery, and a variety of skin infections.

The U.S. Thirty-second Division entered its first battle with many men already weakened by sickness. Rations, medical supplies, and engineering equipment were lacking and, to make matters worse, the troops had not been trained in jungle warfare.

While Americans were slugging it out on New Guinea and other islands in the Pacific, the Imperial Army rapidly became isolated on New Guinea, but showed no indication of planning to leave. Instead, the Japanese regrouped in certain areas and constructed a complex variety of defenses including bunkers concealed by tropical vegetation.

But Japanese troops also suffered from disease and, as supply lines were severed, food and medicine stocks dwindled.

The Imperial infantrymen had only a few months' experience in the jungle, and though they adapted quickly, they too had no previous jungle training. (There are no jungles in Japan.) Their equipment, adequate for the China campaign, was, in general, poorly designed for a war in the swamps and jungle. The long Arisaka rifle was clumsy and constantly became entangled in brush. A rattling dust cover for the weapon presented other problems. (Most soldiers removed it.) Ammo packets lacked water protection; early leather gear deteriorated rapidly in the wet climate and had to be replaced with more durable "web" equipment. Their troops had no reliable submachine gun, which was needed for rapid, close firing in dense underbrush. By contrast, every U.S. combat unit either had or soon received carbines, tommy guns, and "grease" guns.

As the fighting continued in the Salamaua area, MacArthur became impatient with the slow progress and demanded a quick victory. He ordered Lieutenant General Robert L. Eichelberger to take command.

By January 22, 1943, General Eichelberger's men had cleared the enemy, killing about thirteen thousand Imperial soldiers. But the victory cost 8,546 American and Australian lives. In addition, 2,334 U.S. servicemen were forced out of action, disabled by disease.[1]

To counter MacArthur's advance, the Japanese planned attacks with ships and aircraft from the island of Truk, but Admiral Halsey, supported by carriers provided by Admiral Nimitz, destroyed a large percentage of those reinforcements. What was left retreated back to Truk. MacArthur's forces then began to push west across New Guinea and farther north along the coast.

For another year the sounds of war echoed through the jungles of New Guinea. The Japanese were fighting a losing battle. They knew it and Tokyo headquarters knew it. There were no plans to reinforce, supply, or even evacuate the remaining Imperial forces, which were now scattered throughout the central mountains and down the slopes to the western shore. "You must hold western New Guinea for the Empire" was the last message received by Imperial units in the field.

And while the Japanese dug in and prepared to fight to the last man, General MacArthur perfected his "leapfrog" attack tactics of amphibious landings up the coast of the island.

* * *

The Thirty-third Infantry Division arrived at Finschhafen, New Guinea, in mid-May 1944, expecting to be moved into combat in a few days. While disembarking, they paid little attention to the more than fifty cargo ships waiting in the bay for the chance to unload.

Finschhafen really wasn't a port city at all. It was nothing more than an outpost of government buildings, tents, and hundreds of jeeps and trucks grinding their way through deep mud along the narrow strip of land that separated jungle from ocean.

American forces under Sixth Army Commander General Walter Krueger had passed through Finschhafen months before, and were now engaging the Japanese farther up the coast in the Maffin Bay area.

There may have been no Japanese left to greet the Thirty-third, but there were other enemies. Mud and constant rain presented a new challenge for the men, especially the engineers who struggled to maintain drainage facilities. Clothes and blankets became mildewed and weapons required constant attention.

A division "post" consisting of pyramidal canvas tents and, in some places, thatched grass huts erected by the New Guinea natives would become living quarters for the Thirty-third for the next few months.

The natives, once fierce headhunters, had already proven themselves valuable allies. The Australians devoted considerable effort to civilizing and educating the people with kindness and rewards of needed goods. When the Japanese arrived, they set about stirring up hatred and resentment through needless torture and slaughter, as they had in all the lands they'd conquered in the Pacific. And the result, as usual, was the population turning against the Imperial Army. New Guinea natives became willing guides and bearers for the Allies, and assisted in a great number of laborious chores.

Private John McKinney's 123rd Regiment established its camp about twelve miles up the coast. Within a few days the troops were involved in serious combat training once again. There were more bayonet drills, bunker assaults, and advance amphibious training, all more intense and complex than they had experienced in Hawaii. The American

Army had already been exposed to months of fighting the Japanese in the jungle, and knowledge of every known enemy tactic and trick would be drilled into the Thirty-third's riflemen.

But the Thirty-third Golden Cross Division was about to be assigned the most distasteful duty in its World War II history.[2]

That backlog of more than fifty ships waiting offshore for docking had no manpower to unload them.

The men of the Thirty-third had been training since 1942—two years—to fight, first in the desert, then in the jungle. They were not dockworkers, yet someone had to do the job. Unfortunately, the task of unloading and sorting all the supplies from those ships fell to the Thirty-third. Forward combat and service units needed the supplies, and Americans in factories in the States had worked around the clock to provide them.

One regiment manned the docks on a twenty-four-hour schedule while another trained in the field. Then, after a few weeks, they rotated. Men on the day shift worked in driving rain and boiling sun and rested in tents in the cool of the night. Others slept in the midday heat.

Although very few of the men had previous experience in dock work, they quickly became proficient at it. Some learned how to operate wenches and cranes; others worked in the ships loading wooden pallets; still others assisted the loading and unloading of trucks that hauled freight to canvas or crude corrugated-metal warehouses.

But there were some rewards for all that hard work at the Finschhafen post. Fishing and swimming near the camp were permitted on some occasions. The engineers cleared fields and constructed baseball diamonds and basketball and volleyball courts.

John McKinney told his mother, "These fish ain't near as tasty as the ones in Georgia rivers."[3]

He never revealed just how much fishing he did or what he caught.

The men even received warm beer, though its distribution was tightly controlled. And, of course, letters could never state their exact location. Army "censors" scrutinized letters carefully, clipping or inking out information that could be valuable to the enemy. There were other benefits—Coca-Cola, frozen chicken, chocolate, and a variety of "home-grown" vegetables and frozen beef were made available to the men.

Certain times were allocated for relaxation, and popular radio stars performed (often in heavy rain) before thousands of cheering troops. Famous personalities like Jack Benny, Carole Landis, Larry Adler, and Martha Tilton, originally entertaining only at air bases, now donated their time to appear for men in combat areas. Their shows at Finschhafen could, in part, be credited to the USO.

Members of the Women's Army Corps (WACS) arrived to assist with clerical and a number of other duties, relieving men for the more strenuous work. Once women were at the post, the "Special Services" organized dances with big bands. Some musicians were provided by military units, but many came all the way from the States.

Life for the men of the Golden Cross was not really bad between May and September 1944. They worked long, hard hours at the docks, trained over and over again in the field in both rain and blistering sun. But the quality of food was good, and they had plenty of recreational activities and leisure time to relax, watch movies, or even pursue a hobby.

At the headquarters of the 123rd Regiment, an office of "Information and Education" was created. One of the most important duties was the publication of a unit newspaper (actually a few mimeographed sheets of paper stapled together), which they called *The Flying Dinosaur*. The first issue, dated May 22, 1944, contained headline news of the world, sports, and information from the home front. Special announcements pertaining to their regiment also appeared. The 123rd's *Flying Dinosaur*, often the only accurate news received by troops, continued to be published and distributed until the end of the war.[4]

Every soldier would remember his days at Finschhafen for his own personal reasons. Some recalled the beautiful flowers and parrots, wild pigs, movies, warm beer, and huge snakes. And each rifleman in the 123rd soon possessed a little ring made by natives (and some of the soldiers) from Australian silver florins. The fad of wearing one of those rings spread from company to company in a matter of days.

A 1945 photograph of Private John McKinney posing with a captured Japanese machine gun and wearing a ring on his left hand resulted in some believing he had married. He had not married. The ring was one of those made from a florin in New Guinea.

During some leisure time, McKinney, normally one to shy away from organized sports, showed an interest in baseball. He had watched a few games in Georgia, but was never given the opportunity to actually play. His family could not afford sports equipment such as baseball bats or gloves, but the Army seemed to have an ample supply of those treasures and encouraged each man to participate.

Some members of John's platoon convinced him to give the game a try, and he became instantly fond of the sport, so much so that baseball was listed as his sports interest in military records.[5]

Regardless of the comforts the military provided the Thirty-third, the men's morale began to fall drastically. They had been trained to fight, and they knew battles were being waged just a few hundred miles away in northern New Guinea.

Morale has always been a concern of command. As a result, General Clarkson, the Golden Cross commander, toured the base speaking to each battalion. He praised their work and honored them for their vigorous efforts while serving as "laborers." The men were assured that they were, indeed, contributing to the war effort and that their day to meet the enemy would come soon.[6]

PFC John "Mac" McKinney sat on a palm tree log one day in early July 1944, staring at the remains of a Japanese fighter plane that had been shot down a year earlier, crashed, and skidded on its belly into the bank of a slow-moving muddy stream. Its twisted fuselage and tail section remained partly submerged in the dark water. Its shattered canopy and the scattered bullet holes in its aluminum skin under the cockpit suggested something unpleasant had happened to the pilot.

McKinney's attention focused on the nose section of the plane. The missing cover revealed a large engine that appeared in surprisingly good condition, despite the fact that one blade of the propeller was missing, the other bent into an irregular, backward position indicating it had been turning at impact.

PFC Eugene Maziarz and Ed Colwell came upon McKinney studying the plane.

"Hey, Mac," said Maziarz. "Think you could have done a better job of flying that thing?"

"Nope," replied McKinney. "I ain't no pilot."

John McKinney got up and walked to the fuselage for a closer look at the engine compartment.

"Wonder what happened to the pilot," said Colwell. "Any blood in the cockpit, Mac?"

"Nope. Maybe washed away with all the rain." He turned to face his friends. "Everything I need is right here. I'll get busy tonight. I need some tools."

Adolph "Red" Barrette approached the group. "What tools?" he asked. "You gonna make it fly again?"

McKinney looked at his friend with a grin. "You fellows been complaining. The only alcohol you got is warm beer. I'm gonna make you some *real* whiskey . . . white lightning!"

"What!"

"He means moonshine, right, Mac?" Red added.

"Yep."

"You know how to make it?"

"Yep," McKinney assured him. "I gotta take some parts off this good old airplane."

Word spread rapidly through Company A about McKinney's project, but only a few were privileged to watch the construction phase. They gathered the tools he requested—hammer, hacksaw, wrenches, sheet-metal cutters, and screwdrivers.[7]

In a remote section of jungle, not more than a few hundred yards from A Company's camp, John McKinney constructed perhaps the only moonshine still ever to service the 123rd Infantry Regiment during World War II.

As John had envisioned, the still was assembled totally from parts of the wrecked Japanese plane. The copper oil and fuel lines were per-

fect to form a condensing coil, an aluminum wing fuel tank served as
the aging vat, and funnels were assembled from the plane's aluminum
skin, rolled, and hammered into shape.

It didn't take long for the story of McKinney's still to reach his
squad leader, Sergeant Sol Rocke.

It was mostly the report of unusual activity that caught his attention. The mess hall had been asked to save potato peelings for the next
few days. McKinney had promised to pick them up. To the mess sergeant, peelings were garbage, so no one bothered to ask what McKinney planned to do with them.

Then word circulated. Mac needed hard rock candy. Pure sugar
was in short supply, but rock candy, popular in the tropics because it
did not melt in the humid heat, was available in the chow line and also
could be found in C rations.

Sergeant Rocke visited John McKinney's construction site and noticed a pup tent shelter, half of which had been stretched above firewood to keep it safe from rain.

"Hi, Mac," said Rocke.

"Hello, Sergeant," John answered while adjusting something on the
copper coil with a wrench.

"What is this thing, Mac? Looks like a moonshine still."

"Ain't talking, Sarge," replied McKinney.

Sergeant Rocke was not offended. He and the men of his squad
were familiar with John McKinney's reply to a question he either did
not know the answer to or did not want to answer. It was a standard
reply with no insult intended.[8]

The sergeant knew very well what was going on. He also understood that the project had to remain a secret from the officers, or else
they might all be court-martialed. The questions on Sol Rocke's mind
were, would the thing actually produce alcohol, and how long could it
all remain secret?

J.R.'s uncle produced moonshine with good sugar, corn, and a few
"secret" ingredients. Lacking those raw materials, McKinney followed
a simple procedure his uncle had taught him, but employed necessary
substitutes.

He cleaned his still by boiling alcohol (from the dispensary) through the system. Then, several cycles of salt water, followed by good, clean water.

Rock candy, practically 100 percent sugar, was dissolved in boiling water and strained through hospital gauze pads to remove the color from the solution. He added this "sugar" to the slurry of potato peelings.

No one knows just how long John's "aging" process lasted. And he never told anyone the length of his evaporating coil made from copper fuel lines. That, the fire temperature, and a number of other procedures remained a family secret.

The actual production capabilities of the still were never known either, but it did produce at least a quart or two of very strange, foul-tasting alcohol. Years after the war, men still debated its exact color. Some claimed it was clear; others said that it had a pale yellow or even beige cast in different light. But everyone agreed, "It was the strongest stuff I ever tasted . . . only fit to drink when mixed with grapefruit juice or Coca-Cola."[9]

Regardless, Private John McKinney's popularity soared around A Company for a few weeks. Then he wisely stopped production and destroyed the still, removing all evidence of its existence.

John McKinney personally changed little while stationed in New Guinea in spite of those few days of fame. He remained a laid-back young man, but that description fit many soldiers in World War II.

Through his buddies' encouragement, John became more involved in some activities. Baseball was a good example. His friends were those with whom he felt most comfortable. As expected in the military, they consisted of a variety of different personalities from various backgrounds.

During those few months in New Guinea, the men of the 123rd Regiment would cultivate friendships, some lasting long after the war. But what they knew about each other, in the beginning, was generally superficial. Deep feelings, beliefs, and desires were seldom revealed. When they entered combat, there would be no time to share those things with one another.[10]

McKinney considered a dozen men, perhaps a few more, as "friends," and many of these would say later, "I knew McKinney," but they understood very little about him; rather, they remembered certain traits. "He was a crack shot." "He was shy and polite." "He never complained and always did his job."

Men in war knew it was better not to have close friends. The death of a buddy would be difficult, and the more feelings one had for the man killed, the more that could make life unbearable and ultimately affect one's combat efficiency.

John McKinney learned from his friends in A Company. There was his platoon sergeant, Al Johnson, a professional, a tough man from Chicago, outgoing and aggressive, perfect for the job. His squad leader from a Chicago suburb, Sol Rocke, was a fast-thinking, intelligent, college-educated soldier who made good, sound decisions. He is remembered as genuinely caring about each man in his unit. Rocke described John McKinney as a "skinny, polite, easy-to-like fellow with powerful arms and hands."[11]

Sol had developed a friendship during boot camp with a small, slender, easygoing soldier, a former office clerk from Pittsburgh, Pennsylvania, Eldon Homan. Both men were married, and their wives also became very close.

Rocke moved up to the position of squad leader and Homan continued to increase his proficiency with the .30-caliber light machine gun.

PFC Adolph Barrette, nicknamed "Red" for his wavy locks of auburn hair, is particularly credited for getting McKinney involved in baseball. Red, a rifleman, was fond of hunting and had worked as a farmer before the war near Cheboygan, Michigan. So he and Mac certainly had mutual interests. Although usually quiet like McKinney, Red did have the reputation of clowning around from time to time.

An example of this can be observed in two photographs provided by Chicago native and BAR expert PFC Eugene Maziarz. In one photo Red Barrette is in the foreground pretending to be practicing with his M1 and bayonet with another soldier. A smiling John McKinney is standing in the background observing the fun. Red convinced John to join in and pose for a second photo.

PFC Maziarz and John McKinney both had a buddy who was liked by every man in the company, Edward S. Colwell. Each unit had a Colwell, the kind of fellow that, regardless of months of drilling and training, still could not march or go through the manual of arms ("left shoulder, arms," etc.) correctly.

They called these soldiers "sad sacks." (Years later, they called them "Beetle Baileys" after a cartoon soldier who was constantly screwing up.)

America's "most decorated soldier," Lieutenant Audie Murphy, described such a man in his book *To Hell and Back*. "He cannot get the knack of the Army, though he tries hard. His gear is forever fouled up. It drips from his body like junk."

PFC Edward Colwell tried hard. He drilled and practiced and still fell out of step in a march, constantly having to skip to catch up and try to return to the correct pace.[12]

Of course, Ed was teased during the first few days of boot camp, but then the men helped him to improve his military skills. John McKinney coached Ed with M1 rifle marksmanship, and Eugene Maziarz, Sol Rocke, Red Barrette, Eldon Homan, actually all the men in his platoon worked with him until his marching improved, somewhat.

Ed Colwell came from Hull, Illinois, where he worked as a rural mail carrier after his father died. He and his brother Bob were extremely close. Bob joined the Navy and would eventually serve as Ensign Colwell aboard a ship on weather patrol in the Pacific.[13]

But now, Ed's "brothers" were the soldiers in his unit. Those men learned that Ed Colwell might have trouble marching, but otherwise was an excellent soldier. Thanks to his friendship with John McKinney, Ed fired good scores with the M1, and proved to be a friendly, sincere man who never complained about their situation on New Guinea.

That situation changed drastically on August 20, 1944, four months after they arrived on the island.

The 123rd Regiment was separated from the Thirty-third Division and sent up the east coast to the Maffin Bay area of Dutch New Guinea in LCIs (landing craft, infantry). John McKinney and his buddies of A Company boarded U.S.S. LCI #748, and arrived at Maffin Bay on August 28. The entire regiment was on shore by September 1.[14]

The mission of the 123rd was to guard the Wakde Airdrome (airfield), set up its security, and protect a series of ammunition and supply depots from Japanese infiltrators.

To accomplish this, the 123rd would need to establish and maintain a tight perimeter. They relieved the Thirty-first Division, which had already cleared most of the enemy from the area . . . most except for an estimated 1,400 Imperial Army combat troops hiding a few miles to the north and west. The fighting for the Thirty-first was far from over. They received orders to begin an assault on the island of Moratai more than 1,300 miles to the north—and 1,300 miles closer to Japan.

The 123rd would finally be in a combat area. Perhaps that was the good news they had long been training and waiting for. The bad news was the fact that they now had to hold a perimeter with their regiment's 1,750 men . . . a perimeter once defended by the entire Thirty-first Division of more than thirteen thousand men.

CHAPTER 10

*"I had been sent to this island to fight, only to
find that the troops I was supposed to lead
were a bunch of good-for-nothings, quick to
profess their willingness to die but actually
concerned only with their immediate wants."*

Second Lieutenant Hiroo Onoda

Japanese Imperial Army

No Surrender (Translation, Charles S. Terry)

Maffin Bay
Dutch New Guinea
September 1944

Imperial Japanese units on New Guinea may have been demoralized, shot to pieces, and starving, but they still had plenty of weapons and ammunition to welcome the U.S. 123rd Infantry when they arrived at Maffin Bay in September 1944.

Some Japanese stragglers, most of them suffering from infected wounds and tropical illnesses, managed to surrender; however, officers and NCOs reorganized shattered units to ensure that their men continued to fight by the code of Bushido. There would be no surrender permitted.

For soldiers on the island, Japanese and Americans, each day became like a recurring nightmare of rain, mud, dead bodies along jungle trails, and the constant echo of cracking rifle shots punctuated by machine-gun chatter.

The mission assigned the 123rd Regiment, to hold a perimeter formerly manned by an entire division, was not going to be easy. It was an impossible task unless a good plan of defense could be devised immediately.

First, the 123rd requested reinforcements. The Second Battalion of the 136th Infantry—less than six hundred men—arrived to help, but this did not resolve the problem.

The 123rd headquarters came up with another idea. First, they pulled the defense lines back, tightening the perimeter closer to the shore. This required the destruction of old fortifications and constructing a line of new "pillboxes."

One battalion anchored the right flank of the perimeter; one held the ground directly inland from the bay. A third held the left flank, while the remaining battalion worked the docks and stood ready as a reserve to rush aid to any point on the defense line experiencing a major attack. Then the battalions rotated, so each took a turn at dock duty.

Japanese units observed all this, and almost immediately began small nighttime harassment attacks—shouting and shooting into the U.S. perimeter without actually charging the defensive positions.

What, no doubt, had the Japanese curious was the fact that the reinforced 123rd lacked sufficient manpower to defend even the new, tightened perimeter.

There remained about a seven-mile gap, only lightly protected, between the Americans' left flank and its right.

Knowing the Japanese would not resist the temptation to attack through this gap, the 123rd's plan was to defend the area (actually using it as bait) with aggressive patrols and ambushes.

Every rifle company went out on at least one five-day patrol and an unending number of two-day patrols.[1]

New Guinea natives who worked previously with the Sixth and Thirty-first Divisions proved extremely valuable again to the 123rd. Nothing in U.S. Army manuals could equal their knowledge of the terrain, plants, and animals (especially poisonous snakes).

Though the Japanese were starving in many areas and resorting to living off the land, the GIs on patrol in the Maffin Bay area were well armed and well fed; perhaps not as nourished as at the Finschhafen base, but still, for frontline combat troops, their supplies were sufficient. But someone had to carry all that stuff. The job fell to the natives, as reported by Captain Otis B. Rowland, Jr., a graduate of Louisiana State University. He and his wife, Faye, were both from Louisiana. On November 2, 1944, the captain commanded a large patrol on reconnaissance. They were to engage and "destroy any Japanese troops encountered."[2]

His report reads, in part:

Subject: Report of 5-day patrol
           13 Officers
           204 Enlisted men
           67 Native bearers
           4 Native scouts
           2 Japanese scouts

Weapons: 132 M1 rifles
         9 BARs
         60 Carbines
         6 Light machine guns, .30 caliber
         2 Mortars, 60mm
         2 Rocket launchers, 2.36" (Bazookas)[3]

Observations: Reconnoiter west side of Woske River to the mouth of the Tilfe River. Area covered by rainforest. Visibility about 25 yards.

Clearings covered with grass and banana trees. Creek bed 10 feet deep and 10 feet wide. Good water, crossing on log, poor.

Rations: 47 cases, C Rations
           150 lbs. Rice
           12 lbs. Tea
           1 sack, Salt

7 boxes, Pepper

3 cases, D Rations

7 cases, Grapefruit juice

. . . It was found that the river was too deep for fording, so all men were crossed in one rubber boat using a rope on each shore. To speed up the process, the natives constructed a raft, but this went to pieces after three trips, and so much noise was made in construction, the disadvantages far surpassed any small amount of time gained.

Nothing interesting until 2 Jap skeletons were found. An American helmet with two bullet holes was also found at this point. We took a break and a ration of one canteen cup of grapefruit juice was given each man.[4]

In spite of all the equipment carried by the patrol, Captain Rowland did complain in the Remarks section of the report. "Foot powder was not available at the time of the patrol. It is believed that subsequent jungle rot cases would have been materially decreased if the article could have been used during the five days."

The captain also reported poor radio communication with the SCR 684 (later replaced with the SCR 694, which had an improved transmission range of twenty miles).

But the immediate solution to poor radio communication was a technique employed by armies for over one thousand years—carrier pigeons. Messages were sent back to headquarters in tiny containers fastened to the bird's leg. Light, single-engine, fabric-covered aircraft such as Piper Cubs from the 122nd Field Artillery unit dropped the return messages.[5]

Captain Rowland would later be promoted to major, and suffered wounds in a battle on Luzon on March 18, 1945.

The Maffin Bay area was more humid than Finschhafen and the terrain was swampland, making every mission difficult for even the men of the 123rd, who were, by now, in top physical condition. Patrols often splashed through ankle-deep mud for hours, then thigh-to-waist-deep swamp water, and back to packed sandy soil.

* * *

On another part of New Guinea, Sixth Army commander Lieutenant General Walter Krueger reviewed the mission results of a special group of men that had become known as the Alamo Scouts.

In late 1943, with his campaign progressing well in New Guinea, General Krueger and his staff faced an "intelligence" problem. Regardless of Allied victories, there were still plenty of Japanese troops on the island. His headquarters knew approximately where they were, but exactly how many, their physical condition and morale, was not known. The total enemy situation, essential in combat, could be determined only from captured documents, POW interrogations, or air reconnaissance.

General Krueger, unlike most high-ranking officers in the Pacific, had come up through the ranks and understood hardships endured by soldiers in combat. He'd immigrated to the United States from West Prussia, and volunteered as an enlisted man in 1898 during the Spanish American War. While serving on Luzon in 1901 during the Philippine Insurrection, Krueger was commissioned as a second lieutenant. World War I found him serving in the newly formed tank corps. Now, World War II and his commander, General MacArthur, seemed to be pushing him once more toward Luzon.

On New Guinea, General Krueger had become fascinated with the results of a secret, experimental unit formed by the Navy and called "Amphibious Scouts." It was a small, highly trained group of men who volunteered to land at night in enemy territory, reconnoiter for days, and bring out information.

Krueger concluded that his Sixth Army needed such a unit on a permanent basis.

By December 1943, a training site was erected on a small island off the east coast of Furgusson Island. Here, isolated but only a thirty-minute boat ride from Sixth Army headquarters, the first group of volunteers began their six weeks of training in secrecy.

Swimming tests, rubber-boating, marksmanship, and familiarization firing with every known small weapon in the U.S. and Japanese arsenal all were easy compared to hours of hand-to-hand combat training in the tropical heat.

Blinker signaling, radio operation and repair, map and compass reading, and coded message sending were rehearsed, sometimes on a twenty-four-hour basis. Simulated missions were conducted on deserted islands after being dropped off by Patrol Torpedo boats (PT boats).

Those who failed to qualify were returned to their original units; the graduates organized into Scout teams consisting of one officer and six men.

For the next several months, Alamo Scout teams, dropped off by PT boats, investigated Japanese positions and returned with valuable information. Within nine months, various Scouts had earned nineteen Silver Stars, eighteen Bronze Stars, and four Soldier's medals for bravery without losing a single man. In fact, Sixth Army continued to assign Scout teams to hazardous missions until the end of World War II. Though they successfully completed them all without losing a man, unfortunately, the same could not be said for other special units briefly trained by Alamo Scouts.

The Alamo Scouts' gallant deeds, even their existence, remained secret for the duration of the war. Their military descendants, however, became famous as the United States Army Special Forces—the Green Berets.[6]

Once the Sixth Army felt comfortable with field intelligence now pouring in from a variety of sources including the Alamo Scouts, they believed they needed a larger special assault unit that could travel swiftly, carry light weapons, strike, then move on to the next assignment. The U.S. Army in Europe already had such battalions. They were called "Rangers," carrying the designations of First Ranger Battalion through Fifth Ranger Battalion. Appropriately, the Sixth Army in New Guinea would have the Sixth Ranger Battalion.

But where was Sixth Army to find enough men to form a full battalion of Rangers? Luckily for General Krueger, they already had a unit of big, husky soldiers waiting for something to do.

In February 1943, the Ninety-eighth Field Artillery, Pack, found themselves left out of the war when they arrived in New Guinea. The Army had planned to use the Ninety-eighth in the Salamaua campaign, but by March those battles were practically over and what was left of the Japanese units had scattered deeper into the jungles.

The one thousand mules accompanying the Ninety-eighth were needed, though, by Frank Dow Merrill in the rugged Burmese mountains. So the mules were reassigned to "Merrill's Marauders."

Now, an entire battalion of "mule skinners" was left to sit around and wait for the Army to find them a home. With the exception of the officers and a few men, most everyone in the Ninety-eighth was at least six feet tall. Considering the laborious tasks confronting a pack artillery outfit, the Army had established a minimum height requirement of five-ten, and drafted these healthy men from rural farms and mountainous areas of America.

No one thought how perfect it would be to convert these soldiers into Rangers until early 1944. In April, the Ninety-eighth received a new commander, thirty-three-year-old West Point graduate Lieutenant Colonel Henry A. Mucci.

Colonel Mucci informed his men that the Ninety-eighth would become the Sixth Ranger Battalion of "volunteers." A dynamic leader, Mucci trained with his men until they became a unique fighting team.

The Sixth Rangers consisted of approximately six hundred men. Each of the former artillery "batteries" became a company of sixty-four men. A company was composed of a headquarters (one officer and three men) and two platoons with one officer and thirty-one men each. A platoon had its own headquarters, a special weapons section of six men, and two assault sections.

The "assault" had a headquarters of one man and an assault squad of five men armed with Browning automatic rifles (BARs).

The firepower of a Ranger company (sixty-four men) with their M1 rifles, BARs, M1 carbines, and Thompson submachine guns (tommy guns) equaled that of a 108-man regular infantry company.

Ranger training began with grueling hours of calisthenics, five-mile runs, and twenty-mile hikes. Endless hours of firing weapons and bayonet training were interrupted only by practice attacks on simulated Japanese pillboxes and other fortifications. Created as a highly mobile strike unit, the sixth lacked machine guns and mortars, and had to draw bazookas from other outfits if they needed them. Thus, the Rangers were never considered for a "dig-in" type of defense.

Their communication section spent weeks training with the SCR 684 radio, only to have them replaced with the state-of-the-art SCR 694.

The soldiers of the old Ninety-eighth finally had a home and were busy training while Private John McKinney and Company A of the 123rd conducted patrols in the Maffin Bay area. In less than a year, the war would bring Company A, the Alamo Scouts, and the Sixth Rangers together at a beautiful spot on Luzon known as Dingalan Bay.

* * *

From the beginning of World War II to present, American GIs have quickly developed slang words for practically every new military item encountered. In recent times, for example, the High Mobility Multi-Purpose Wheeled Vehicle has become better known as the Humvee.

In World War II soldiers not only had special names for their own equipment—"grease guns," bazookas, etc.—they also named enemy weapons, sometimes by their appearances or the sounds they made.

"Woodpecker" brings forth an image of a bright-colored little bird tapping away on a tree trunk searching for insects. But in the Pacific, the shout "Woodpeckers!" caused one's stomach to turn and a nauseating feeling in the throat as you dove for cover or tried to dig under a fallen tree.

The Type 92 Japanese machine gun designed by Nambu fired a 7.7-millimeter shell, recycling slowly, causing a *tap-tap-tap* sound that resembled that made by a woodpecker. It was a heavy weapon, usually fitted with a bipod, requiring two or three men to operate it. Though slow-firing, they were especially deadly because the enemy deployed them in clusters of ten (when possible).

The 92 was replaced by the Type 99, also a 7.7mm, but lighter and faster-firing and it could be operated by one man. There was also the revised "96"—fast-firing, weighing thirty pounds, and firing a smaller (6.5mm) cartridge from a thirty-round magazine. Oddly, all these Japanese machine guns produced a firing sound similar to that of a woodpecker, but the Type 92 came closest to duplicating the bird.

Another deadly weapon employed by the Japanese was the Type 89 Knee Mortar. This strange-looking device, carried and fired by one man, was about two feet long, consisting of a launch tube attached to a narrow pipelike shaft (which contained the trigger mechanism) and a bottom curved plate. This plate gave the impression that it should be placed against the thigh just above the knee to fire. Some GIs tried firing the mortar by actually pressing the plate against their legs, with bad results. The recoil from the launch was enough to cause severe bruising, and in some cases, a fracture.

The correct method of firing was to place the curved base plate over a small tree trunk or a log and pull a lanyard, which activated the trigger. Knee mortars were effective in close-quarter jungle fighting, providing a small soldier with the capability of launching its grenade-type projectile for a considerable distance. Though normally used to support attacks within two hundred yards, the weapon did have a maximum range of seven hundred yards.

* * *

PFC John McKinney was sharing his foxhole with PFC Adolph "Red" Barrette on a humid October night near the Woske River less than a mile inland from Maffin Bay.

The perimeter along the river consisted of three pillboxes constructed of logs and sandbags, each armed with a .30-caliber light machine gun manned by two men. A series of "rifle pit" foxholes reinforced with sandbags completed the line of defense.

PFC Morris Roberts and PFC Eldon Homan manned the pillbox closest to McKinney's position with a machine gun. To his left, squad leader Sol Rocke and PFC Ed Colwell occupied a foxhole. They, like McKinney, were armed with M1 rifles. Next to them, PFC Eugene Maziarz peered down the barrel of his BAR in the darkness toward the river's edge.

None of them could actually see the river, but they knew that the men of Company C were patrolling the other side about two miles up the beach near Sawar airstrip.[7]

A few minutes before midnight, the rain, which had fallen with a vengeance since late afternoon, abruptly stopped. Now the only sound came from rainwater dripping off leaves. For a few moments, a stillness settled in the jungle.

Suddenly, the peace was broken by shouts and screams that seemed to be coming from their side of the river.

The men of A Company had been told the Japanese were noisy fighters, especially when they were preparing to attack. Small explosions began to rock the American positions, followed quickly by the constant *tap-tap* sound of the enemy's "woodpeckers" as they went into action. The blasts from the knee-mortar projectiles indicated that this was no harassment, but a full-scale assault.

Flares burst in the sky, lighting up the entire area. For several seconds, the scene was a mixture of bright flashes, smoke, and eerie shadows—then, darkness.

Were the flares fired from the Japanese or by someone in A Company? McKinney and the men around him would never know the answer. But in those seconds of light, he glanced to his left. He could not see Sergeant Rocke, but Ed Colwell was firing his M1 carefully, spacing two seconds between shots. This left John McKinney feeling comfortable. Maybe Colwell would never learn to march correctly, but he surely had nerves of steel and was performing like an experienced rifleman.[8]

In the first few seconds of the battle, A Company answered the Japanese with a barrage of rifle, BAR, and machine-gun fire. Within about thirty seconds, bright flashes seemed to "bounce" near the river, followed by the sound of muffled explosions. American 60mm mortars had begun to rain death on anyone near the water.

After fifteen minutes, the woodpeckers fell silent. The Japanese knee mortar barrage had lasted only a short while at the beginning. There was another five minutes of A Company blasting away at the unseen enemy, then shouts of "Cease fire! Cease fire!"

Squad leaders moved, crouching low, from foxhole to pillbox, checking for casualties. None. A Company had survived its first major firefight without losing a man or anyone suffering so much as a scratch.

At dawn, patrols moved out cautiously to check for enemy casualties. They had been warned to remain especially alert for "booby traps," knowing the Japanese often placed grenades and other explosives under their own wounded. But the patrols found no wounded, nor did they find any bodies, only "pieces of bodies, blood, and torn bits of clothing." The Imperial Japanese soldiers may have been starving, but they still had enough strength to carry away their dead comrades.

Now, the 123rd Headquarters decided they had to have an enemy prisoner to interrogate if they were to learn the exact (or even approximate) Japanese strength in the Woske River area.

Obviously, a patrol the size of the one commanded by Captain Rowland would not be capable of moving quietly through the jungle and surprising or capturing a prisoner.

The mission would fall upon the newly formed Thirty-third Division Scout Team, a handpicked unit of volunteers trained for special assignments such as this. Men from every regiment of the Golden Cross had volunteered for the Team, and once the 123rd took on patrol duty in the Maffin Bay area, the Scout Team went into action with eight-to-twelve-man patrols. They had received training from the Alamo Scouts, and quickly established a reputation in the Thirty-third of being capable of penetrating deep behind enemy lines.

For the prisoner-snatching mission, Lieutenant John L. Durant, a tall, slender former platoon leader in the 123rd, would lead, with the slightly shorter, baby-faced Lieutenant Francis E. Peebles of the 136th Infantry Regiment serving as second in command.

Lieutenant Durant believed their best chance of taking an enemy soldier alive was to stage an ambush just across the Woske River. But Headquarters of the 123rd decided Durant's team needed reinforcements, so they attached one platoon from F Company led by Lieutenant Raymond R. Utke. That decision may have been a fatal mistake. Rather than a small team of eight or ten, a thirty-one-man patrol forded the Woske River at 0400 the morning of October 20, 1944.

At 0500, Lieutenant Peebles, carrying a tommy gun, and Lieutenant Durant, with his M1A1 folding stock carbine, had their ambush in place only three hundred yards west of the river and seventy-five yards inland from the shoreline.

Lieutenant Utke, armed with an M1 rifle, held his men closer to the river, ready to reinforce the ambush party.

They waited for five hours for the Japanese to walk into their trap. Finally, Lieutenant Durant gave up and decided to relocate their ambush closer to the Sawar airfield.

Lieutenant Utke and five riflemen of his Fox Company led the way along the beach tree line, followed by Lieutenant Durant and his scout team and the large group of the infantry platoon.

Apparently, the Japanese, alerted by the large enemy unit on the move, had been watching the American patrol since dawn and had their own ambush well established. They let Utke and his five men pass, then blasted the American column with knee mortars and ten well-hidden "woodpecker" machine guns. Lieutenant Durant and his men were trapped on the open beach between enemy machine guns and the ocean.

Lieutenant Peebles managed to rush from the rear with fifteen F Company men, and began to rain return fire upon the Japanese. Their reinforcing attack forced the Japanese to break off the ambush and scatter into the jungle. Squads of Americans retreated from the battle and rushed to the Woske River. They crossed to safety on the other side. Both Lieutenant Utke and Lieutenant Peebles, along with nine members of the patrol, suffered wounds, but still managed to escape across the river. Lieutenant Durant and five other Americans were not so lucky. They had been killed by mortar fragments or machine gun fire and were left behind on the beach.

On January 25, 1945, almost six months after their arrival at Maffin Bay, the 123rd Infantry was relieved and replaced by units from the Ninety-third Division.

Although John McKinney and his buddies of A Company survived those months with no serious wounds, ten men of their regiment had been killed and fifty-five wounded by the Japanese.[9]

The 123rd had proven themselves in combat. They gained confidence and experience in skirmishes with the enemy. General MacArthur's headquarters knew the 123rd was now ready to engage in larger, more difficult battles and shed their blood on another island.

The war in the Pacific had moved on toward the Philippines, while units like the 123rd remained on islands to slug it out with members of the Imperial Army who refused to give up. In 1955, ten years after the war officially ended, the few remaining Japanese soldiers on New Guinea finally surrendered. Others chose suicide rather than commit such a dishonorable act.

CHAPTER 11

*"American soldiers! We are determined
to engage you in the Philippines for any
length of time . . . ten years, twenty years, or
even longer if you like. Are you sure
you can stay fighting that long?"*

Japanese Propaganda Leaflet
January 1945, Luzon

October 1944

General MacArthur's leapfrog assaults through the Pacific had narrowed the distance from Australia to the Philippines by October 1944.

While the 123rd Infantry exchanged fire and ambushes with Imperial Army forces at Maffin Bay, New Guinea, the American Third Fleet's carrier-based aircraft, along with the Fifth Air Force, pounded enemy land bases and ships throughout the South Pacific.

Mindanao, the large southern island of the Philippines, had been accepted as MacArthur's first target for his promised "return," but a series of Allied successes produced such a profound effect that a different plan developed.

In a change of strategy, General MacArthur and Admiral Halsey agreed on a bold new plan. The Americans would invade the 115-mile-long narrow island of Leyte right in the middle of the Philippines. The date set, October 20, 1944.

Imperial Army General Tomoyuki Yamashita arrived in Manila on Luzon in early October to assume command of the massive 500,000-man Fourteenth Area Army. Over 200,000 were scattered throughout the southern islands, and most of those were concentrated on Mindanao, where they expected the invasion to come. Twenty thousand were based on Leyte.

Yamashita's air force defense for the Philippines consisted of only 150 combat planes and a few obsolete reconnaissance aircraft. But he did have "reinforcement" fighter aircraft on nearby Formosa (Taiwan). Essentially, the Americans had proven themselves masters of the sky in two years of combat.

General MacArthur had promised to return, and now he was ready to keep that promise. Only, he brought with him almost 200,000 soldiers, including General Walter Krueger's Sixth Army. To protect the invasion army, MacArthur could count on 2,500 combat aircraft from the Far East Air Force and an additional 1,500 planes from the Navy's Seventh and Third Fleets.

It was the airfields on Leyte that had the Allies' attention. From those valuable bases, air strikes could be launched against any island in the archipelago, and Formosa as well.

Guarding Leyte Gulf and the main island were three small islands covered with thick woods and rugged hills—Dinagat, Homonhon, and Suluan. Almost five hundred Imperial soldiers defended Dinagat, but no enemy troops were thought to be on the other two.

The Japanese were known to be operating radar stations, and perhaps had some artillery on the islands with other military installations. All of these had to be destroyed. The GIs would erect their own radar and seize and hold lighthouses, important for signaling inbound U.S. ships. General Krueger now had a unit perfect for assaulting the Leyte islands—the Sixth Rangers. They would land three days before the main invasion, performing as they had been trained.

On October 17, the weather turned against the invaders as a storm set in. High winds, dark skies, and hard rains, along with Japanese gunfire, greeted the Rangers.

Company D landed on Suluan with orders to take and hold a lighthouse. The island was not unoccupied. The Japanese killed one Ranger and wounded another in the first few minutes of fighting.

Companies A and C landed on Dinagat, and began to annihilate the enemy with remarkable skill and precision.

B Company landed on Homonhon with a mission to set up a large light to help American ships navigate.

About twelve days later, Company B, led by their commander, Captain Arthur "Bull" Simons, followed up with an invasion of Suluan to finish off the remaining Japanese soldiers still refusing to surrender.

Captain Simons and a small group of Rangers, including Captain James Fisher, M.D., climbed a coral cliff by the light of a full moon and attacked the enemy holding up in a sixty-foot-tall lighthouse. Four small buildings nearby concealed a larger Japanese force.

Once Simons and his men captured the lighthouse, they found themselves trapped. Then the balance of B Company, led by an aggressive, outspoken lieutenant, Leo Strausbaugh, sprang into action and breached the Japanese perimeter. Lieutenant Strausbaugh, followed by a squad of Rangers, smashed through the lighthouse door to find Simons, Fisher, and their men unharmed but understandably stressed from the battle.

Captain Simons barked at the young lieutenant, "Strausbaugh, you son of a bitch! I thought we were all going to be killed! You almost had me believing in God, but here you are!"

The Rangers, now a combined force, shot their way out of the lighthouse and tracked down the retreating Japanese. No Imperial soldier survived.[1]

On October 20, General Douglas MacArthur set foot on a beach of Leyte and announced over a hastily erected portable radio: "This is the voice of freedom, General MacArthur speaking. People of the Philippines, I have returned! By the grace of the Almighty God, our forces stand again on Philippine soil . . . the hour of your redemption is here!"

By the end of October, the Allies had practically secured Leyte and enjoyed the exclusive use of her valuable airfields. But still, fifteen thousand Imperial soldiers, no longer fighting as functional units, held out in small groups, similar to their tactics on New Guinea. Short of ammunition and food, they would fight for another twenty-five days until finally hunted down and killed by American patrols or Filipino guerrillas.

Imperial Army Commander Yamashita had argued with his Tokyo headquarters that his men should be held on Luzon, not Leyte, to await MacArthur's invasion. He believed, with good reason, that Luzon would be the "great battleground." But headquarters overruled him, demanding reinforcements be furnished for the twenty thousand-man Leyte garrison. The result was another disaster for the Imperial Army.

On Christmas Day 1944, General Yamashita advised the scattered forces on Leyte that they had been written off as lost. They were to "seek an honorable death."

By January 1, 1945, almost seventy thousand Imperial Army ground forces were dead. Very few survived. Most of those did not surrender; they had been wounded and captured.[2]

The tenacious stand by the Japanese on Leyte cost the United States 15,584 soldiers killed between October 17, 1944, and January 1945.

During the battle for Leyte, the Japanese also lost a substantial number of warships and planes, but introduced a new type of warfare in a desperate effort to slow the American advance—suicide bombers.

An Imperial Air Corps called Kamikaze, or "Divine Wind" (named after the typhoons that destroyed the Mongolian invasion fleet heading for Japan in the thirteenth century), was established using suicide pilots flying explosive-laden aircraft. Their mission: crash into American ships.

These pilots, usually with only six weeks of training, were instructed to seek out the especially vulnerable U.S. carriers. Unlike British carriers, which had decks of steel, the U.S. ships were decked in wood.

Over the next ten months, as the kamikaze suicide aircraft dwindled in number, they managed to sink thirty-eight Allied ships and kill 4,907 American sailors.[3]

Despite heavy losses of infantry and sailors on Leyte, the Americans were determined to push on toward Luzon and the Philippine capital, Manila.

In late 1944, the war raged throughout the Pacific as MacArthur's forces leaped from island to island, destroying Japanese men, ships, and bases where they found them.

Some Japanese leaders still held hopes that the United States would tire of the war and seek to negotiate peace. Nothing much was left of the Imperial Air Force or Navy by December. Only the Imperial Army could stall MacArthur, and the best way to do that was to tie up his 200,000-man army and their supporting units on Luzon.

On December 4, 1944, while the 123rd Infantry was still tied down by a few hundred fanatical Japanese at Maffin Bay, the rest of the Thirty-third Division continued its duties at Finschhafen. Then, leaving the 123rd at Maffin, the balance of the Golden Cross shipped 1,500 miles to the jungle island of Morotai.

The Thirty-first Division had invaded Morotai back in September, but the Japanese began to reinforce their garrison.

Morotai had major airfields the Americans needed from which to launch fighters and bombers to support other South Pacific operations.

The 136th Regiment of the Thirty-third engaged strongly fortified Japanese positions, and encountered tree snipers who used rifles or dropped short-fused explosives on patrols. Thus, trails became unsafe and the Americans had to resort to cutting (literally) through heavy jungle. They found the vegetation so thick that machine guns and mortars were useless. Fighting broke down to the squad level, the GIs using carbines, M1s, BARs, bayonets, and trench knives in hand-to-hand combat.[4]

A hatred for the Imperial soldier developed as members of the 136th experienced the horrors of combat for the first time. It wasn't the war itself, rather the unfamiliar tactics employed by the Japanese. Night harassment had been perfected by the enemy, who used shouts, screams, and shots to terrorize exhausted troops.

In the minds of American infantry, the Japanese fought a totally different war from the GIs' scenario of "fairness" and "stand up and fight."

Now the Americans encountered an enemy who butchered civilians and wounded, including their own, with bayonets and swords. Their own wounded were sacrificed with "booby traps," grenades, and other explosives.

Some of the Japanese snipers were actually wounded men tied on limbs, and had to be blasted from the trees before it was safe to continue a patrol.[5]

On January 14, 1945, Armed Forces Radio announced that Mac-Arthur and his Sixth Army had invaded Luzon a few days earlier. The 136th, like the 123rd, was now battle-hardened and anxious to enter the fight for the Philippines.

Luzon had the attention of the world in January 1945. General Mac-Arthur had returned.

After almost four years of preparation, the Thirty-third Golden Cross Division was ready to become part of the big picture and the final drive to Japan. For the first time since September 1, 1944, the entire division would assemble and advance toward the enemy as a consolidated unit. Troop ships carrying PFC John McKinney and his 123rd Regiment sailed north from New Guinea and rendezvoused with the remainder of the division moving out from Morotai.

By February 9, 1945, as the Thirty-third reached Lingayen Gulf on the west coast of Luzon, more than 1,297 of MacArthur's men had been killed and 4,500 others were out of action due to wounds. During those same four weeks of fighting, Yamashita had already lost more than fifteen thousand killed.[6]

* * *

Most of Tomoyuki Yamashita's sixty years had been devoted to military service for his emperor. His brutal but brilliant victories in a jungled part of Asia earned him the title "Tiger of Malaya" as his troops smashed Singapore, dealing the British one of their worst defeats in history early in the war. He understood, to a degree, the American and British mentality, and knew the secret of breaking the Allied spirit by permitting his army to commit atrocities. He and his army had once thrived on taking the offensive, but now the situation had changed. The Japanese had failed to break the American fighting spirit, and U.S. troops continued to receive 100 percent support from civilians on the home front. Knowledge of atrocities infuriated the Americans, and the taste of revenge became sweet on the lips of men who at one time did not embrace such desires. Americans had been pushed too far and nothing, not kamikazes and not suicidal holdouts by any size units, would stop their determination to obtain all-out victory.

The Imperial Army was essentially doomed. The awesome capability of American industry and American soldiers' fighting spirit would cost the Japanese the war. Mostly, the Japanese had greatly underestimated America's will to fight for islands and people so far from their continent.

General Yamashita no longer commanded the elite army that had destroyed the British in Southeast Asia. Luzon had, for some time, become a training ground for the Imperial soldiers destined for assignment on other islands. Men were constantly rotated in and out.

Of the 250,000 men still under his command on Luzon, most were poorly led by young officers recently sent from Japan or noncombat areas and a few old veterans of the China and Manchuria wars ten years earlier.

Imperial General Headquarters continued to insist that Luzon was indefensible, but Yamashita argued that his plans to retreat into the mountains would allow him to prolong the struggle. Yamashita also wanted to abandon Manila, reporting that he needed the seventeen thousand sailors and marines stationed there for his mountain strongholds. He ordered the Naval commander, Rear Admiral Sanji Iwabuchi, at Manila to put up a brief resistance, then retreat north to link up with the main force.

The admiral would disobey those orders and defend the city, mostly for the reason of Japanese prestige. The suicidal stand of Admiral Iwabuchi ultimately cost the lives of practically all of his seventeen thousand men as well as almost 100,000 civilians. During the final days, Naval commanders turned their men loose on the Filipinos in Manila to rape and massacre, partially as a reward for their loyalty, but mostly in keeping with their modified "warrior code" and the right to seek revenge for their situation.

The central plains area would be defended by a small delaying force; six thousand men were assigned to hold Corregidor, and only one thousand spread out through Bataan to give the Americans trouble there. General Yamashita had no intention of being trapped on Bataan and Corregidor as the Americans were in 1941 and 1942, nor did he plan to sacrifice men to hold MacArthur on the Lingayen beaches.

With the exception of Admiral Iwabuchi's force at Manila, General Yamashita actually had twice as many troops on Luzon as U.S. intelligence calculated.

Yamashita divided his army into three "groups" or areas.

The first area, the Shobu Group, commanded by himself, would be located northeast and east of Lingayen Gulf.

The second area, the Kembu Group, guarded the approach to Clark Air Force Base and the entrance to the Bataan peninsula. It was commanded by Major General Rikichi Tsukada.

The third area, the Shimbu Group, commanded by Lieutenant General Shizuo Yokayama, would defend the mountains east and northeast of Manila and southern Luzon.

After each fought a delaying action, inflicting as many casualties as possible, they were to withdraw to three mountain strongholds, which included the fertile Cagayon Valley, from which they planned to draw food during their long stand. Years of fighting might pass before U.S. morale would collapse and the Imperial Army could rush down to retake Manila.

Yamashita's strategy to make a final stand in the practically roadless, jungle-covered mountains was basically a good one. The U.S. would be denied (because of the terrain) the complete use of their tanks and heavy ground weapons. Rains and low-hanging clouds limited the use of airpower.

Therefore, the battle was to be fought mostly by riflemen against riflemen, which is exactly what Yamashita knew would tie down the Americans for a long time.

But his plan did have one weakness. The ground Yamashita chose to fight on also favored the Filipino guerrilla operations. Those men were eager to fight the Japanese, as were the Huks. The guerrillas knew the local dialects, the native (natural) food, and the trails and caves. At least for a while, the Northern Luzon Guerrilla Force and the socialist Huks would fight a common enemy. In some cases, even civilians thirsting for revenge turned on the retreating Japanese.

The battle for Luzon was to become the largest in the Pacific, and troops locked in combat would number six times those engaged there in 1942. Against the largest Japanese army ever assembled on one island, the Americans would commit more troops than employed in the North Africa or Italian campaigns.

But what would General Yamashita's plans accomplish? First, he believed that the U.S. might negotiate a peace if the war dragged on much longer and cost large numbers of American lives. If that did not unfold, then at least the Japanese mainland would have more time to prepare its defense—a defense that many Imperial staff members were certain would completely destroy any invading enemy.

* * *

Professor Yoshio Nishina continued to work with his staff at Kyoto University to develop a functional atomic device. The target date for them to provide the military with two bombs remained late summer 1945.

But the professor still needed one thousand pounds of uranium, promised by Nazi Germany but not yet delivered. It seems that by February 1, 1945, Germany had its own problems with Allied bombing raids. But the Germans, in true obedience to their promise, assured the professor that a submarine would depart with the uranium sometime in March.

* * *

In Handa, Aichi Prefecture, Japan, sixteen-year-old Hitoshi Miyaki left his job where he worked on the B6 bomber and started home for dinner. Along the way, as was customary, he talked with some former classmates who worked on a different assembly line producing reconnaissance planes.

The topic of conversation that night of December 6, 1944, was the same as a few of the previous evenings—what was that strange, dart-shaped aircraft under construction in a nearby building?

Hitoshi and his friends knew they should not discuss that odd project openly. They assumed it must be an Imperial Navy secret weapon—a logical conclusion since armed Naval guards were posted about the building and military vehicles with Navy markings constantly darted about town.

The next day, (coincidentally) December 7, 1944, at 1:36 in the afternoon, an earthquake with a magnitude of 8.0 struck the Handa area. One of the buildings where Hitoshi worked completely collapsed killing thirteen of his friends. In all, ninety-six workers were killed that day. In the chaos that followed the earthquake, those participating in the Navy project, along with all their equipment and the strange-looking plane, disappeared. Some said the military moved into a cave a few miles away. No one would dare ask questions.[7]

What Hitoshi and his friends had seen was a prototype of a new rocket-powered aircraft designed by Navy Ensign Mitsuo Ohka. The first Ohka rocket, as it was originally called, had been difficult to maneuver, so with corrections made in design, production of the modified "Model 22" began in December 1944.

The Ohka was designed to be carried into the sky by a Mitsubishi "Betty" bomber, then released for the pilot to guide the craft and crash it with its explosive warhead into U.S. Navy ships. Basically, the Ohka rocket was another example of the kamikaze, since the rocket pilot would not survive.

Even some Japanese pilots and Navy commanders thought the Ohka rocket ridiculous and nicknamed the aircraft the Baka (Fool).

Nonetheless, production of the Model 22 Baka continued, with the Navy being promised at least 750 rockets by March 1945. Everyone involved in the project agreed that the best place to conceal the Baka would be in caves. When American ships came close to Japan, the Fool could be released.

Far more threatening than the Baka, a practical aircraft project was under way in a factory at Gumma.

In June 1944, Kazuo Ohno and Kenichi Matsumura completed their prototype of a plane code-named the Nakajima Kikka (Orange Blossom). A Naval attaché to Germany had returned with plans for a marvelous new type of aircraft. The Germans called it a Messerschmitt (ME) 262.

This revolutionary aircraft was jet-powered, capable of taking off from a runway unassisted carrying a 1,100-pound bomb, and could maintain speeds of 432 miles per hour for a range of 127 miles. At that speed, it matched the best piston-engine fighters the U.S. had put into the sky.

The Orange Blossom was a beautiful, sleek, bullet-shaped aircraft with twin engines to be flown by a crew of one.

The Japanese redesigned the ME262 to make the Blossom a little smaller. They were certain the speed would increase to over five hundred miles per hour. No American fighter could keep up with that.

Unknown to American military intelligence, twenty-five Orange Blossom fighters had been constructed by 1945 and hidden in caves. Plans were to have hundreds of the Blossoms ready for combat by August 1945.

Once American bombers and fighter escorts appeared in the sky over Japan, something would be needed to meet that threat.

In January 1945, as General Yamashita began his defense of Luzon and plans to delay the American Army, Japanese engineers near Tokyo came up with an even more frightening type of aircraft known as the Mitsubishi Shusui—a solid-fuel, rocket-powered interceptor-fighter capable of reaching American high-altitude bombers. The plan would be for the Shusui to either shoot down American B29s with air-to-air rockets, or crash into the enemy planes.

Capable of performing at speeds of over 576 miles per hour, the little rocket fighter was destined to be the master of the sky. Nothing flying in the world at that time could equal that speed. There were plans for full production to begin in mid-1945, with combat fighters ready by August.[8]

CHAPTER 12

"You'll never get a war movie authentic
until you put smell *into it!"*

Leon Beck, American guerrilla

Luzon, 1945

Everywhere the horrible stench of burning wood, grass, and human flesh hung in the humid air. A light breeze cooled Private John McKinney's face, but it brought the nauseating smell of manure and decomposing bodies from a nearby barrio.

McKinney lay on his stomach, his irritated eyes straining to see through the smoke. A few feet away, Private Red Barrette tilted a canteen to his mouth. He gargled, then spit the warm water out. Mac had already done that, and still the acid, oily taste of burnt gunpowder remained. And the smells would remain, saturating battle uniforms and hair. No one had changed his sweat-soaked clothes for over two weeks. No one had time or extra water to bathe or even wash his hands.

The 123rd Infantry's A Company, facing the enemy that scorching morning in late February 1945, could not dream of being rotated to a rear area for rest like some soldiers fighting in Europe enjoyed from time to time. In central Luzon, there wasn't much of a rear area to relocate to. Even if you were pulled back from the front line for a while, your life still hung by a thread. Japanese snipers peppered the rest areas, and suicide bombers, satchels of explosives tied to their bodies, infiltrated the perimeter and blew themselves up next to tanks and jeeps.

The insects, snakes, dust, dysentery, malaria, jungle rot, and that terrible smell of death was always there, a constant reminder of what man must pay for his freedom.

Elsewhere, the American offensive continued throughout Luzon, pressing feverishly ahead, driving the Japanese farther into the mountains or surrounding and squeezing them into small pockets. Then the enemy was systematically annihilated.

During the night of January 30, Sixth Army Rangers, guided by Alamo Scouts and supported by Filipino guerrillas under Captains Juan Pajota and Edwardo Joson, attacked a Japanese POW camp at Barrio Pangatian near Cabanatuan. Their raid liberated over five hundred U.S. and Allied prisoners, many held since the fall of Bataan.[1]

A few days later, on February 5, U.S. troops sliced into Manila and a savage house-to-house battle began. GIs broke through the gates of the ancient Santo Tomas University and freed more than four thousand Allied prisoners (mostly civilians and dependents of the Bataan defenders).

The struggle continued for almost a month while Japanese troops, realizing they were trapped, went on a rampage, raping women of all ages, mutilating babies and small children, setting hospitals on fire, and murdering civilians.

Manila had been devastated, much the same as Warsaw and Stalingrad, but finally, the American flag was raised over the ruins and General MacArthur announced, "My country kept the faith. Your capital city, cruelly punished though it be, has regained its rightful place—citadel of democracy in the East."

As the struggle for Manila reached a climax, U.S. forces, again assisted by Alamo Scouts and Filipino guerrillas, attacked another Japanese concentration camp at Los Baños on February 23 and liberated Allied prisoners.

Imperial Army troops, surrounded in areas south of Manila, were slowly being destroyed. Those east retreated into lines of defense in the southern Sierra Madre Mountains, while northern forces withdrew along with General Yamashita and his staff to Baguio and the high hills surrounding the city.

The Japanese may have planned to hold the American Army at bay for months, maybe years, in the Philippines, but they could not prevent the Allied advances throughout the Pacific.

While the Sixth Army battled the Imperial Army in the Philippines, American marines stormed the black sand beaches of Iwo Jima on the morning of February 19.

After days of bloody battle, the marines captured three valuable airfields, but the struggle would continue until the end of March. Iwo Jima cost the lives of 6,821 Americans along with more than twenty-eight thousand men wounded. Twenty thousand Japanese soldiers died, including their commander, who committed suicide on March 22. Only about one thousand Imperial soldiers were still alive on March 26 when the island was declared secure. Those airfields became emergency landing strips for crippled U.S. bombers returning from raids over Japan and bases for their fighter escorts. Tokyo was now less than seven hundred miles away.

* * *

As the war seemed to sweep around the Philippines, General Yamashita's Luzon forces were doing exactly what he demanded of them. They surrendered nothing, fighting to the last man on every hill and making the Americans pay dearly for each inch gained.

The Imperial Army's morale began to slip. In some areas on Luzon, starvation and disease claimed as many men as death from combat.

When some Japanese were captured, most had wounds so severe that they could no longer fight; they didn't even have the strength to commit suicide.

Most Imperial Army units on Luzon had recently been pieced together from remnants of others. They were down to practically no aircraft cover, and by February 1 had less than a quarter of the number of vehicles as the U.S. Gasoline became almost nonexistent. Precious reserves were saved for tanks. They too soon ran short of fuel and were buried into hillsides with only the gun turrets visible, thus becoming excellent "pillboxes."

But Japanese mechanics had adjusted what remained of their troop trucks and other vehicles to run off ethyl alcohol (made from sugar cane).

The advantage of ethyl alcohol for some was the fact that they could drink it as well as use it for fuel.[2]

Adding to all those problems was a shortage of reliable ammunition. Often, ammo supplies were in the wrong place at the wrong time.

By early February, the Imperial soldiers' battle tactics had become more desperate. Any plan that killed or delayed Americans seemed worth a try.

Playing dead and blowing up an enemy with a hand grenade was nothing new in their repertoire, but they added a cruel twist by having a sniper ready to shoot the medic who rushed in to help. Killing a medic ensured that other Americans would eventually suffer.

Japanese soldiers often hid in unexpected places, including hastily dug holes, and waited for the GI. Others left sandal tracks or abandoned campfires to lure their enemy into an ambush. Their favorite tactic was to face their snipers in the opposite direction and let the Americans pass, then shoot them in the back.[3]

McKinney's Golden Cross Division landed at Lingayen on February 10, a full month after the main invasion. General Krueger had plans for the Thirty-third. On February 13, they were moved in to the battle lines and relieved the 158th Regimental Combat Team.

Facing the Golden Cross front were the Imperial Twenty-third Division and the Fifty-eighth Mixed Brigade, key units of the Fourteenth Area Army sent by General Yamashita to block the Americans from reaching Baguio. Many of these men were combat veterans from the China campaign. They had succeeded in constructing well-concealed gun emplacements, establishing easy and effective fields of fire, all designed to take advantage of the rugged natural terrain.

The 130th Infantry Regiment took a position to the right of McKinney's 123rd. All units began to send out patrols to determine the strength and exact location of the enemy.

No longer would the Americans see the happy faces of Filipinos who greeted them on the beaches, holding fingers up in a V and shouting, "Victory, Joe!" and, "God Bless America!"

The brief glimpses of smiling men carrying "game cocks" (fighting roosters) and young ladies standing in clear streams, their beautiful raven-black hair glistening in the sun as they washed clothes, pounding the cloth on large stones with wooden paddles, were now in the past for McKinney and his pals. The war had left those Filipinos ravaged, but finally in peace. The war now waited up the trail for the 123rd. All the trails for the American Army led to their goal—the Japanese command center at Baguio and the destruction of General Yamashita's forces.

From Damortis, at the northern coast of Lingayen Bay, to Baguio by air is only about twenty miles, but on winding roads through the hills the distance is more like sixty miles. In clear weather on those danger-ous curving trails, a drive from the Bay to Baguio would have required no more than four hours. But that was assuming no one had destroyed the roads with explosives and soldiers firing rifles, machine guns, mor-tars, and artillery were not interrupting things along the way. A peace-time trip of four hours became a horrible foot march for the 123rd, a cruel, long, bitter trail requiring more than thirty days.

First, the patrols sent out by the 123rd searched for shortcuts to Baguio that might have been less defended or even overlooked by the Japanese. If such routes had existed, the battalions might have gotten close to Baguio without detection.

Finally, at the end of February, the Thirty-third decided on a direct move, cross-country from Rosario to Pugo, thereby positioning them-selves for a siege on Baguio from the west.[4]

Captain Harry L. Ice, Jr., commanded First Battalion, A Company of the 123rd. This twenty-seven-year-old Pennsylvania native, a 1942 graduate of the University of Missouri, had been an All-American foot-ball player, starring as a running back in the 1941 Orange Bowl.

Graduating as a Reserve Officer, he joined the Thirty-third Division in the war's early days while they were still at Camp Forrest. Time off was given so Ice could play football in the game between the Army All Stars and the Chicago Bears in 1942.

Captain Ice had previously served as Able Company's executive of-ficer, then liaison with their battalion, where a two-year friendship de-veloped between himself and another former football star, from New

York University, Major Robert V. Connolly, the executive officer for the battalion at that time.

Harry Ice was a small, trim officer, naturally fast on his feet and a quick thinker. Most important, he had worked with the men of A Company since the beginning and through the New Guinea campaign. They understood one another and the men trusted their commander.

Private John McKinney, his sergeants, and buddies followed Captain Ice along a high wooded ridgeline that, in some places, reminded J.R. of his old hunting grounds in Georgia. He told his sister after the war, "I realize the trees and bushes were different, but for a moment it made me think of home."

A Company fought their way up one hill and spread out on the ridge waiting for a signal to start the advance up the next one. The Army had already given a name to their objective—"Twin Peaks." These were two hills side by side, towering perhaps seven hundred feet, dwarfing the surrounding smaller hills that lay nestled at their slopes. Clouds seemed to cling to the summits, producing gray-brown shadows on the hillsides.

Battalion headquarters issued orders for A Company to attack one hill, C Company the other. Their mission was to find the best route to the top, then attack Japanese emplacements, hopefully driving the enemy off.

Even the approach to the Twins was a dangerous mission. Surrounding the mountains was a deep, moatlike "draw" that had to be descended into, its bottom crossed, and its opposite side scaled before each hill itself could be climbed.

The terrain and tactics were something new for the men who had been first trained to fight in the desert, and had spent the last several months fighting in the jungle.

The climb would demand that the men sling their weapons over their shoulders so that both hands could be free to hold on and pull themselves up by grabbing rocks, vines, and shrubs.

The Japanese had been waiting for the opportunity, and began to rain rifle fire and grenades down upon the attackers. The Americans tried to split and move in from the left and right flanks. Imperial soldiers saw this coming and kept them pinned down. Because of the hill's sharp slope, it was impossible for A Company to return fire with any decent effect. The company backed down the hill and tried a full attack on the left side. Again, the Japanese forced them away.

C Company, attempting to take the other hill, met similar resistance.

The men retreated and rested for the night. At dawn, Captain Ice ordered another attack. This time they tried the opposite north side, and managed to fight their way only one hundred yards before being turned back by machine-gun fire. The men carried their wounded back down the hill for another night's rest.

Just before dawn the next day, a patrol managed to make their way past dozing Japanese sentries, and returned to camp reporting they had heard conversation in a banana tree grove on a wide natural ridge on the side of the hill near the top.

Technical Sergeant Alfred W. Johnson recruited a squad of some of his best shots. His small assault unit would include riflemen Private John R. "Mac" (aka J.R.) McKinney, Private Adolph "Red" Barrette, and Corporal Gerry "Ramp" Rampy. Private Gene Maziarz's BAR would be the only automatic weapon.

The plan called for another squad to move around to the right while Johnson's men rushed the grove from the front.

Johnson's team caught the Japanese totally by surprise. Before they could pick up weapons, M1 and BAR fire cut them down. In seconds, twelve Imperial soldiers lay dead in and around a large foxhole. Private Maziarz reported later, "We all fired so fast, it was over in a few seconds. No one knows who shot who. It didn't matter. That job was done!"

The GIs found a large radio in the foxhole at the grove of trees. Sergeant Johnson destroyed it with a hand grenade.

The job was done, but now "every Jap on the hill was awake and came at us from two directions. They were using knee mortars for support. We didn't have enough firepower to fight it out for long!" said Gerry Rampy in a later interview.

The support squad distracted one flank of Japanese long enough for both units to withdraw down the hill. Everyone made it back unharmed.

Captain Ice was not about to give up. He had his orders. His men must clear the hills. All night, two artillery battalions blasted Twin Peaks, and at dawn, the chemical battalion launched white phosphorous mortars. Through this smoke, Companies A and C once again climbed the hills to seek out the Japanese who might have survived the artillery shelling.

Company A passed the banana tree grove, stepping over the bodies of the enemy killed the day before.

But what they didn't know was that the Japanese defenders had protected themselves by hiding in caves and bunkers during the night.

Suddenly, Company A ran into well-entrenched Japanese infantry armed with rifles. These men were only decoys, luring the Americans into a trap. Beyond lay the true defenses waiting in bunkers.

Captain Ice heard the high-pitched "woodpecker" sounds of Nambu machine guns open up on his men. His radio message to battalion headquarters told the story in two chilling words: "We're stopped!"

Moments later, the C Company commander reported, "We're stopped, too!"[5]

Captain Ice gathered a squad of riflemen, moved through the gully, and started up one of the hills. He planned to get a close look at the enemy's emplacements and give a personal report by radio to headquarters. Then and only then could he offer his assessment and recommend the next course of action.

They had just crossed the first ridge when rifle shots, like a string of firecrackers, popped in the distance. Bullets ricocheted from the dirt at their feet with familiar "zinging" sounds. The men dove for cover, thrusting rifles forward as they hit. But Captain Ice, still clutching his carbine, fell backward. He rolled over and struggled to his knees. His right hand grasp at the wet, red spot on his shirt.

"I'm hit!" the captain shouted. "Return fire!"

There was no need to issue the order. Through training and instinct, his men had begun to rake the front with a constant barrage of M1 fire.

The Japanese shooting ceased. Captain Ice stood up and opened his shirt for a closer look at the wound. He could feel the bullet just under the skin.

"I'll be okay," he assured his men. "I'm really blessed. This round must have been spent.[6]

"You men spread out. Gather as much info as you can, then head back within an hour."

The captain insisted that he could make it to camp unassisted. Alone, he staggered down the hill, through the gully, and finally collapsed on a stretcher when he reached the camp. Though it was not a serious wound, Harry Ice had lost a considerable amount of blood and the medics worried about infection. They held the company commander on a cot for a few days. Then Captain Ice was permitted to return to his A Company.

Battalion Headquarters ordered A and C Companies to fall back farther. Artillery began to pound the "Twins," while aircraft blanketed the slopes with flaming napalm.[7]

A report classified "Secret" until late 1946 summed up the battle for Twin Peaks: "The nature of the mountainous terrain was a great aid to the Jap in defending his position. We had an uphill fight all the way. Each ridge was higher than the preceding one. Thus, as we drove the Jap from one, he would take up another prepared defense position on the next higher ridge which gave him good observation of our positions and movements. From these ingeniously prepared positions the Jap soldier fought suicidally to the bitter end."[8]

McKinney and Barrette tried to clear their mouths and noses of the stench as the napalm did its job of burning every organic thing it struck to a cinder, including the Japanese soldiers.

But on March 3, the First Battalion troops were ordered to pull out. They were moved by truck to the Tubao area, just east of Agoo. Captain Ice's Company, having taken a beating for two weeks, was relieved by the Second Battalion of the 130th Infantry at Twin Peaks. It would be up to the 130th to search for Japanese wounded and stragglers on the hills. Some might have escaped the shelling and napalm.

Now the entire 123rd Regiment had to clear a huge tract of low, rolling hills between the little village of Pugo and some ridges held by other units. Especially important were two five-hundred-foot hills labeled "X" and "Y" and believed to be used by the enemy as observation posts.

Once again, the Japanese would be "able to look down our throats all the way to Baguio," as one battalion commander reported to the 123rd headquarters. Someone had to come up with a special plan on how the GIs might take X and Y and all the other hills between them.

As strange as it may seem, the solution actually came as an idea generated from documents removed from the body of a dead Japanese.

The Americans became very cautious of night movements in the thick jungles of New Guinea. But in the hills of northern Luzon, the underbrush and foliage was not nearly as dense as a jungle.

The enemy documents and battle notes indicated that the Japanese truly believed that the American infantry would not attack or even move at night.[9]

Typical of their mentality at the time, once convinced that the GI feared night movements, the Japanese were certain the GIs would never change under any circumstances. Consequently, the Japanese lost night alertness altogether.

***

Mortar and machine-gun expert, Sergeant Gerald Nutt, twenty-three years old, had a fascination with electricity and looked forward to returning to his home in Carthage, Illinois, for a career involving "anything electrical."

Sergeant Nutt had poor eyesight. One might think that his condition would have classified him as 4F with the draft board. "Gerry," as his buddies called him, could be physically unfit for the military. But during World War II, one had to be "damned near blind" for a medical deferment. For many soldiers, there was the horrible thought of what they would do if they lost their glasses during combat.

Sergeant Nutt had been wearing prescription glasses since the third grade. He, like so many other men in a similar situation in combat, never worried about the handicap. His glasses, it seemed, were a part of him.

But at 3:00 A.M. near Hill X, things were about to change for Sergeant Nutt.

Capitalizing on the knowledge obtained from those Japanese documents, the entire 123rd Regiment launched their first large-scale night attack.

With only a little light from the moon, Sergeant Nutt, carrying his 60mm mortar, moved out near John McKinney and the rest of their A Company buddies.

They worked their way through the brush in the darkness, Nutt cursing silently the problems he was having with the long mortar tube. "It constantly got hung up in bushes" and bounced off tree trunks as he turned and twisted his way up the narrow trail. Then it happened. The mortar tube broke loose from a large bush and swung around, smashing into Gerry's face. The shattered glass and frames fell and disappeared in high grass.

"I'm through, boys," Sergeant Nutt muttered.

"What?"

"My glasses broke. I can't find them. What the hell am I going to do if the Japs attack?"

"Hold on to my belt, Gerry," the man in front said. "I'll move slow."

Gerry Nutt admitted years later that, for a few moments, he thought he might get sent to "the rear," wherever that was, and rest the next few days.

"But it didn't work out that way." Before the morning ended, Sergeant Gerry Nutt had a new set of glasses, compliments of the Regiment's Medical Aid Station.

"All through Army training, New Guinea, and until that moment, I never thought or worried what might happen if I lost my glasses in combat."[10]

The Aid Station had traveled with the 123rd Regiment Headquarters to the town of Damortis. From there, the medics moved forward through the rugged terrain to be in the fighting and provide frontline treatment to the wounded.

Evacuation was extremely difficult and dangerous in the steep hills of

Northern Luzon. It was accomplished mostly by Filipino litter bearers. Through their efforts, more trained medical personnel were relieved to render aid to the wounded.

The Army naturally anticipated problems with eyeglass replacement, and was ready with prescribed backup pairs of glasses for the men on the front line.

Sergeant Nutt missed the first attack, but he and his mortar team would be in the next battle and the next and the next as they inched their way toward Baguio.

As a result of the night attacks, Hills X and Y fell to the First Battalion. The 123rd Infantry learned some good tricks in night tactics, and went on to drive the Japanese from Hill 3000 and Hill 4980.

* * *

American aircraft conducted their first fire bomb raid on Tokyo on March 9, followed by a second bombing on the tenth.

Military Intelligence had suggested sometime before that fire bombs could easily create an inferno that would essentially burn "Tokyo to the ground." The fact that so many civilian homes and small businesses were constructed of wood and paper made them perfect targets for fire bombs. Only the Imperial Palace was to be spared.

The first raid was successful. It killed over a hundred thousand people.

Nagoya became the next target on the eleventh, then Osaka on the thirteenth, Kobe on the sixteenth.

The B29s returned to rain fire on Nagoya once again on March 19, 1945. Even with tens of thousands of Japanese civilians being burned alive during the fire bombing, the Japanese spirit did not break and there was no talk of surrender. The U.S. Air Corps knew they had to plan to fire bomb every city on each island.

In America, some began to question if the B29s were simply dumping gasoline on hundreds of thousands of innocent (noncombatant) Japanese, including children who were too young to work in factories. They were wrong. It was not gasoline. It was napalm, gelled gasoline.

CHAPTER 13

*"Ninety percent of war is having good
intelligence; if you know where the enemy is
and what he has, you can figure out how to
deal with him."*

General Douglas MacArthur

(To American Guerrilla Colonel Bernard Anderson, 1945)

Luzon

April 1945

Who will remember the names of the barrios or even the towns? Those
who fought and bled there and saw their buddies blown apart there.
And when they are gone, who then? The loved ones who knew they suffered somewhere. And when they are gone, who then?

The men of A Company, waiting to move up and attack the Imperial
soldiers, lay quietly on the south side of Hill X with unknown thoughts.
Since leaving New Guinea, there had never been much time to really get
to know one another. When the opportunity came, they would talk in
little groups for a few moments. Conversations were limited to subjects
like where one was from—countryside or city—and what they wanted to
do when the war finally came to an end.

Every man had his own good-luck charm or special personal item—
some connection to the peaceful world they once knew. Some carried
rosaries or a religious medal, many a small Bible, a photo of someone
loved, or any little thing "from home."

Emotions peaked and ran heavy. It was not unusual to see big men, tough little men, farm boys and city guys, break down and cry, then go on fighting.

Sadness disappeared suddenly like a spring rain, only to return again and again, sometimes replaced by anger and hatred—hatred for the enemy, hatred for the Army that had put them in that awful, stinking, miserable hell called battle.

Often the rifleman knew the only things he had left to trust were his buddies and his M1 rifle.

Now Hill X; another hill to cry on, to bleed on, to die on. There were a hundred Luzon hills that GIs were fighting for that day. This one happened to be called X because it had never been named by anyone.

"It sure seemed bad to die in a place that ain't got no name," John McKinney told his sister Betty in a letter. "But some boys did."

PFC Gene Maziarz checked the magazine in his "Beautiful BAR," as he affectionately called his weapon, and waited for the order to advance. His thoughts flashed back to a few days before, April 1st, when his "drinking buddy" and ammo man, Tony "Chippy" Ciepelewski, was wounded. He remembered the chill he felt and how he wondered if he would ever see Chippy again, then the relief, almost joy, when he got the message: Chippy would be okay and back on the front lines soon.

"Looks like another one got it!" the man crouching nearby said.

Gene glanced around. "Where?"

"Over to your left. On the hillside."

PFC Maziarz could see men carrying the body of a GI down the hill slope about fifty yards away. "Wonder who it was," Gene muttered.

The rifleman stared straight ahead and did not answer.

Minutes crawled by. Still no order to advance. Rifle fire from the Japanese lines diminished except for an occasional "crack" of a single shot, assuring everyone that the enemy was still up there waiting.

A soldier with his rifle slung over his back carried four canteens of water by their chains and dropped down next to PFC Maziarz.

"Brought some extra water from camp," the man said. "Figured you guys could use it."

"Thanks."

After a brief pause, the man added in a soft voice, "Mickey got it. A few minutes ago. In the head just below his helmet. Sergeant Rocke is with the body."

"Mickey!" Gene replied. "What a lovable guy. He was the nicest fellow in the whole battalion."

"Yeah," the soldier agreed. "The sniper got it too. McKinney was near Mickey at the time, raised up and killed the Jap with one quick shot."[1]

In their camp at the foot of Hill X, Sergeant Sol Rocke had covered the body of PFC Michael W. "Mickey" Danielewsky with a canvas pup tent, and was about to return to his squad when he saw PFC Henry F. Wietecki racing toward him.

Sgt. Rocke knew that Mickey and Wietecki were from the South Side of Chicago, the same age, and had been good friends since the early days of the war.

PFC Wietecki, cradling his M1 and out of breath, halted as he reached the canvas. "Mickey?" he asked, his body beginning to shake. "Is he dead, Sarge?"

Sergeant Rocke answered soberly, "Yes, he's dead. Killed instantly. He didn't suffer."

Henry Wietecki sobbed uncontrollably, his entire body shaking. "No! Is he *really* dead?"

Sergeant Rocke nodded. "Yes."

Henry's crying became hysterical for almost a minute, then abruptly stopped. He shifted his rifle to his left hand and wiped at the tears with his right arm. With eyes locked on the ground, he slowly walked back up the hill.

Riflemen learned to accept death each in their own way. They had to. Death was with them every day and through the night. Those who knew Mickey Danielewsky would remember he was killed on April 4, 1945. Soldiers remember the death of a pal forever. In combat, during that fatal moment when a friend is taken, there is shock, disbelief, sadness, and anger, but the deep sorrow for those who survive comes later and never goes away.[2]

Several days after Mickey's death, PFC Henry F. Wietecki performed with exceptional courage in another battle and was awarded the Bronze Star for bravery.

* * *

On March 27, the First Battalion had moved to the Asin Valley and set up their headquarters at a power plant town known as Galiano.

Two huge mountains flanked the valley, Mt. Bilbil on the north and Mt. Lomboy on the opposite side.

The battalion's mission was to fight their way to Asin by taking the most direct route along a dirt road running between the mountains. Military intelligence apparently did not know that the Japanese had heavily fortified those mountains and their surrounding hills.

The enemy permitted the First Battalion to proceed a short distance out of Galiano. From the vantage points in the highlands, the enemy was, no doubt, surprised to see the Americans were walking into a trap so easily.

Japanese mortars and mountain artillery began a ruthless shelling, which continued through the first week of April.

It is unknown if the Japanese defending the Asin hills were aware that their homeland had just been invaded. On April 1, more than fifty thousand GIs landed on the island of Okinawa and were making progress, advancing cross-country.

First Battalion, including John McKinney's A Company, received the invasion news as the shelling of their positions continued. Japan had been invaded? Maybe the war would be over soon. Maybe it would not be necessary to fight all the way to Baguio. Maybe some would be going home soon. Maybe . . . maybe. But Company A's war was right there on the trail from Galiano, and the battalion had been stopped by Japanese shelling. Advancing even another hundred yards would bring heavy casualties. A new plan was desperately needed.

A long knoblike hill with a ridge separating it into two parts ran down the southern slope of Mt. Bilbil. Since it had no name on the map, it became Hill X.

In a switch of tactics, the battalion, led by A Company, moving to the left, would assault the hill.

Drinking water became more precious than ammunition. Salt tablets saved lives as the men began a steady climb, some on narrow trails, some struggling through the brush.

Heat trapped inside their battle fatigues drenched the men in perspiration. Web equipment and leather boots became soaked in sweat, feeling like a heavy rain had just passed over. Men, strong experienced men, fell to the ground, too exhausted to continue. With what energy remained, they ripped open their shirts in an attempt to expose skin to any cooling breeze.[3]

A Company covered three hundred yards, three times the length of a football field, fighting against Japanese rifle and machine-gun fire. Then the Americans were stopped.

Seven times A Company tried to push farther up the hill, and seven times the enemy stopped them, inflicting more GI casualties each day.

About midday on April 9, men in Sergeant Rocke's squad heard a shout. "Captain Ice is down! The captain's hit!"

For the second time in a month, A Company Commander Captain Harry Ice was wounded. His luck held out. He would return to duty in three days.

In prewar times, Baguio was at its zenith of popularity as a summer capital of the Philippines. This mile-high city had an abundance of natural beauty, including tall pine trees. It was also noted for its golf courses, swimming pools, nightclubs, tennis courts, and a mild, often cool mountain temperature; a welcome relief from the sweltering tropical heat of the lowlands.

Now the beautiful scenic routes winding up the mountains to Baguio were death traps. The roads went between rocky bluffs, perfect for Japanese riflemen, mortars, machine guns, and light artillery.

Against the Japanese mountain fortifications, American armor and heavy artillery was practically useless—until engineers, continually exposing themselves to enemy fire, cleared the sabotaged roads and rebuilt bridges.

After being chopped to pieces for seven days at Hill X, Company A, and what was left of their battalion, was ordered to pull back to Galiano and rest. Fresh troops were sent in to continue the attack until the hill and its mountains were finally in U.S. hands.

PFC John McKinney did not actually see the body of PFC Mickey Danielewsky. But he did pause at the canvas that covered the Chicagoan.

"Them boys are the *real* heroes!" he exclaimed to his sergeant. "Them boys that die up here; not us who walk away."

The Japanese also lost men at Hill X; most on the front lines, plus a few who had attempted to circle behind A Company to attack from the rear. They never made it. Their bodies littered the trails and the road back to Galiano.

"I felt bad for them Jap boys," John McKinney wrote to his mother a few weeks later, "when I saw their bodies lying along the trail. No one knows who they are. Their families don't know where they died. They was my enemy, but they were doing their duty, like me."[4]

John McKinney had been "just another foot soldier who always did his job," as Captain Harry Ice would later describe the Georgian.

Members of Company A, First Battalion, 123rd Infantry Regiment, Thirty-third Division remembered John McKinney sixty years after those 1945 battles on Luzon during interviews with the author.

Gerry Nutt, mortar and rifleman: "Where there was food you would find McKinney. He just seemed to quietly appear out of nowhere at the smell of chow. But I'll tell you, that slow-talking boy was one hell of a shot with the M1."

Gerry "Ramp" Rampy, staff sergeant, usually carried a carbine, but sometimes an M1: "John mostly was sitting around by himself just a-watching the other fellows who were always messing with one another. A nice guy. I never got to know him real well, but it's that way in war. Not much social time. What we knew about him, we liked. If you needed help with some little chore, he was right there to lend a hand. You didn't have to ask him."

Gene "Maz" Maziarz, Browning automatic rifle (BAR) man: "Mac was soft-spoken, kinda skinny, like all of us, I guess. He was sure deadly with that rifle. He didn't say much, and I never heard him say a real vulgar word during it all."

Sol Rocke, sergeant (and John McKinney's squad leader), carried rifle, carbine, or tommy gun: "One lasting memory I have of Mac was his deep Southern accent and polite manners. He had more patience than any soldier in the outfit, and he seemed to have a natural instinct for moving about those hills on Luzon. One more thing, he made good moonshine! Can you imagine someone constructing an entire still from a wrecked Japanese plane?!"

Henry Van Westrop, sergeant, photographer for the Thirty-third Division: "I only met him [McKinney] once, briefly. I had been called over to headquarters and saw this young skinny soldier sitting on the grass next to a .30-caliber machine gun. I went over to him and asked if he minded if I took his picture. He looked up, smiled slightly, and replied in a slow drawl, 'Sure, go ahead.' He wasn't much for making conversation. Mostly, I asked questions and he would reply with 'nope' or 'yep.' A few minutes later someone told me I had just taken a picture of *the* McKinney."

Jesse Frazee, sergeant, carried carbine or rifle: "I loved to tease Mac on some subject to get him to respond with one of his favorite replies, 'I ain't talking!' And he really didn't talk much, but we had fun with one another that way. Glad he was one of us. I sure would not have wanted to be in his rifle sights. He never missed!"

From desert training to Hawaii to New Guinea and through mid-April 1945 on Luzon, PFC John McKinney had, indeed, been "just another soldier who always did his job." Perhaps the performance of all the men in A Company from a military point of view had been outstanding. But they were trained and knew what was required of them in combat. Their job: destroy the enemy and try to stay alive in the process.

* * *

Once back in Galiano, A Company was assigned the task of guarding a huge stockpile of ammunition, food rations, and other supplies trucked in for the forces fighting in the hills. That should have been something of a restful duty compared to frontline combat.

But rest remained elusive. The moment they set up camp and placed guards on the perimeter, the Japanese began to attack in small raiding parties firing rifles, machine guns, and knee mortars. Galiano became anything but a sanctuary for the weary. From the ninth to the eleventh of April, Japanese artillery pounded the little city from their positions in the mountains.

I Corps Headquarters and the 123rd commanders finally agreed: A Company and its battalion had suffered enough. They were brought back to the town of Sison to serve as a reserve unit. This would mean at least a few combat-free days. It also gave time for commanders to present overdue awards for bravery.

Fifty-eight men in Company A received the Order of the Purple Heart (sometimes called the Badge of Military Merit) for combat wounds inflicted by the enemy. Six men killed in action were awarded the Purple Heart posthumously.[5]

The Bronze Star, a medal awarded for heroic service in action ("not involving aerial flight") was awarded to a few men, and even fewer were awarded the Silver Star, the Army's third-highest combat medal for gallantry (after the Distinguished Service Cross and the highest award, the Congressional Medal of Honor).

All the men of the 123rd had performed bravely during those difficult days, but certain conditions had to exist for a medal to be awarded.

A Company's Captain Ice remarked, "If the Army gave out medals to all those brave men who earned them this past month, they wouldn't have enough medals in the warehouses."[6]

Most combat veterans will say that the system for awarding medals for bravery can never be fair. That unfortunately is true. So many brave deeds go unnoticed, or the correct number of witnesses is not present at the time to testify later.

Men did extraordinary things, of course, not for medals, but because they were doing their job.

No one can satisfactorily explain all the motivations for acts of bravery, especially those performed beyond what is expected of every soldier. Each case is different.

In April, not far from where John McKinney's A Company engaged in battle, Captain George Lindsay's L Company was hit by two hundred Japanese probing their defense lines. It was 3:00 A.M. Lindsay's machine guns and BARs cut down a large percentage of the enemy, who, by the second attempt, had changed their tactics to a full "banzai" (suicide) charge in the darkness. Survivors reported the terrible, shrill battle cries of the Japanese and the moans of their wounded that could be heard above the noise of the weapons.

PFC Burton J. Lee repelled one enemy flank attack with his BAR. Unable to get good aim at the attackers, the private leaped from his foxhole, blazing away with the BAR. Six Imperial soldiers fell dead in front of him.

The next morning at dawn, the Japanese charged again, bayoneting their way through the American defense lines, and fought toward L Company's command center. One man stood in their way—PFC Lee. Again, he climbed out of his foxhole and walked toward the charging enemy, firing his BAR, pausing only long enough to reload with a fresh magazine. The surprised Japanese hesitated, then hit the ground. For a moment, Lee and his BAR had stopped the charge.

Lee continued to advance, pumping round after round into the prone enemy. Men rushing to his aid saw PFC Lee "stagger as several puffs of dust burst from the back of his fatigue shirt." Nambu machine-gun fire had caught him in the chest.

But Lee didn't fall. He stumbled and regained his footing as he continued on toward the screaming Japanese, the BAR still spitting fire.

He managed another six yards, stepping over those he had just killed, and shot several more who were charging at him. Then he dropped his BAR and "pitched forward" into the grass, dead.

Inspired by PFC Lee's bravery, his buddies rushed at the remaining Japanese. L Company won the battle that day.

Captain Lindsay recommended PFC Lee for a posthumous Medal of Honor—recommended by an officer, witnessed by more than twelve soldiers. General MacArthur's headquarters denied the recommendation and reduced the award to a Distinguished Service Cross.[7]

At Sison, the men of A Company enjoyed rest, hot food, and a change of clothes (for the first time in three weeks). I Corps's plan was to prepare the entire First Battalion for the final assault on Baguio.

But A Company would be denied that opportunity.

I Corps headquarters, thanks to reports from guerrilla leader Colonel Bernard Anderson, learned that Japanese infantry, retreating from the hills around Manila, were making their way north to join up with General Yamashita by following a route along Dingalan Bay.

The bay was located on the east coast of Luzon, the opposite side from where Company A had been fighting.

Aerial reconnaissance confirmed Colonel Anderson's reports—small groups of Japanese had been spotted along the Umiray River. They were moving north at the point where the river empties into Dingalan Bay.

I Corps quickly dispatched a team of Alamo Scouts to the Umiray River for an up close investigation. Now, with that done, the corps planned for a special task force to move into the area and put a stop to the Japanese retreat.

Company A, enjoying their short R and R, was to become the key unit in that task force. But Sergeant Sol Rocke would not accompany them. Suffering from a bad case of jungle rot, Sergeant Rocke was sent to a field hospital to recover. Rocke protested. He wanted to remain with his men whom he had trained and fought with side by side. The doctors, however, had different ideas. Sol Rocke would be out of duty for a while, and PFC John McKinney had lost his favorite sergeant and squad leader.

* * *

On April 11, German Admiral Doenitz supervised the loading of his submarine U234 and, through an interpreter, briefed two Japanese Naval officers who would accompany him on their long sea journey from Europe to Japan.

Aboard the U234 was 1,120 pounds of uranium promised to the

Japanese for their atomic bomb project. It would only be enough to make two bombs.[8]

Hitler's Germany was now days away from total collapse. U.S. bombing in Japan had caused a delay in the Japanese A-bomb program. Most scientific equipment and related raw materials were moved to Korea, out of the range of American planes. There, they had to wait for the U234 and the precious uranium.

CHAPTER 14

"Prevent the enemy from breaking through
to the north. Patrol and kill!"

I Corps Orders to the Dingalan Bay Task Force

April 1945

Long ago, Luzon's Dumagat people were mostly nomadic, moving from one mountain to another at the southern end of the Sierra Madre range.

They hunted wild pig and small deer, gathered fruits and root crops, and fished the clear rivers with spears.

These peaceful people had no weapons to make war. Their language did not even have a word for "war," nor did they have words for or understand the meaning of "rape" or "hate."

Yet they named everything in their world, which was enclosed by a river on the south, the Mingan Mountains on the north, and the Pacific Ocean to the east.

The Dumagat's productive hunting was in the mossy forest of tall hardwood trees beneath the majestic mountain peaks. There were seasons for the hunt, which varied depending on the migration of animals. Their land was blessed with a year-round mild climate refreshed by ocean breezes. Unlike other parts of Luzon, there was no distinctive rainy or dry season (though they did receive "harvest rains" between October and December).

Trees in the lowlands provided coconuts, bananas, mangoes, and avocados, and the streams always had plenty of *bulig* (mud fish) and catfish.

The Dumagats called the river that formed their southern boundary Galan, and they named the beautiful bay it flowed into Dingalan or "By the Side of the River Galan."

Dingalan Bay was their holy place, a place for worship. Its eighteen miles of coastline is protected by two major coral reefs, and the blue waters had an abundance of marlin, yellowfin tuna, salmon, mackerel, lapu-lapu, sap-sap, and scrod. But the Dumagats did not fish in the bay. Spear-fishing in the shallow streams produced all they needed.

Like most primitive people, they believed in magic. Large bats, monitor lizards, hawks, and eagles in the forest had souls and shared valuable secrets about survival with them. And the waters of Dingalan Bay also spoke to the people, giving advice for the future, warning of storms, and promising wonderful things, which today we might call miracles. They believed those "miracles," or "holy gifts" as they called them, would only come to those who loved and respected their land and valued the gifts from hunting and fishing.

Through reverence to the waters of the bay, the Dumagats never lived on its brown, sandy beaches. They remained in the mountains and forests, visiting the sandbars from time to time to give thanks to the power that brought them life, a power they did not understand, yet never questioned.

It all had to change for the Dumagats, not because they desired it, but because others wanted their world, or at least what was *in* their world.

In the early 1900s, farmers from the provinces of Quezon, Nueva Ecija, and Ilocos migrated into the paradise, mostly to harvest fruits. In the 1930s a logging operation began with a sawmill complex erected on flat land at the northern end of Dingalan Bay and the name of the Galan River was changed to Umiray.

The Dumagats moved to a higher altitude and remained a safe distance from the intruders.

In 1942, the Imperial Japanese soldiers came to take over the sawmill. They needed lumber for barracks and other construction projects scattered about Luzon.

When a few brave Dumagats tried to return to their sacred bay, the Japanese soldiers shot them.

In early 1945, as the Americans pushed across Luzon from the west coast, the Japanese deserted the sawmill and things were peaceful at Dingalan Bay for a few months.

Then, in March, Japanese soldiers began to travel along the Umiray River. They turned north, following the tree line near the ocean. Again, the Dumagats found safety high in the mountains. But the lowlands and beaches of their Dingalan Bay paradise were about to become a place of violence and death.

* * *

In mid-April 1945, a Japanese Army launch traveled slowly north, slicing through the clear waters of Dingalan Bay. It remained close to the shore, zigzagging here and there, trying to avoid scraping its bottom on submerged sandbars and boulders.

At 9:00 A.M. it turned into the mouth of the Umiray River. Its engine throttled back and the little boat moved at a slower speed.

The Umiray is fifty yards across at its mouth and three to five feet deep at that point. But less than a quarter mile west, it narrows to thirty yards, then twenty, and eventually, far upstream, to only ten yards.

Likewise, the depth changes rapidly, but that and the current depend mostly on the amount of rain that has fallen in the mountains.

When the launch struck the gravel bottom, the engine stopped and the launch coasted quietly to a sandy bank.

Had the Japanese been watching the boat enter the river, their spirits might have been lifted. They were waiting for the food and medical supplies badly needed by the soldiers on that movement north. And they were hoping for mail and a message from some headquarters assuring them that more boats were coming to help evacuate them, or even word that planes would soon be dropping supplies.

There were no more boats coming, and the Imperial Army's air force on Luzon had essentially ceased to exist. The Japanese would have been disappointed for another reason that morning. When soldiers leaped from the boat and rushed for the woods, it was obvious that they were not from the Imperial Army. They were Americans and Filipinos!

Using a captured Japanese military launch, an Alamo Scout team of three men plus guerrillas, under Sergeant James Farrow, had successfully deceived snipers along the coast and completed the first phase of their mission to land at the mouth of the Umiray River.

This group, according to historian Lance Zedric, had become known as the "Farrow Team," and had three enlisted Scouts, First Sergeant Frederico Blambao, Sergeant James Farrow, Jr., and Sergeant Peter Vischansky.

Since early February, Scout teams had spread all over the Philippines on a variety of assignments. At the time Sergeant Farrow departed on his mission, all officers were leading other teams operating mostly in northern Luzon. Throughout their vigorous training, emphasis had been placed on "assuming command." Should any officer be unable to perform his duties, every team member knew exactly what had to be done, and would take over command. The same held true with availability. If an officer was not available, a noncommissioned officer assumed those duties. In this case, Sergeant Farrow was chosen to lead the mission.[1]

The total assignment was to "land at the mouth of Umiray River. Move southwest along river. To contact Japs moving from Antipolo northeast along the river. To capture prisoners, eliminate small patrols, prevent Japs from crossing to north side of river. To locate all possible trails that could be used by Japs in this area. To set up radio station and OP [observation post] covering all trails and observe Japs moving north."

The first report from the Farrow Team ignited a fire that would become the "Umiray River—Dingalan Bay Mission." Colonel Bernard Anderson's guerrillas already had I Corps Intelligence Section's attention. There was little doubt that the Japanese were "streaming" in retreat up the east coast of Luzon. With all the fighting on the west coast and the American push up the center of the island, there was only one avenue of escape for the Japanese: march to Dingalan Bay, then north and west.

Determining just how many enemy soldiers there were, where they were, and exactly which route they traveled was a perfect job for the Scouts.[2]

I Corps Intelligence realized that to adequately cover Dingalan Bay from south to north would, no doubt, require two Scout teams. But all teams had other assignments at the time. At least, I Corps selected the perfect location to send the available team—the area where Farrow would be likely to gather the most valuable information on enemy movements—the Umiray River.

After waiting an hour, Sergeant Farrow led his men up a trail along the south side of the river, traveling slowly all day until they reached the tiny village of Balete. It was 7:00 P.M., near dark. They discovered the barrio already had visitors—two hundred Imperial Army soldiers preparing to rest for the night.

A Japanese sentry spotted one of the Filipino guerrillas and a firefight began. The Scouts had no alternative but to engage the enemy, and hopefully trick them into believing they were under attack by a much larger American force.

The battle lasted almost six hours; then suddenly the Japanese broke off from the fight and retreated north into the darkness. No Alamo Scouts were hit and enemy casualties are reported as "unknown."

After a brief rest, the Scouts continued west along the river until they reached Maroraqui Creek, where they came upon an enemy force of fifty camping at the intersection of the creek and river.

Now it was late in the second day. Without hesitation, the Scouts attacked, and in a few minutes succeeded in killing three Japanese soldiers, capturing three "United Nippons," and scattering the remaining.[3]

Oddly, the next day the Scouts again ran into "the same two hundred Japs as before." The enemy was still moving as a somewhat organized unit. The Scouts ambushed the Japanese, determined to break their ranks into nothing more than squads. A battle lasted over four hours, resulting in six dead Japanese and one captured. Enemy survivors fled southeast. All members of Sergeant Farrow's team had performed with outstanding courage, making intelligent decisions while employing techniques learned from months of training.

To say that the Japanese soldiers along the Umiray were surprised to encounter the Scouts would be an understatement—*shocked* more likely describes the enemy reaction.

The retreating Japanese had no idea where the Americans came from or how they'd arrived so far up the river, and they did not know how many GIs were in the Dingalan area.

Only a few weeks before, Japanese planners of the withdrawal had assured them that there were no Americans at Dingalan Bay, only a few Filipino guerrillas. The word of alarm passed from one group of stragglers to another. It would be safer to remain in small squad-size units and cut through the woods. Many others did not receive the suggestion or ignored it.

Having accomplished most of their mission, the Alamo Scouts returned to Balete with their prisoners and planned to move on to the river's mouth. At the village, they came upon three Japanese and quickly killed them. Maps and documents were found on their bodies.

A day later, two thousand yards upstream from Dingalan Bay, the Scouts attacked yet another party of Japanese and killed them before they could escape into the woods.

Now, with captured maps, documents, prisoners, and a good knowledge of Japanese troop strength, the Scouts were ready to send another radio report to be relayed on to I Corps. Their conclusion—on any day as many as three hundred Japanese soldiers could be along the Umiray, but they were now scattering into small groups.

Sergeant Farrow was told to remain at the Umiray River and await orders to evacuate; estimated date of withdrawal May 10. The Scouts would continue reconnaissance patrols and report any changes in the enemy situation by radio. The sergeant elected to move back up the river to the Maroraqui Creek and set up camp there.

A few guerrillas escorted the enemy prisoners along with documents back to the American lines in the Japanese launch. Two days later, they returned with supplies of food and ammunition.

Meanwhile, Sergeant Farrow was advised by I Corps Intelligence that a special "Task Force" was on the way to Dingalan Bay to block the Japanese escape.

The task force planned to establish their headquarters at the old sawmill, abandoned by the Japanese and now in the hands of a unit of Colonel Anderson's Filipino guerrillas.[4]

From that base at the north end of the bay, they would have good radio contact with the Alamo Scouts and future patrols operating at the southern end of the Umiray River.

* * *

General Tomoyuki Yamashita and what was left of his Fourteenth Area Army were virtually sealed off in the mountains of northern Luzon. He'd expected that situation and, on April 8, 1945, counted on his men to continue to fight bravely and delay the ever-advancing Americans. He also expected reinforcements, not from Japan, but remnants of his own army breaking out of pockets east and south of Manila and slipping north to join him.

But the final offensive for Baguio had begun. The Thirty-seventh Division pressed in from the northwest while the Thirty-third, led by the 123rd Regiment, continued their yard-by-yard advance from the southwest.

American guerrilla Colonel Russell W. Volckmann left his mountain stronghold far north of Baguio and with eighteen thousand men, including some reinforcements landing on the coast, began to fight south and east through the mountains, squeezing General Yamashita even more. The Japanese staff had nowhere to retreat but to another mountainous area northeast of Baguio.

* * *

Captain Harry Ice's weary A Company would not be given much time to rest at the town of Sison. American troops continued to gain ground, but the number of casualties increased as the Japanese fought back, determined not to lose another hill. But they were losing. One hill, then another, one cave, then two, and the mangled bodies of more GIs were brought back for temporary burial.

On April 10, 1945, the Thirty-third Division was ordered to turn over all reserve units to the direct command of I Corps.[5]

I Corps was ready to launch an all-out assault on Baguio in an effort to finish off General Yamashita. Then, as often happens during war, concurrent with ordering the First Battalion (in reserve) back into service, a special request arrived at the Thirty-third headquarters. The G-3 section of I Corps needed one rifle company—the toughest they had—and the battalion executive officer to report to the town of Rosales located about twenty miles southwest of Baguio. The request only stated that they were needed for a "high-priority mission."

Captain Harry Ice, his two wounds barely healed, and PFC John McKinney, along with his battle-hardened buddies of A Company and Major Robert V. Connolly, the battalion's executive officer, were trucked to Rosales.

Through the chain of command, Major Connolly had established a reputation as an intelligent, calm, and aggressive officer. His physical appearance and his military bearing had left a lasting impression with division officers in staff meetings.

At a time when the average American soldier stood about five-seven to five-ten, Connolly was a giant of a man at six-three and weighing over 220 pounds. His years as an "aggressive tackle" at New York University certainly prepared him for future challenges. After graduating, he joined the Army as a private at age twenty-six in February 1941. When the war broke out in December, he was already assigned to the Golden Cross Thirty-third Division, training at Camp Forrest. He entered Officers Candidate School (OCS) and received his commission as a second lieutenant in May 1942. Later, he became A Company commander.

As a captain, Robert Connolly received the Bronze Star for bravery while fighting with the 123rd in New Guinea.

Now Major Robert V. Connolly, at age thirty-one, would be given a mission that carries his name in U.S. military history—the Connolly Task Force.

Since he had grown up with the 123rd since its birth, it was only logical for Connolly to select his friend Captain Harry Ice to be second in command of this force.

The two officers may have been different in size, but they were team players, aggressive, persistent, and possessed the natural ability to be dynamic leaders.

When Connolly and Ice along with A Company arrived at I Corps Headquarters on the tenth, the major was ushered into the G-3 office. Able Company was deployed around the area for additional security.

Major Connolly was informed that he would be responsible for blocking the escape route used by the Japanese at Dingalan Bay. The combined group from A company (First Battalion), Colonel Bernard Anderson's First Battalion, and the Second Philippine Regiment would be called the Connolly Task Force.[6]

The staff reviewed reports received from Anderson's men operating in the Dingalan area. The Second Anderson Regiment had, according to them, "secured" and were "holding" the sawmill at the north end of the bay. Some of their men had secured a second sawmill some three or four miles north and inland at Bitolok. But the only reliable information came by radio from the Alamo Scouts at the Umiray River.

Though it had been reported to I Corps that the Japanese were "harassing" the Filipinos at the Dingalan sawmill, the question remained just who was harassing whom?

Colonel Anderson was in another area responding to orders from Sixth Army. His knowledge of the enemy and the terrain continued to be of great value. He would not be released to help organize his troops at Dingalan. But previously he had trained most of his junior officers, who, to this point, had little or no combat experience.

Anderson's guerrillas patrolled from the sawmill and managed to conduct a few ambushes, which were successful. Fortunately for the guerrillas, their units outnumbered the Japanese. Yet, the fear remained that the enemy would group and become organized into a two-hundred-, even four-hundred-man force. Dealing with that would, indeed, be difficult for the inexperienced guerrillas.

The guerrillas watched the flow of Japanese soldiers continue, and worried that the enemy might "launch an attack on these valuable installations" (the sawmills).[7]

On April 11, Major Connolly set about choosing his staff. I Corps simply told him to take what he needed from his First Battalion.

Major Connolly had already decided that his rifle company would be Ice's outfit. Captain Ice became the task force executive officer and passed on command of his company to Lieutenant William B. Roop, who had been wounded only two weeks earlier in the battle at Galiano. There, he'd earned the Bronze Star for bravery.

The assistant battalion surgeon, Lt. Howard "Will" Foley, joined the Force as their surgeon. The assignment made Will Foley very happy. He now had the opportunity to talk about Hawaii party days with his old buddies of A Company.

Lieutenant Daniel J. Ferrone, the Battalion S4, was called upon to be the supply officer, and Staff Sergeant Robert V. Easton would serve as the battalion operations sergeant, assistant to the intelligence officer.

Major Connolly had long admired the work of twenty-six-year-old Lieutenant John F. Reardon, whom he considered outstanding. Lieutenant Reardon was born in Spokane, and graduated from the University of Washington, where he received a reserve commission. In 1943 he enrolled at Fort Benning for additional infantry training. Early in the war he served as a platoon leader of Company C, but soon moved into Battalion Headquarters, joining the Connolly Task Force as Intelligence and Operations Officer. There, Lieutenant Reardon demonstrated his own "intelligence," interpreting data from patrols and other units and applying it into plans for each of the First Battalion's combat companies.

Connolly knew that John Reardon would be the perfect man for his task force. Someone had to analyze all the data coming in from patrols, Alamo Scouts, and guerrillas, and recommend plans for battle.

Major Connolly requested supporting weapons from D Company (the heavy weapons section), which would include a few troops to man their heavy (water-cooled) machine guns and 81mm mortars. Then he added a sprinkle of medical aid men, clerks, and drivers.

On April 12, trucks furnished by I Corps provided transportation for the Connolly Task Force, which now totaled twelve officers and 137 enlisted men. The all-day trip from Rosales to the northern shore of the C-shaped Dingalan Bay was uneventful, so much so that some of the men managed to catnap en route.

Connolly and his staff attempted to organize the First Anderson battalion at the sawmill, and declared it his "Command Post—Task Force Headquarters."

It required several hours for the jubilant Filipino guerrillas, celebrating the arrival of Americans, to settle down and begin to function as a serious part of the Force.

On April 13 (April 12 in America), came news of the death of President Roosevelt. Men of the task force gathered in small groups as word spread rapidly through the camp. Some eyes were wet, some discussed their loss, and then all went back to their duties.

The official announcement came over Armed Forces Radio, and was relayed by a company clerk from the sawmill headquarters.

The news overshadowed announcements that Hitler was holding out in a Berlin bunker and that the Russians claimed the bombed-out German capital would fall any day. The war was practically over in Europe.

But the only president most of the men of the Connolly Task Force had ever known was dead of a cerebral hemorrhage three months into his fourth term in office.

This was the man who'd given the soldiers and their parents hope, spirit, and guidance to survive the Great Depression. The longest-serving president in American history was gone.

It would be a few weeks before PFC John McKinney had time to write to his mother. He mentioned the president's death, remembering the family had discussed the radio "Fireside Chats" just after Pearl Harbor.[8]

The men at Dingalan Bay, indeed in every combat area, welcomed any news from the outside world. Mostly, it arrived by shortwave overseas broadcasts and the Armed Forces Radio Network.

Germany was finished, and American forces were fighting their way slowly across Okinawa. Everyone knew the fall of Okinawa would open the way for an invasion of the main islands of Japan.

Now, all news was important, and each piece had to be discussed and analyzed. Was the war in Europe over at last? Would the Japanese surrender the remaining islands, avoiding an American invasion? Could a soldier dare let his thoughts wander to things like going home and love?

Home! American servicemen on Luzon believed that maybe they should begin paying closer attention to what those static-filled radio broadcasts reported. They learned that, in a few days, jockey Eddie Arcaro would ride the Kentucky Derby favorite, "Hoop Jr." The price of gasoline was holding at twenty-one cents per gallon, with limited amounts available to those lucky to have gas ration stamps and the right identification sticker on their windshield. The minimum wage was forty cents per hour, and women were making good money working in defense factories.

Back home, sentimental songs saturated the airwaves. Even though Jack Benny, Edgar Bergen and Charlie McCarthy, and the Great Gildersleeve remained popular entertainers, people longed to hear the crooners. Bing Crosby with Xavier Cugat had a big hit, "You Belong to My Heart." Frank Sinatra, sponsored by Old Gold cigarettes, introduced two new dreamy songs on his radio show—"I Should Care" and "Put Your Dreams Away for Another Day."

In Japan, radio stations were required to broadcast only patriotic music, public information announcements, and news of Imperial Army or Navy war progress. By April 1945, in reality, there was no Japanese military progress. However, propaganda continued to report victories.

Broadcasts of sentimental or love songs were forbidden. In fact, the Japanese people were discouraged from singing or even discussing love songs in public. Such bans had existed since the military seized control of the government long before 1941.[9]

For many generations, the Japanese had equated sentimentality with weakness. Individuals were sentimental about any number of things. But that was personal and they were reluctant to admit it openly.

All of this would probably have mattered little to the men of Company A as they set up their command post at Dingalan Bay on April 13, 1945, and prepared for the first assignment. They had been fighting a brutal enemy face-to-face for a long time with little rest. Warriors had no time, nor could they afford, to think of sentimentality.

CHAPTER 15

*"We must defend routes of withdrawal
to the mountains around Baguio. There
we can hold the enemy for years."*

Captured Japanese Divisional Document

December 1944

Along the Umiray River
Mid-April 1945

Colonel Muto Masayuki's left hand grasped the brown metal scabbard
of his sword, which hung loosely by the side of his dusty uniform. The
right hand moved slowly around its long hilt. His fingers seemed to be
enjoying the pebblelike feel of its stingray skin cover.

He suddenly forced the hilt down and forward as if he was ready to
draw the blade.

A girl knelt before him on the sandy trail. Her walk that morning
had deteriorated into a stagger, punctuated with an obvious limp. She
had fallen, but somehow managed to stand and continue on, trying
desperately to keep up with the Imperial soldiers leading the way.

When she fell a second time, she tore her cotton kimono, and
sprained or broke an ankle. With her strength gone, only determination
and pride enabled her to crawl a few more yards. Finally, she collapsed
for a moment, then raised up on her knees and sat on her legs. Long
black hair fell straight as she bowed her head. With one last courtesy to
the colonel, she brushed the hair at the back of her neck with her hand,

exposing a white target for the blade to strike. Then she clasped her hands in her lap and waited for the death blow she knew must come.

But Colonel Muto did not draw his sword. Agonizing moments passed. The colonel spoke, almost in a whisper.

She tilted her face upward slightly, acknowledging his voice. A woman about to die by ritual execution was forbidden to gaze at her executioner, even though the two had shared cups of sake a few weeks before at the officers club near Manila.

Her sunken eyes fixed on something far away, the expression that of one already dead. The pale, gaunt face, once known for shy seductive smiles, now revealed nothing. Dry, cracked lips locked and did not move to beg for mercy.

She was proud to be pure Japanese, not an inferior mixture. Her family had worked for generations at the home of a superior class of samurai. There she'd learned much about Japan's history from the other servants. At fourteen, her parents sold her to a famous geisha house recommended by their samurai master. Her training included not only music, song, and dance, but the art of intelligent, sometimes flirtatious conversation.

She undoubtedly knew as much about the Code of Bushido, the "way of the warrior," as Colonel Muto. She must have accepted the fact that, by that code, there could be no mercy or compassion. Her true thoughts and feelings, like those of most Japanese women, remained hidden. She had lived her twenty-one years with that tradition, and now faced death holding secrets deep inside. No woman of class would bother a Japanese man with talk of feelings. Her life, as the officers knew it, was a façade, for a geisha existed in two worlds, one known to a few and another hidden behind a screen of song, conversation, cosmetics, and beautiful kimonos.

This geisha had done no wrong, broken no rules, offended no Imperial soldier. But injured and exhausted, she was now a burden, a useless thing endangering the group's survival as they struggled each day to stay ahead of the American Army.

A few paces from Colonel Muto, combat-hardened Sergeant Morii Fukutaro and Sergeant Yamashita Yoshi stood statuelike, feet spread apart, left hands on their saber hilts. Their once-highly polished boots, like the colonel's, had become scratched and dirty during the journey. Both sergeants were ready to draw their blades and step forward to complete the execution should the colonel give the order. It was common for an officer to pass on such a privilege to a noncommissioned officer.

The sergeants probably expected Colonel Muto to call on one of them, for he hesitated, and even had spoken to the girl. Something must have disturbed the colonel. His behavior had not been typical that day.[1]

Beheadings were a common practice to elevate morale and the fighting spirit of Imperial soldiers. Bushido taught that a good warrior must remain familiar with blood and death. But no soldier cherished the thought of decapitating a Japanese girl.

She was called Chiyo, a common name, and all that they would remember her by. She, along with five other geishas, was from Kyoto. For over six hundred years, Kyoto had produced the most talented geishas in all of Japan. At least, that is what the majority of businessmen and military officers believed.[2]

Traveling on orders of the High Army Headquarters, the girls had arrived at General Tomoyuki Yamashita's Fourteenth Army Area at Manila in November 1944. They were a gift to the general's staff, and a rare one at that.

The war was not going well for the Japanese. American forces had already captured Leyte in the middle of the Philippine archipelago. The Imperial Army knew that an Allied invasion of the main island of Luzon would come soon. This had General Yamashita busy making plans for a strategic withdrawal to the northern mountains of the island, while fighting delaying actions along the way. But morale had begun to slip. Yamashita's staff needed an emotional lift, something to help them cope with their stress from war. They already had a variety of girls for entertainment who spoke Japanese, cooked meals favored by the soldiers, dressed as geishas, and were familiar with traditional ceremonies. But these were *ianfu,* "accommodating women" or "comfort girls" from Korea. The *ianfu* at Manila were reported to be beautiful, but they were not Japanese. The girls were good for sex perhaps, but by Japanese belief, they were of an inferior race.

In Japan, throughout the war, true geishas remained in demand as spirits declined even among the most fanatical officers. Many geishas had to be placed in factories as laborers, Japan's answer to America's "Rosie the Riveter." Some were killed with other civilians during Allied bombing raids. The six geishas arriving in Manila were all that could be spared.

When General MacArthur returned to Luzon with his massive army of over 200,000 men in January 1945, General Yamashita already had his plans of withdrawal in motion. The Japanese moved their headquarters to the Philippine summer capital of Baguio along with their largest force, 140,000 men, the Shobu Group.

Colonel Muto, a staff officer in the Shimbu Group, received orders from someone supposedly speaking with direct authority from the Fourteenth Headquarters. He was instructed to evacuate Manila with Miss Chiyo and the five geishas. A few comfort girls were taken along to carry the geishas' belongings and accommodate the platoon of infantry he was to recruit as guards.

More than fifty comfort girls had to be left behind. Most disappeared, swallowed up in the chaotic, bloody battle for Manila during February 1945.

Colonel Muto never located a full platoon, managing only to gather ten young riflemen and two older sergeants.

Though somewhat vague, the colonel's orders did emphasize certain points. He must deliver the geishas to Baguio by following the Umiray River east to Dingalan Bay. There they were to turn north, hugging the tree line along the beaches to the next bay, known as Baylor. With the ocean at their backs, they would head west through mountain passes and the central plains to Baguio, a foot journey of over two hundred miles.

Fourteenth Army Area Headquarters expected the Americans to divide their forces, sending some toward Manila while the others pursued the Japanese north. The east coast of Luzon, including Dingalan and Baylor Bays, they theorized, would be safe for retreating soldiers.

Another part of Muto's orders stated that, should the Americans catch them during the withdrawal, he must execute all the women, including the geishas. American soldiers, Headquarters informed him, had the reputation of raping and slowly torturing Japanese female captives to death. No one questioned what facts that information was based upon. And, of course, there was no mention of surrender. All Japanese civilians and military knew that, in the Code of Bushido, surrender was a dishonorable and criminal act, punishable usually by death.

The women did not need to be told of their fate if captured by the enemy. They had heard rumors of how horrible the American GIs treated prisoners. Under the Code of Bushido, Japanese soldiers could torture and rape. This was considered part of the reward of victory. It was logical to assume that other armies behaved the same way.

But the geishas were more educated than the others. Because of their profession, they had been privileged to overhear conversations of wealthy businessmen in Kyoto, men who had traveled to the United States. They told of a different moral and military code followed by American soldiers, one of compassion for noncombatants. The geishas doubted if American soldiers behaved the way the Imperial Headquarters wanted everyone to believe.

On January 29, 1945, Colonel Muto commandeered four trucks evacuating to Cabanatuan City. They planned to link up with other convoys heading north. On January 30, the vehicles dropped off the colonel and his unusual group at a village called Norzagara. The comfort girls carried the geishas' ensembles on their backs—kimonos, cosmetics, small musical instruments, tea ceremony supplies, and an assortment of Western-style dress, negligees, and undergarments.[3]

As the hot, exhausting days crept by, the colonel's determination to accomplish his mission never seemed to falter. Stragglers encountered in the third week were instantly absorbed into their unit. The colonel's pride grew as his numbers increased. But problems also mounted. The new men, an assortment of infantry, clerks, and engineers, were in poor health and suffered from malnutrition. All the soldiers constantly squabbled over the small amounts of food found around deserted villages. The tough sergeants knew that the men could easily slip into depression as morale deteriorated. The bickering was the first sign of more trouble to come. Despite differences, the soldiers craved to be part of a unit. Each had been trained to obey orders without question, and to work, fight, and think as a group.

Four weeks into the march from Norzagara, the food rations they carried were exhausted. Progress had been slowed by the pace of the women, who were hampered by the kimonos and sandals the colonel demanded they wear.

At the western base of the Sierra Madre Mountains, the Umiray begins as a small stream flowing north swiftly in a bed of polished stones, visible through clear waters.

The well-worn path they traveled was dusty in some places, but changed to damp, sandy earth in others when it followed closer to the river. On their left, or north side, heavily wooded mountains rose sharply, broken here and there by bald, rocky cliffs.

For the first forty miles, the river was shallow and its water appeared safe to drink. Small fish darted about, but no one had equipment to catch one. The men tried using their hands as traps, with little success. Spears and gigs quickly improvised from bamboo produced more favorable results.

Still, hunger remained a problem. In the Philippines and other conquered islands, the Japanese Army carried very few rations on a mission. Each soldier was expected to live off the land, buying food with "occupation peso" scrip, but mostly stealing what they wanted from the natives.

Colonel Muto sent squads of men on trails that led from the river to raid nearby barrios for food. But the Filipinos had learned long ago to hide such valuables as rice, dried fish, and vegetables. Normally a hospitable, friendly people with a reputation of being extremely generous and accommodating, especially to visitors, the Filipinos had experienced nothing but viciousness from their Japanese conquerors. Filipino hospitality had been answered with brutality.

Muto's men found nothing but scraps to eat in the villages. Japanese soldiers who'd passed their way earlier had already taken everything edible. His men resorted to eating wild vegetables, mangoes, coconuts, grass, and the bark of young trees. By the sixth week, some of the soldiers were experiencing difficulty keeping up with the pace of even the women as hunger and dysentery took their toll.

Everyone feared falling out of the march. That was treated the same as desertion in the Imperial Army. A court-martial was not required, for the colonel had the authority to decide who would live or die.

Escape was not an option to consider. The soldiers knew that would bring a slow death from starvation and disease, or perhaps a faster one if discovered by Filipino guerrillas. And no one wanted to leave the security of the group.

Colonel Muto and his sergeants often discussed their evacuation route, but with each other. No information had been shared with the women or soldiers except the fact that they were traveling to join General Yamashita. The general's location and how they would get there was not information for subordinates. If something happened to the leaders, the rest of the group would eventually be doomed.

Frustration must have continually haunted Colonel Muto. After six weeks, three men collapsed along the road. They died where they fell, probably from a combination of heat exhaustion and hunger. And two nights after he lost those men, the Korean comfort girls disappeared into the shadows of the jungle.

One girl known as Sung, too weak to join the escape, was left behind. For more than a year, she had performed her duties as a sex slave and servant for the Imperial soldiers in Manila. Now, by failing to warn those men that her comrades were planning an escape, she had committed a crime against the Emperor of Japan.

Sung's last morning along the Umiray was miserable, like each day had been on that journey. The days were hot and humid with very little breeze. Nights brought little relief and swarms of insects. By 9:00 A.M., sun rays broke through the green canopy of tree leaves that covered the trail, but still, most of the path remained in dark shadows.

Moments before her execution, she became hysterical, crawling and clawing in the dirt. As a Korean, she understood that her life had never really had value to the Japanese. The soldiers had once enjoyed her, and maybe she thought that at least one man might step forward and plead for her life. That would have only been a fantasy. No Japanese soldier would dare speak to an officer on the subject.

Two soldiers lifted Sung and forced her to her knees. No one offered a blindfold. Colonel Muto moved to her side. He raised his sword straight up, elbows bent slightly, both hands firmly grasping the hilt. Confidence was his only expression. This execution would be like others he'd carried out in China and the Philippines. Suddenly, the blade cut through the air and down upon the back of her neck.

His first blow was successful. Sung's head rolled into the trail and her body crumpled forward.

The colonel quickly swung the sword at his side to remove drops of blood, then traditionally wiped the blade on a piece of her clothing before returning it to its sheath. He barked an order and strutted up the trail, followed by his little army.

Sung's frail, headless body remained on the path. Since she had committed a crime, there would be no burial.

Carrying the geishas' belongings had now become the unwelcome task of the remaining soldiers.

Days later, the group no doubt wondered if they were about to witness another execution of a woman.

Minutes had passed while Colonel Muto, hands at his sword, stood before Chiyo. Beads of perspiration rolled from beneath his service cap to narrow-slit eyes, then down to a fat, sunburned chin.[4]

He must have been wondering how he would explain his losses to Headquarters. The *ianfu* were of no concern. They were expendable and could be replaced. Even the loss of a few soldiers was expected. Comfort came to the others as they thought of how all would be honored at the great Yasukuni shrine in Tokyo upon giving their lives for the Emperor and Japan. But a geisha? Explaining the death of a woman he was supposed to protect and deliver would be difficult, perhaps unforgivable.

Six soldiers stood at the trail's edge about thirty feet north of Chiyo. They held their long, bolt-action Arisaka rifles ready and, even though exhausted, they appeared alert. Bayonets laboriously polished during rest stops glistened when the blades occasionally caught sun rays.

Between Chiyo and those soldiers, five geishas, wearing faded, thin kimonos, squatted Asian-style, waiting for Muto's next move. Chiyo probably could not hear her girlfriends crying.

Thirty feet to the south, three younger soldiers stood at a classic "parade rest," rifle butts on the ground, bayonets pointing skyward. Colonel Muto's squinting eyes remained on Chiyo. Still, he did not draw his sword. Then his hand released its grasp on the hilt and moved along his wide, brown belt. It paused at a leather holster containing a Nambu automatic pistol. Muto shouted an order at Sergeant Morii, who quickly snapped to attention. Then the colonel repeated the command in a deep, strong voice. Did any man have a *tonto*? No response. The men remained stone-faced and silent. Apparently none had a knife like the one the colonel demanded.[5]

Colonel Muto Masayuki barked again. The rigid Sergeant Morii turned and with long strides moved past the sobbing geishas to the first soldier. With mechanical movements, the soldier detached his bayonet and handed it to the sergeant.

Morii returned and, holding the bayonet in both hands, parallel to the ground, presented it to his colonel.

Colonel Muto nodded toward Chiyo. The sergeant slowly placed the bayonet in the dust next to the girl's knees. Then he stood and bent his body at the waist in a deep bow. After that respectful gesture, he took his place next to Sergeant Yamashita.

The colonel had solved the dilemma. An execution of a geisha had been avoided. He would permit Chiyo a different honorable death, *seppuku,* ritual suicide.

Should Allied forces find her before she died, she could reveal nothing important of their mission because she had so little information about it.

Chiyo knew what to do. The ceremony for *seppuku* had been part of her cultural education. And she also knew that her death would come slowly. Colonel Muto was not concerned with that fact.

Colonel Muto continued toward Dingalan Bay, proud the problem was solved.

He revealed later that he had been assured fishing villages existed where the Umiray emptied into the ocean, now only a three-day march to fresh fish and maybe rice. But Headquarters had also promised there were no American soldiers at Dingalan and none could be expected there until mid-June. The east coast of Luzon was supposed to belong to the Japanese for a while longer.

But unfortunately for Colonel Muto, the battle lines had changed. MacArthur's army had pressed ahead during the past thirty days, faster than Imperial Headquarters projected. American soldiers were waiting at Dingalan Bay.

As Muto's group moved up the trail away from Chiyo, one of the geishas turned for a last glance at her friend.

She started to wave good-bye, but Chiyo's glassy eyes were frozen on the bayonet. Then the geisha witnessed something she would always remember.

As the last three soldiers passed in front of Chiyo, two paused briefly and placed their extra canteens of water at her side. The third dropped something into her lap. It appeared to be a ball of rice, the remains of rations he must have hoarded for days.

The young men, no doubt, thought their small act of compassion went unnoticed by the others. Whether they intended their gifts for the living or the spirit of the dead, the geishas did not know, for Chiyo, another fragile casualty of war, was never seen again.[6]

CHAPTER 16

"If the Japs come up that sandbar,
you men got to stop 'em here, or they'll run
right through us!"

Sergeant Al Johnson to PFC John McKinney

Umiray Outpost

April 22, 1945

Twenty-nine-year-old Lieutenant Max Ladin stood at five-three and weighed only 130 pounds. He might not have resembled a Hollywood version of a dashing infantry officer, but he had proven to be qualified as a leader.

His parents were Jewish-Russian immigrants who'd worked hard to send their son first to Allen Military Academy for five years, then the University of Texas at Austin. Max finished three and a half years at the university before dropping out to help his family during the final years of the Great Depression.

When the war began, the Army sent Max to San Antonio for training to become a combat medic, but the staff learned of his early military education and recommended him for Officers Candidate School (OCS).

Graduating as a second lieutenant, he entered "heavy weapons" training and obtained a proficiency in the use of heavy 81mm mortars and the .30-caliber water-cooled (heavy) machine gun.

On April 9, 1945, First Lieutenant Max Ladin reported to his battalion headquarters expecting to learn that the staff had approved his request for an emergency leave. His mother was seriously ill at their home in Houston, Texas, and not expected to live much longer.

The lieutenant had seen enough combat on New Guinea and Luzon to qualify for the leave, but that had no effect on the Army's decision.

The Connolly Task Force requested another section from a heavy weapons company to reinforce those of Company D, 123rd Infantry heading for Dingalan Bay.

Max Ladin commanded such a section, but he was in the 136th Infantry. Why were he and his men needed for a mission assigned to an entirely different regiment? What became of the leave request to see his dying mother?

The 136th headquarters staff offered a typical but understanding, "We're sorry, *but* . . ." type of answer. All other units were massing for that final assault on Baguio, and Ladin's section of mortars was the only one that could be spared to assist Major Connolly.

The staff assured Max that his leave request would be given attention once the Dingalan mission was over.

On April 10, Lieutenant Ladin and his section of fourteen men, including Tech Sergeant Victor J. Wendling of Saginaw, Michigan—"the best NCO on Luzon" Max later labeled him—joined Captain Ice and A Company for the journey to Dingalan Bay.[1]

One of Max's fellow officers remembered him after the war: "We teased Max a lot about being the only member of the Jewish faith amongst all of us officers with Irish, Scandinavian, and English blood, but he had a wonderful, dry sense of humor about it all. That was bad luck for him to get the Task Force assignment. He was the right man for the job—smart, tough, and quick-thinking. What a strange-looking pair, Max and his favorite sergeant!"[2]

Indeed, side by side, Max seemed dwarfed by Wendling's huge six-seven frame.

Max Ladin accepted his fate. Of course, inside he hurt, knowing he might never reach his mother in time. But he knew he had a job to do. The war was far from over, and he was ready to lead his men if that was what the Army needed him to do.

Dingalan Bay
April 15

There was considerable activity around the sawmill as the Connolly Task Force converted their headquarters into a full garrison.

Captain Ice deployed fifteen of his A Company men plus a company of Filipino guerrillas to the tiny barrio of Papaya located almost thirty miles west of their base. Papaya was along the western base of the Sierra Madre Mountains about fifteen miles southeast of Cabanatuan City. Any new units looking for the Task Force Headquarters could be escorted to the bay from there.

Eighteen miles to the south of the Task Force Headquarters, at the junction of the Umiray River and Maroraqui Creek, Sergeant Farrow's Alamo Scout Team, now with fresh supplies, was reinforced with twelve more guerrillas. The team's daily radio reports to Lieutenant John Reardon's intelligence section at the Task Force Headquarters indicated that the Japanese continued to break into smaller groups, but were still moving along the river toward the bay.

At two locations between the Umiray-Maroraqui intersection and the bay where the river was very shallow, small units of guerrillas established listening posts and waited for Japanese stragglers to pass. Major Connolly's plan called for these units to dispatch runners upstream to report on enemy activity to Sergeant Farrow, who could then radio anything important to Major Connolly.

But on April 19, disagreements developed among the guerrillas and they abandoned one of the fording areas. Those men traveled cross-country to the safety of Connolly's headquarters.

The exact cause of the problem was never determined, but some reports blamed superstitions. Still others stated that the arguments were between loyal followers of Colonel Anderson and Huk sympathizers.

An area where the water was only ankle-deep remained unprotected. The Japanese could safely wade across the river at that point, and maybe others.

* * *

At the sawmill, two perimeters of defense were established. Some reports state that there were a total of three, if one counted the Huks who unofficially represented Colonel Anderson.

The first ring of protection was provided by the guerrillas who were definitely part of Anderson's unit. These were mostly foxholes with riflemen and machine guns. Some had reinforced protection from logs; many did not.

The next ring was rather irregular or fluid and provided by Huk members. Anxious to impress the Americans, they worked hard and long digging foxholes, and appeared to be very efficient and "military" in their performance. But some of those men simply disappeared from time to time, returning with claims of ambush successes. When their NCOs were questioned, they explained that these men had been "out on patrol," a phrase they'd quickly learned from the GIs.

Major Connolly and Captain Ice became uncomfortable with the presence of the Huks, who claimed they were no longer associated with the communists or the socialist movement. Still, the American officers did not fully trust even "former Huks," and issued orders to the men not to discuss any plans, technical information, or become too friendly with the Huks.

Connolly had Captain Ice deploy the bulk of his A Company in a tight perimeter closest to the headquarters buildings. The heavy (81mm) mortars were set up near the buildings, the light mortars closer to the perimeter.

Upon personal inspection of their lines, Major Connolly concluded he needed more men to adequately defend and protect his headquarters. Soon, small patrols would be sent out to seek the enemy, and one rifle platoon already had orders to prepare for a movement to the Umiray River. This would leave his lines looking more like "a piece of Swiss cheese," as Captain Ice later reported.[3]

Major Connolly was aware that practically all infantry units were already assigned the task of taking Baguio and attacking Japanese strongholds in the northern mountains. Nonetheless, he sent his request to I Corps Headquarters. The Task Force mission might fail if they did not receive more men.

While the major's request for reinforcements was processed through channels, Lieutenant Reardon, the Task Force intelligence officer, had alarming news. Alamo Scouts radio had reported that enemy movements continued. They remained mostly in small groups of twelve or less, and seemed to be in poor physical condition. The Filipinos were reporting, however, that the Japanese were massing here and there. Not all were moving north out of the Dingalan area.

With conflicting information, Connolly and Ice agreed that their plans must be activated at once. The time had come for aggressive action against the enemy. They had already selected a triangular-shaped, flat, open sandbar on the north side of the mouth of the Umiray River to be their outpost. A rifle platoon under Sergeant Al Johnson prepared to march some eighteen miles around the bay to reach that area.

From the outpost, American patrols would comb the surrounding hills, engage and kill the enemy, and return with reliable information for Lieutenant Reardon. A confirmation of Japanese massing could indicate they were planning an attack somewhere.

* * *

Staff Sergeant Roy Potts, a six-four, two-hundred-pound Sixth U.S. Army Ranger from Tennessee, described his B Company commander, Captain Leo Strausbaugh, this way: "Leo was just an outspoken kid at the time, but he was smart, cared about each of us, and was willing to try anything that was good for the cause."

Potts carried a Japanese bullet in his chest, two inches from the heart. Army doctors were afraid to operate, and the sergeant was given a forty-five-day leave to visit the States. Thus, Roy Potts would miss the next B Company assignment . . . a mission to Dingalan Bay.[4]

On April 22, Captain Leo Strausbaugh, carrying his favorite M1 carbine, reported to Sixth Ranger Battalion headquarters for a new mission.

A number of changes had transpired within the Sixth Rangers since their success on the Leyte islands back in October 1944 and the POW Camp Cabanatuan raid in late January 1945.

The Rangers remained the pride of Sixth Army Commander Gen-

Top left: The remains of a sharecropper's home near Woodcliff, Georgia, identical to the one in which John R. McKinney was raised in the 1930s. *Author's photo*

Top right: The peaceful waters of Cannon Lake near Sylvania, Georgia, one of John R. McKinney's favorite fishing spots. "My idea of freedom is to catch one of them good Cannon Lake fish and cook 'em on the bank," said J.R. *Author's photo*

Left: Pvt. John R. McKinney on leave in Georgia in 1943. J.R. loved dogs. To him, each one was good for hunting something.
Courtesy of Danny Lynn and Sue Derriso

Types of World War II Japanese Weapons used in Umiray-Dingalan attack

Top to Bottom:

1. Sword, military issue, commonly called a samurai sword because of its similar appearance to those ancient weapons.

2. Rifle, bolt action, Arisaka Type 99, 7.7mm, 5-round clip. A 15½″ bayonet was almost always attached for combat.

3. Light machine gun, Type 96, 6.5mm, full automatic with a 30-round magazine. The Japanese also had at least one Type 99, 7.5mm in the battle at Dingalan Bay. Both types can be operated by one man and appear similar at a glance.

4. Grenade Launcher, Model 89, 50mm, commonly called the "knee mortar," though it was not to be fired from the knee. Effective range: about 700 yards.

Author's photos. Weapons shown in 1 and 2 are from the collection of Ted Pribnow, Lt. Col. USAF (Ret.)

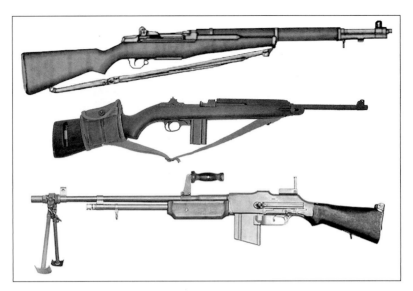

TYPES OF WORLD WAR II AMERICAN WEAPONS USED IN UMIRAY-DINGALAN ATTACK

Top to Bottom:

1. M1 Rifle, Garand, .30 caliber, commonly called the "M1." Semiautomatic, 8-round clip. Clip ejected after last round fired. Effective range: 400 yards.

2. Carbine, M1 (a three-quarter scale rifle) 15- or 30-round reusable magazine, semi- or full automatic. Effective range: 250 yards.

3. Browning Automatic Rifle, commonly called a "BAR," air cooled, 20-round magazine, 550 rounds per minute, semi- or full automatic, .30 caliber. Effective range: 600 yards. Magazine can be changed in 2–4 seconds but averaged 7 seconds in combat. Operated by one man.

Author's photos

Light machine gun, model 1919A4 Browning, air-cooled, 250-round belt-fed, .30 caliber, 400–550 rounds per minute, full automatic. Weight: 41 lbs. with tripod. Effective range: 1100 yards. Operated by one man, usually assisted by another.

Author's photos

Expecting to be deployed to North Africa, the 33rd Division trains in the Mojave Desert near Needles, California, in March 1943. Standing, left to right, Sgt. Bill Kinney, Lt. Richardson, Sgt. Al Johnson. Kneeling PFC Jack Loveland and Sgt. John Bailey. *Courtesy of Gene Maziarz*

Above: PFC John R. McKinney, bottom left, clowns with some of his 123rd Infantry Regiment buddies shortly before the Dingalan Bay assignment. Bottom right, PFC Ed Colwell, wounded during the Dingalan Bay battle. Top row, left to right, PFC Earl Frates, Roy Philips, William F. Gowne. *Courtesy of Bob Colwell*

Right: Standing, left to right, Pvt. Eldon M. Homan, killed in the dawn attack on the Umiray River outpost on May 11, 1945. Michael W. Danielewski, killed at Twin Peaks, Luzon, six weeks earlier. Pvt. Louis Gabany. Seated, left to right, Sgt. Sol Rocke, Lt. Robert B. Mayhew. *Courtesy of Dr. Sol Rocke*

Top left: Gerry Nutt (left) and Sgt. Gerry Rampy in New Guinea. Rampy visited McKinney at the outpost only hours before the Japanese attack. He reported having a "funny feeling" they were being watched by the enemy. Nutt became part of a security guard assigned to protect John McKinney in late May 1945.
Courtesy of Gerry Nutt and Gerry Rampy

Top right: Col. Bernard Anderson, American guerrilla commander on Luzon awaits a U.S. supply submarine in 1944. Some of Col. Anderson's guerrillas were assigned to the Connolly Task Force at Dingalan Bay, but without Anderson they lacked combat discipline.
Courtesy of Col. Bernard Anderson

Left: Like most GIs fighting on Luzon during World War II, Roy "Punchy" Phillips, a professional boxer, lost weight due to a diet of combat rations and the daily stress of combat. *Courtesy of Gene Maziarz*

Top: Connolly Task Force headquarters. The sawmill at the north section of Dingalan Bay. *Courtesy of the National Archives*

Middle: B-25 Medium Bomber, similar to the one shot down near Dingalan Bay with Lt. Reardon on board. B-25s were called "Mitchells" for Gen. Billy Mitchell who was court-martialed in the 1920s for his outspoken promotion of air power. The Mitchell gained attention in 1942 when Lt. Col. Jimmy Doolittle flew a squadron off the carrier Hornet to bomb Japan. Top speed: 284 MPH.
Courtesy of the National Archives

Bottom: 60mm mortar position. The emplacement at the Umiray River outpost was less permanent. *Courtesy of Gerry Rampy*

Top: Bayonet practice. Posed for photo, John McKinney (center) watches as Pvt. Adolph "Red" Barrette (left) clowns with another G.I. *Courtesy of Gene Maziarz*

Bottom: McKinney (left) joins the fun. "Red" Barrette on right. *Courtesy of Gene Maziarz*

Pvt. John McKinney poses with a captured Japanese light machine gun. This Type 96 has a magazine that holds 30 rounds of 6.5mm ammunition. Photo taken a few days after the Umiray battle. *Courtesy of Gene Maziarz and the National Archives.*

Above: Pvt. Edward Colwell, wounded in the arm while rushing for more rifle ammunition during the early moments of the Japanese attack at the Umiray Outpost, May 11, 1945. *Courtesy of the National Archives*

Right: Capt. Leo V. Strausbaugh, commanding B Company, 6th Ranger Battalion. Blunt and outspoken, he would not permit his men to be sacrificed unnecessarily at Dingalan Bay.
Courtesy of Leo Strausberg, Colonel, USAF (Ret.)

Sgt. Leroy Nix, one of four men awarded the Silver Star for bravery during the Umiray River outpost battle, which lasted thirty minutes. *Courtesy of Gerry Rampy*

Gene Maziarz with his "beautiful BAR." To better control the weapon during rapid fire, Gene modified it by attaching a machete handle to the forearm grip. *Courtesy of Gene Maziarz*

Back from a patrol, Gene Maziarz (left) and guerrilla Jessey Mercado display a captured Japanese battle flag. It reads, in part, "*Takada Yoshiro*. Be forever a brave warrior."
Courtesy of Gene Maziarz

Filipino HUK guerrilla Jesus "Jessey" Mercado with a pet monkey. Mercado often impersonated a female to obtain information from the Japanese.
Courtesy of Gene Maziarz

Some of the Japanese soldiers killed in the hand-to-hand battle with Pvt. John McKinney lay scattered near his machine gun position. This photo, taken less than an hour after the attack, by Lt. Max Ladin shows weary U.S. soldiers on the left and Filipino guerrillas on the right. Camera faces Dingalan Bay with the rising sun at the right causing the side of the photo to blur. Enemy jackets were removed to search for weapons, documents, and explosives. *Courtesy of Max Ladin*

Weapons platoon leader Tech. Sgt. Victor J. Wendling (left) stands next to an unidentified guerrilla captain, in front of the Umiray outpost command tent. Sgt. Wendling was awarded the Silver Star for risking his life to save Lt. Max Ladin. Photo taken by Lt. Ladin about one hour after the battle at Umiray River.
Courtesy of Max Ladin

Above: Japanese survivors of the battle at Umiray. These starving soldiers surrendered several days after the battle. *Courtesy of the National Archives*

Below: A Company commander Capt. Harry Ice (kneeling) and PFC John McKinney pose with the .30-caliber light machine gun a few days after the Umiray River battle. *Courtesy of the National Archives*

This eerie scene with snowlike ground fog and clouds was taken by 33rd Division photographer Henry Van Westrop near hill KP21 just north of Baguio, Luzon, in June 1945. The 210th Field Artillery Battalion gathered to pay final respects to Lt. Col. Thomas Truxtum, the division's highest-ranking officer killed in action. He and Maj. Balch had been shot in the head by a Japanese sniper. Security was immediately increased for Sgt. John R. McKinney. *Courtesy of Henry Van Westrop*

September 3, 1945. General Tomoyuki Yamashita (second from the right) officially surrendered all Imperial Japanese forces in the Phillippines at Baguio, Luzon. Some Japanese soldiers, either unaware of the surrender or refusing to accept it, continued fighting as guerrillas for another thirty years. *Courtesy of Henry Van Westrop*

Betty McKinney prepares her brother John for his Medal of Honor ceremony. This photo was taken by a member of the military who had the McKinneys pose in front of a mirror. The picture of the reflection accounts for John's military decorations appearing on the right side of his uniform rather than the left.

Courtesy of Bob Colwell and the National Archives

A faded 1946 photo shows John McKinney posing with his old single shot .22 rifle a few days before his trip to the White House. His family, seated around him, are, front left, brother Ralph, top row, left to right, brothers Dewey (D.H.) and Jack. Father Dewey, sister Betty, John (J.R.) and mother, Mattie. Not present is brother Hank, who was still in the army. *Courtesy of Bob Colwell and the McKinney family*

Promoted to sergeant, John R. McKinney receives the Congressional Medal of Honor for his bravery at the Umiray River. President Harry S Truman presents the medal at a White House ceremony in January 1946. Upon hearing some of the details of Sgt. McKinney's "one-man stand" against the enemy, President Truman, a combat veteran of World War I, commented, "I would rather have earned one of these than be president!" *Courtesy of the National Archives*

John R. McKinney granted a rare media interview years after the Umiray battle. A return to favorite foods produced a heavier J.R. compared to the skinny rifleman of 1945. The interviewer reported that during the entire meeting, McKinney's eyes "never lost the terrible stare of sadness."

Courtesy of Atlanta Magazine, 1966

John R. McKinney attended only one military reunion, with the 33rd Infantry Division in 1995, two years before his death. The hat, given to him by his nephew Danny Lynn Derriso, became his "fishing hat."

Courtesy of Danny Lynn and Sue Derriso

The people of Georgia honored their little-known hero with the dedication of this highway in 1995. It is a section of State Route 21 stretching to Effingham County (from Sylvania to Savannah). *Author's photo*

eral Walter Krueger, and continued as the honor guard for his head-quarters, waiting for special assignments. The Ranger Battalion answered directly to General Krueger, not to a division or corps commander. They could request the Rangers' help with the approval of Krueger.

When Major Connolly's request for reinforcements came through I Corps to Sixth Army, Captain Strausbaugh and his B Company were selected for that mission. Major Robert "Woody" Garrett had moved up to battalion commander, replacing Lieutenant Colonel Henry A. Mucci, who was transferred to a new command. In another month, Garrett would receive the Silver Oak Leaves of a lieutenant colonel.

Captain Strausbaugh's friend and fellow warrior Arthur "Bull" Simons had been promoted to the rank of major and assigned to Ranger Headquarters.

Captain Strausbaugh's only orders were to report to Major Connolly at Dingalan Bay with sixty-five men of his Company B. Naturally, the captain assumed his unit would be assigned an assault mission, which they were trained for (and already had experience in gained during the Leyte invasion).

Connolly explained the entire Task Force mission to the B Company commander, who was then told to "dig into the south side of the hill and prepare to protect headquarters' flank."[5]

Puzzled at the unexpected order, Leo and his men obeyed and dug in on the hillside. He was certain the real mission would be revealed soon. Perhaps they were there to attack a Japanese-held beach or some special fortification. The Rangers followed orders and waited.

Twenty-six-year-old Staff Sergeant James Robbins, born in California, was working near Las Vegas, Nevada, when drafted at the beginning of the war. He'd grown up with the Sixth Rangers since its creation in New Guinea.

"We were talking amongst ourselves as we dug in that day," James Robbins reported. "We had been trained and operated as a special strike force, hit with surprise and destroy. We were not qualified or equipped to stand and fight in a defense situation for any length of time. Ranger companies had no machine guns and no mortars. We were sure no one explained to General Krueger what was expected of us at Dingalan, or he would have never let us go over there."[6]

April 22, 9:00 A.M.

Sergeant Gene Maziarz had just returned from a night patrol and finished cleaning his "beautiful BAR" when PFC John McKinney, Ed Colwell, and Red Barrette approached his foxhole carrying their M1 rifles and "full web equipment" (pistol belt with canteen, first-aid packet, etc.).

"You guys leaving for patrol?" Gene asked.

"Nope," answered McKinney with a grin, "going fishing."

"We're on the way to set up a camp at the mouth of some river . . . about eleven miles south across the bay. Going by boat. Mac's dreaming. Won't be any time for fishing," Red added.

"Beats walking," Gene replied, slapping parts of the BAR back together. "How many?"

"Don't know for sure," said Red. "Maybe twenty-four . . . they alerted one full platoon, but I haven't seen that many getting ready yet; a few fellows from the 136th and a bunch of Filipinos going along."

Gene laughed. "Where they gonna get boats for all those guys?"

"Who knows?" Ed Colwell injected. "Captain Ice and Sergeant Johnson told us we'll go by boat and set up an outpost."

"Outpost!" Gene worked the bolt on the BAR, assuring it functioned correctly as he puzzled over his buddies' report. "What kind of outpost?"

"Guess we'll find out," said Red. "Looks like we'll be seeing you there. Ice says that patrols will soon move out from our base camp. . . ."

"Outpost!" Colwell corrected.

"Yeah," Red went on. "We'll be shoving off in about an hour. Supply fellows are stacking up boxes of C and K rations. Guess they plan for us to stay there awhile."

As the men started to walk away, Red turned and said, "By the way, Gene, there's a girl been a-standing over there watching. Think she wants to meet you!"[7]

"Sure, sure!" Gene Maziarz replied as his friends headed toward the headquarters building.

Then Gene saw her. She was walking directly toward him with a slight twist to her stride, her loose-fitting fatigue pants appearing to almost float just above the ground. Her wavy black hair surrounded a long neck and fell in curls about the shoulders. But it would be the Filipino's bright, friendly smile that Gene would always remember.

Then the Filipino spoke with a soft, high-pitched voice. "Hi, Joe! I am Sergeant Jesus Mercado of Colonel Anderson's Second Regiment. My friends call me Jessey."

Then, in a deeper voice, the guerrilla added, "You can be my friend. Call me Jessey."

Sergeant Gene Maziarz was stunned. The Filipino walked, looked, and at first, spoke like a woman, but obviously was a man.

Jessey's big smile broke into a laugh. "Sorry to fool you, sir. I wanted to show the American how I sometimes trick Japanese!"

The two men sat down and began to share stories. Jessey explained that he'd survived Bataan and joined the Huk movement to fight the enemy as a guerrilla. Later, as feuding intensified amongst the Huk leaders, he'd left and joined up with Colonel Anderson's guerrillas, eventually finding himself assigned to the Dingalan Bay area. He had successfully used his long-hair female impersonation to talk his way through Japanese lines and obtain information. But now, there were no actual lines, only groups of stragglers moving through the area.

The conversation continued for a while until Jessey excused himself, promising to return with his pet monkey.

Sergeant Al Johnson paused on the way to join the men assembling at the beach. He saw Sergeant Maziarz talking with Mercado. Johnson walked up to Gene.

"Don't let the smile fool ya," Al Johnson said. "That long-haired guerrilla is a die-hard commie! He's with the Huks. I seen him up on their perimeter."

"Ahh, Sarge, he seems friendly, speaks good English. Maybe I can learn a few things," Gene replied.

"Yeah," Johnson shot back. "Just be careful what you tell him!"[8]

Several minutes later Jessey returned, this time with two younger guerrillas and his pet monkey.

Sergeant Maziarz had picked up an extra trench knife a few weeks earlier. He presented it to Jessey. The gift bound a friendship that lasted through the next month.

During another conversation, Jessey had a warning for his new friend. "I know the Americans have a radio at the Umiray River already." The Filipino spoke almost in a whisper. "The men gossip. They say many of you will be hunting Japs along that river. I know the river well! Be careful! At one place the trail is very narrow . . . about three hundred meters from where the river empties. The trail is close to the river at that point. A hill on the north side of the trail is steep with many large rocks. The Japs hide there to do ambush."

* * *

First Lieutenant Max Ladin was certain his luck had taken another turn for the worse as he stepped aboard the nineteen-foot motor launch.

Major Connolly had just appointed him Outpost Commander, and now he and his mortar men were off to a spot on the map that appeared to be surrounded by nothing but wilderness.[9]

His situation had become more sensitive. There were two other lieutenants heading for the outpost, and the men of the rifle platoon going along were from the 123rd Infantry Regiment. They would all be taking orders from an officer from the 136th Infantry, a man who was totally unfamiliar to them.

But the men of A Company soon learned that the Outpost Commander position was little more than a title when it came to routine duties. They had their own sergeants and lieutenants between themselves and the commander. They also discovered that Ladin was "a tough little officer," but fair, realistic, and "actually friendly at times."

The problem of how to move Lieutenant Ladin, his fourteen men of D Company (136th Infantry), fifty Filipino guerrillas, and twenty-five riflemen of A Company to the outpost area had been resolved.

Major Connolly's original plan called for an eighteen-mile overland march through dense, steamy forest, crossing steep mountain slopes and wading through several small swamps. That would require at least fourteen hours, maybe longer considering all the supplies they planned to carry.

The idea of walking Dingalan's gently sloping beaches from the sawmill to the Umiray River at first sounded appealing, but everyone knew the dangers of moving through open country, especially on a beach. An attack by even a small group of Japanese could be devastating if the Task Force was trapped between jungle and ocean.

The second plan solved the problem. A number of *bancas,* small Filipino fishing boats somewhat resembling canoes, were joined together by rope to form a floating convoy. The lead banca was tied to the nineteen-foot motor launch made available to the Task Force. Now the fourteen-hour journey by land was cut to two and a half hours by water.

PFC John McKinney was part of the first "landing" party to unload on the beach about one hundred yards north of the Umiray River. He later described his first few moments of the arrival to his sister: "We stormed ashore from those shaky canoes, completely unopposed. There weren't nobody there. Weren't nothing there but a bunch of bushes and water lilies. No more than a sandbar with plants all over the place growing out of sand and dirt."[10]

"No doubt the outpost was strategically located, but it was nothing more than a barren tip of a peninsula," said Max Ladin later. "Like an old-time fort, it appeared to guard the entrance to the river. We stood out like a sore thumb. Of course, it must have been a threat to the Japanese seeing us there. If they had artillery or heavy mortars, they would have wiped us all out in a matter of minutes. We were trapped. An ocean on the east side, a wide river on the south, and a fifty-yard stretch of mud and backwater creek on the west. The only way the enemy foot soldiers could attack would be down the neck of our peninsula from the north. This neck was some two hundred yards wide. That strategy seemed too logical, but we sighted our mortars in that direction anyway, just in case. Of course, they could attack up the sandbar from the south. No one really expected that."[11]

By the time the boat convoy's second wave arrived with more men and supplies, the outpost already had its perimeter established. Some of the men were finishing up their foxholes and three machine guns were in place.

The new arrivals said that they had passed by the Umiray's mouth, continuing south in calm water for almost a mile. They reported that the shoreline south of the river consisted of coral reefs and rocks with steep cliffs rising more than thirty feet from the water's edge. Totally different from the dark sand beaches stretching north from the river.[12]

Lieutenant Ladin's men converted the remains of a grass-and-bamboo nipa hut at the center of the camp by covering it partly with a wall tent. This became the outpost "Command Post" (CP). A two-foot-deep pit was dug and supplies—food rations, first-aid equipment, and ammunition—were stashed under the hut for protection from the weather.

The mortar men had their four 81mms in place near the CP and were ready for action in minutes.

Three light mortars (60mm) were placed a little closer to the perimeter. Each mortar was assigned a separate zone of responsibility so that 360-degree fire could be laid in the event that an attack came from all sides.[13]

At least, that was the official report given to I Corps later. Actually, the fire direction was to the west and north. No mortar coverage was planned for the ocean side or Umiray River area. And not one was aimed at the long sandbar to the south.

The perimeter formed almost a perfect triangle—its base running about 150 yards along the ocean, with one two hundred-yard leg along the river and the other two hundred-yard leg blocking the north.

First Lieutenant Ladin, accompanied by Second Lieutenant Edwin Voss and Sergeant Al Johnson, both from Illinois, inspected the perimeter, assuring that the rifle pits were spread apart correctly. Behind the rifle pits, or foxholes, were the quarters, pup tents erected over another foxhole. When a soldier finished his watch and was replaced by another, he simply moved a short distance and slept under tent shelter in the protection of his foxhole.

Sergeant Leroy Nix of Oklahoma had responsibility for the 60mm mortars and Staff Sergeant Neal Cowin supervised all communication. From a field phone base unit at the command post, wire ran to phones along the west and north perimeters. An SCR radio, also at the CP, gave them communication with the Alamo Scouts upriver and Task Force Headquarters at the north end of the bay. Even though the signal was weak and often filled with crackling static, it still gave a sense of security. They were not totally cut off from the world.

During the first few hours, the men discovered a problem with their outpost. No matter where they dug foxholes, they struck water at the two-foot level.

"Don't give us much protection; even a fox wouldn't get in a hole like this," PFC John McKinney mentioned to PFC Ed Colwell.

Though frustrating, the men knew how to compensate for the situation. Dirt was piled up in a mound around the hole to give the soldier an additional one or two feet of protection. But there were no logs and no sandbags, only a pile of dirt separating the men from Japanese bullets.

The perimeter inspection team reached the far south tip of the outpost triangle, which pointed directly to the long sandbar.

Two Filipino guerrillas, PFC Eldon M. Homan and PFC Morris Roberts, were helping PFC John McKinney with their .30-caliber air-cooled (light) machine-gun emplacement.

Sergeant Johnson stepped into the pit and sighted down the barrel of the gun, turning it left and right to check their field of fire. After a few moments, he turned to McKinney.

"If the Japs come up that sandbar, you men got to stop 'em *here*, else they'll run right through us!"

* * *

The skin of the machine gun became too hot to touch as it sat in the tropical sun, so they covered it with branches from small bushes growing nearby. They'd planned to do that anyway to camouflage their weapon—to hide her from the Japanese. And they changed the green cover daily so that the machine-gun position blended in perfectly with the terrain.

The machine gun gave the little group of Americans a feeling of invincibility. It belonged to them—at least for now, it did.

CHAPTER 17

"Be forever a brave warrior."

Battle Flag Inscription
Sergeant Takada Yoshiro
Imperial Japanese Army

Luzon
April 28, 1945

The soldier's bloated corpse floated facedown in the slow-moving Umiray River. Only his uniformed torso was visible, the head and legs hidden beneath dark waters, making it difficult to tell if the remains were Japanese or American. It bobbed next to the sandy shore, then jerked by the current, drifted away, only to return again as if it needed to be near land.

PFC Anthony "Chippy" Cipielowski, burdened with the weight of Browning automatic rifle bandoliers and his own cartridge belt and M1 rifle, stepped cautiously along the narrow dirt trail separating the river from the wooded hillside. His eyes scanned the trees and thick brush, but seldom focused on the river, which flowed silently toward Dingalan Bay. Most of Chippy's patrol was a few yards ahead, but his drinking buddy and BAR man, Sergeant Gene Maziarz, followed close behind. As usual, Gene wore his steel helmet tilted back, revealing locks of wavy black hair covering part of his high, suntanned forehead. Beads of sweat had made little paths in the dust that caked his youthful face.

The Filipinos called it the "dry season." Indeed, there had been little rain. Dingalan Bay was supposed to have no distinctive seasons, yet each day the bright tropic sun burned hot and the air seemed almost supersaturated with moisture. It was as if the sky wanted desperately to rain but could not.

By noon, shirts soaked with sweat had narrow white stripes of crusted salt in the cotton material. Everyone had become familiar with death, but no one ever adapted completely to Luzon's energy-draining humid heat.

Private Cipielowski had been wounded three weeks earlier at Galiano, and his strength disappeared quickly. His thirst was overpowering, and the one canteen of water he carried never lasted through the morning.

Gene Maziarz paused, shifting his "beautiful BAR," and watched Chippy kneel down next to the river's edge.[1]

Chippy rested his M1 on the soft sandy soil and removed his canteen, apparently unaware of the body floating a few feet from where he dipped the aluminum cup.

That morning, they'd passed four dead Japanese along the trail. The patrol did not know if they'd died from wounds suffered in an earlier battle, or even who'd killed them. The human body decays fast in the tropics, often concealing the cause of death. The brain of the living struggled with little success to become accustomed to the stench of the dead. That horrible, nauseating smell hung in the air along the river and almost numbed the senses.

Still unaware of the dead man nearby, Chippy raised the canteen cup overflowing with cool river water to his lips.

"Chippy!" Sergeant Maziarz snapped in a firm voice. "Don't drink!" He pointed toward the floating corpse.

Chippy glanced at the figure. Then his sweat-lined face wrinkled with an expression of disgust.

"Jap officer," Chippy said. "See the wide leather strap across his back!"

Gene nodded in agreement.

Chippy Cipielowski dumped the water from his cup, unscrewed the canteen cap, and glanced at the corpse.

"Oh, what the hell!" he muttered. Then he forced the canteen below the water's surface. In a moment the bubbles stopped. He dropped two "purification" tablets into the container and returned it to its belt case.

"What the hell!" he exclaimed again as he stood up.

Sergeant Maziarz shifted his twenty-pound BAR, once more grasping the customized front grip he had made from the handle of a machete. He glanced around, sensing a strange quietness enveloping the area.

Then the sergeant's thoughts raced to the warning given by Jessey Mercado some days earlier. The description of a favorite Japanese ambush point fit their surroundings. The trail was narrow and close to the water's edge. The hill rising from the north side of the trail was wooded and sprinkled with huge boulders.

Gene told the author during an interview, "By the time I got to Dingalan Bay, I didn't think of being scared anymore. I had already survived so much combat I felt I could live forever."[2]

Suddenly Gene spotted two men making their way up the hill. They were wearing soft caps, not helmets. Both carried M1 rifles and one had a "strange-looking" radio on his back. They moved slowly, making no sound.

Chippy saw the men and shouted in a muffled yell, "Hey! Where you guys going?"

One of the hill-climbers turned. He was close enough for Gene to see his dirt-smeared face.

The dirty face moved his hand and placed an index finger to his lips.

That was enough of a warning. Gene and his patrol spread out and took cover. They held their position for only a minute, then rifle shots cracked from the hillside.

A scream, followed by shouts, then more screaming. Gene could see them. Four Japanese soldiers, charging down the hill, their rifles with long bayonets jutting straight forward.

The Japanese had prepared an ambush exactly where Jessey predicted, only Alamo Scouts had turned the ambush into one of their own.

The Scouts on the hill adjacent to the charging Japanese fired their M1s again. One of the enemy tumbled forward, apparently killed instantly. Another stumbled and began to limp from a wound, but he regained his balance and continued the charge.

A Japanese sergeant had a small white flag with a red circle tied to the epaulets of his shirt. It fluttered behind him like a cape.

Sergeant Gene Maziarz stood calmly at the edge of the trail following the caped man in his sights, waiting like the rest of the patrol for a clear shot.

Up the hill and only fifteen yards from Maziarz, the enemy sergeant screamed one last battle cry: "Banzai!"

Gene Maziarz squeezed the trigger, firing the BAR with rapid short bursts.

The Japanese pitched forward, his rifle flying from his hands. His lifeless body skidded facedown the remaining few yards of the hill and came to a stop at Maziarz's feet.

Once again, the river valley was quiet. Sergeant Maziarz's patrol had all fired the moment the BAR spoke. Dead Japanese lay scattered about the hillside near the trail. A search revealed no documents or maps, only a few photographs of loved ones in their uniforms.

The Alamo Scouts waved and disappeared over the hilltop without saying a word.

Sergeant Maziarz wiped at the sweat on his face with a jacket sleeve and reached down to remove the dead Japanese's *hinomaru yoseguki* battle flag.[3]

He and his patrol returned to the outpost at the mouth of the river. There they had some time to visit with John McKinney and other buddies. They joked about the shallow foxholes, the lack of protection in the area, and how "only the Army could dream up such a place for an outpost." After a night's rest, they enjoyed a boat ride back to the Task Force Headquarters.

The moment they arrived, another squad departed for the outpost as rotation of patrols continued on a daily basis.

Relaxing around Headquarters, Gene and his men learned that

Baguio had fallen the day before. They were proud that their Thirty-third Division had played a key role in the capture of the "summer capital." Nothing much was said about General Yamashita and his staff escaping Baguio. To the men of the Connolly Task Force, Dinga-lan Bay was *their* war.

Gene Maziarz found Jessey Mercado and thanked him for the am-bush warning; then they posed together with the captured battle flag.

Sixty years after surviving that ambush, Gene Maziarz learned the meaning of the inscription on the flag. In part, the translation reads, "Takada Yoshiro, be forever a brave warrior."

"Well," said Gene, "no one can ever say he wasn't brave!"[4]

May 1, 1945

Task Force patrols continued to comb the hills around the sawmill, the mountain slopes just west of Dingalan Bay, and the Umiray River. It was the river area and constant guerrilla reports of Japanese massing together that aroused Lieutenant Reardon's concern.

No A Company patrol or Alamo Scouts had seen any group of Japa-nese larger than ten or twelve since that first day of the Scouts' arrival. The prisoners captured, though, were ill or wounded, and all were starving. None seemed to have knowledge of a large force. Lieutenant Reardon spent several days accompanying patrols, and then pieced to-gether his information at night.

In reports to First Battalion and I Corps Headquarters, Major Con-nolly cited Reardon as "the most valuable single member of the Force."[5]

Lieutenant Reardon was embarrassed by the praise heaped upon him by Connolly's staff. Mostly, his mind was set on finding those "new assembly areas" supposedly being used by the Japanese. Reardon's re-lentless pursuit for information allowed very little time for sleep during those first eighteen days.

The patrols could not locate the assembly areas, and squad leaders began to doubt their existence. No one questioned the *possibility*, though. As the number of Japanese killed by patrols increased, so did the concern that many more might be hiding somewhere in the surrounding mountains.

On May 3, Major Connolly reported to I Corps that their "aggressive" patrols had already killed over two hundred Japanese with no Task Force losses. Another 150 bodies of dead enemy soldiers were reported, men who had apparently died of disease, exhaustion, starvation, or wounds from earlier battles. Twenty prisoners, all in poor physical condition, had been taken.[6]

May 4

Concern for the men at the Umiray River sandbar increased when a Japanese prisoner revealed under the "none-too-gentle persuasion of a guerrilla lieutenant" that at least 150 Imperial soldiers were banding together and planned to attack the outpost.[7]

Why would sick and exhausted soldiers attack the outpost when they could easily go around it? Perhaps their objective was the large supply of food the Americans had stored there. Of course, the honor of liquidating a few more Americans and confiscating their weapons had to be also appealing.

Major Connolly, Captain Ice, and Lieutenant Reardon agreed. They needed more men and weapons. But as those concerns had the staff's attention, another problem, this time from within, appeared.

Sixth Ranger B Company commander Captain Leo Strausbaugh had been waiting to learn of their true mission at the bay.

The captain may have had a reputation of being blunt and outspoken, and patience wasn't one of his virtues, but he never forgot his position and basic military courtesy. He requested a meeting with Major Connolly.

"Sir!" Captain Strausbaugh reported. "We are still standing by for our assignment—"

"I gave you your assignment, Captain," Connolly interrupted.

"Your men were to dig in on the south hill and protect our flank! We are expecting an attack . . . maybe at the outpost or here."

That was the answer Leo expected, and he was not happy with it. "Does the major have an idea of the size of the force that may attack?" the Ranger captain inquired.

"Yes, about two hundred; a little more or less; we're not sure yet."

"Two hundred!" Strausbaugh exclaimed. "Sir, I don't like the sound of this! I have sixty-five Rangers, no machine guns, no mortars, no way to stop two hundred Japanese except with rifles and bayonets. We can stop them, but we'll take heavy casualties doing it. I have an obligation to protect my men. We aren't designed as a frontline defense! We can't—are not supposed to—repel a major attack!"

"I suggest you get back on the hill!" Connolly said sternly.

But Captain Strausbaugh persisted. "Sir! I'm not here to sacrifice my men when there are other companies in our Army trained and equipped to do the job you need done."

"We'll see about this!" Connolly replied. "Captain Ice . . ."

"Sir!"

"Contact Division Headquarters and apprise them of our situation!"

Captain Ice hesitated, not sure exactly what the major wanted. Was he bluffing?

Leo Strausbaugh was not to fall for a bluff. "Sir!" he argued. "We don't belong to your division. We answer to General Krueger, the commanding general of the Sixth Army! Maybe he can help your predicament."

Major Connolly breathed deeply before answering. "I know who General Krueger is, Captain. Okay! You're relieved. But can you get us some reinforcements down here when you report to Sixth Army?"

"Of course, sir!" Strausbaugh said as he saluted and did an about face.

By nightfall, Captain Strausbaugh reported to his Ranger Battalion commander, Lieutenant Colonel Garrett.

"By God, Strausbaugh! I'm glad you had the guts to tell them how you feel . . . the truth! Of course we'll help. D Company is attaching to

a rifle company from the 136th. They'll be at Dingalan Bay by dawn."
Then the Ranger colonel added, "With light machine guns and 60mm
mortars! Now, you and your men get some rest."[8]

May 5

The actual count of men on duty at the outpost on any particular day is
hard to determine.

Twenty-four from Company A were still with John McKinney, and
Lieutenant Max Ladin had his fourteen mortar men. But the number of
guerrillas varied as some joined the American patrols that left the camp
daily. On the fifth of May, twenty-five guerrillas departed with one of
their lieutenants and did not return. That left the tiny outpost with
about twenty-five guerrillas.

Less than seventy Allied soldiers protected the valuable supplies.

Lieutenant Ladin, accompanied by Sergeant Johnson, checked the
perimeter at least once a day. There was really not much else to do, and
the cadre worried about morale.

Actually, morale remained high. No one really worried about the
"uniform discipline," which was a blessing on that hot, humid sandbar.
Some men wore their pants loose, not "bloused," at the boots. Others,
due to personal discipline and concern about insects crawling up their
legs, kept the trousers tucked in. Jackets often remained loose, outside
the pants. Some left the jackets unbuttoned with sleeves rolled up, many
did not.

The men had plenty to eat (C and K rations), and each man had a
good supply of insect repellant and cigarettes. News from Task Force
Headquarters arrived daily with new patrols, and the outpost CP radio
operators maintained routine contact with the sawmill.

So, the men at the outpost spent their time improving their foxholes, sharpening trench knives, cleaning weapons, and waiting.

Each NCO and officer knew exactly how many men he had at the
outpost, but there were no morning reports forwarded to Task Force
Headquarters. Major Connolly and Captain Ice were never very happy

with routine paperwork. Since they were at Dingalan Bay on their own, the recording of routine matters simply did not exist. Connolly, of course, filed a report after his mission, which circulated from the 123rd Infantry Regiment to I Corps, but it concentrated on important information (enemy killed and captured, etc.).

The war on Luzon consisted of one battle after another, one patrol and then another, one attack followed by another—all repeating in hundreds of areas simultaneously. The normal paper reports, because of the combat situation, were often misfiled or, more often, never even recorded.

May 6

First Lieutenant John F. Reardon had been charged with the responsibility of obtaining intelligence of Japanese "capabilities and intentions" in the Dingalan Bay area for Major Connolly's Task Force.

With that information, he was to design plans for measures to prevent enemy attacks and to keep the Japanese from escaping north.

Even with the lieutenant's personal involvement accompanying patrols, interrogating POWs, and interviewing both guerrilla and A Company patrol leaders, still no definite information could be obtained regarding the massing of Japanese troops.

Yet, the guerrillas insisted that their "bamboo telegraph" runners reported that Japanese were assembling south of the Umiray River and moved to new bivouac areas frequently.

Reardon had the reputation of making sound, mature decisions. He knew he must find a better way to investigate those reports. If they were true, the Task Force remained in danger.

Only one way to effectively survey a vast wilderness—from the sky.

Lieutenant Reardon journeyed by truck to Lingayen Strip, a temporary air base constructed by Sixth Army near Lingayen Bay directly across Luzon from Dingalan. There he met other "observers" from I Corps, who would be going on the flight: Major Forrest L. Kennor of Atlanta, Captain James G. Ferrell of Houston, First Lieutenant Robert

Nancolas from Wisconsin. The presence of these officers gave Reardon the opportunity to convince I Corps that the Connolly Task Force needed more men and weapons to effectively battle the large group of Japanese at Dingalan Bay if they existed. Observing the enemy from the plane would give the "brass" the proof needed.

They boarded a B-25Jb "Army Air Force Serial Number 44-29371." The young crew was already proceeding with the checklist in preparation for takeoff. The pilot was Second Lieutenant George B. Kurth of Hannibal, Missouri, assisted by copilot Second Lieutenant Clyde Ames of Washington State. Second Lieutenant Louis Bruno of Pennsylvania would be navigating. Radioman and gunner was Sergeant James F. Kirby of Troy, New York. The other gunners were Tech Sergeant Wilson M. McLawrin of Texas and Staff Sergeant Walter Waskewich from New Jersey; a total of ten—six crew members and four passengers.

The B-25 was assigned to the Seventy-first Bombardier Squadron, Thirty-eighth Bombardment Group, and had the usual .50-caliber Browning machine guns—a total of twelve; eight "fixed" in the nose section, one at the left turret and one at the right, and two at the tail section. Thirty-five hundred rounds of ammunition were loaded for each machine gun.

Their official record stated #44-29371 was sent on a reconnaissance mission to aid the Sixth Army in planning future operations in the Baguio area. However, it wasn't until seven days after takeoff that Lieutenant Colonel Peter Calza, the adjutant general from Headquarters I Corps, revealed in a letter to General MacArthur the plane's true mission; "Destinations were Baguio and Dingalan Bay areas."

On May 6, 1945, at 0837 hours, the B-25 lifted into clear skies and with "visibility unlimited" set its course at forty degrees. From that moment on, there was no radio contact with the aircraft.

In a little more than an hour, the men on board had gathered the visual knowledge they needed over the Baguio mountainous area and set the aircraft's course almost due east toward Dingalan Bay.

They approached the Sierra Madres and, flying at about 150 miles per hour, banked to the south, barely missing the highest mountain peaks. Then Lieutenant Kurth lowered his craft as it streaked over the Umiray River.

Suddenly, the B-25 began to receive fire from the ground. Lieutenant Reardon had found his elusive Japanese force, but it was too late to react. No time to break radio silence and give the location of the Japanese, no time to even radio a distress call.

Lieutenant Kurth and Lieutenant Ames struggled with the controls, attempting to gain altitude, but enemy machine-gun fire had done serious damage to the lumbering aircraft.

The B-25 bomber, its tail number 44-29371 surely visible to the Japanese below, nosed earthward and slammed into a wooded hillside. All ten aboard, including Lieutenant Reardon, were killed instantly, either by the crash or by the fiery explosion that followed.

The information needed by the Connolly Task Force, the actual size of the Japanese force, their bivouac area location, and their weapons, died with Lieutenant John Reardon.

There was another mystery. With no radio communication with the B-25, the Seventy-first Bombardier Group had no idea just where the wreckage was located. Search planes were dispatched, seven on the morning of May 7, three more that afternoon, and two more on the eighth.

At first, the status of the men aboard the B-25 was listed as "MIA" (missing in action), but within a day or two that changed to "KIA" (killed in action).[9]

The news of Reardon's disappearance reached Major Connolly midday on May 8. The staff had already feared the worst when the lieutenant did not return the night before.

Every man at the sawmill headquarters had lost a friend. Voices were hushed for the next two days as the men went on with their duties.

Sometime during the night of the eighth, Major Connolly, with a tone of anger in his voice, remarked to Captain Ice, "Now we have no idea what the Japs are planning, or even where they are!"[10]

Had he lived another two weeks, Lieutenant John Reardon would have reached the age of twenty-six.

CHAPTER 18

"I've got a funny feeling we're being watched!"

Sergeant Gerry Rampy to PFC John McKinney

Umiray Outpost

May 10, 1945

They come at dusk, hovering like a hummingbird, seeking children and pregnant women. Those are their choice victims, but if there are none in the village, anyone will do.

They call them Aswangs, small creatures with only half the body of a man, but unlike a man, they fly. Some say they have small wings, some say no. But then, few who have seen them lived to speak of the experience.

The Aswang uses his long fangs and tongue to puncture the neck of victims, then drains them dry of blood. If he tires of a liquid diet, he simply sucks the breath away and moves on, leaving a lifeless body behind.

The Aswang is a simple killer, usually taking one life at a time. Much more horrible is his competitor, the Manananggal, who may take every member of the family in one night, often leaving his victims with raw scars.

The superstitions embracing these two supernatural creatures dated long before the Japanese snatched the Philippines from the Americans. Fear of the Aswangs existed when the Spaniards introduced Christianity four hundred years earlier.

By the start of World War II, more than 90 percent of the Philippine population was Catholic. The Church struggled for centuries to convince the people to rid themselves of old superstitions, but was unsuccessful.

As with all cultures, superstitions—the supernatural—often explained the cause of death of someone when the priest or government officials could not.

Can the Aswang be destroyed? Some believe that remaining a devout Catholic, wearing a crucifix, and saying the Rosary will keep the creatures away. Others say that is not enough. Some state it is possible to kill an Aswang.

Major Juan Pajota of the United States Army, one-time military governor of Nueva Ecija Province on Luzon, claimed he possessed a "chant" given to him by a witch he met on his home island in the Visayan area. The magic words were to be said over the blade of a bolo.[1]

Pajota reportedly tricked two Aswangs who were flying above a rice paddy at the edge of his barrio. Covering himself with mud, he lay in wait until the creatures came close. Just as they passed overhead, he jumped up and chopped them to pieces with his bolo. He cremated the remains and buried the ashes.[2]

According to the Scouts of Sergeant Farrow's team, the Filipino guerrillas at the Umiray River actually believed Aswangs were nearby. Some of the men became frightened and began to argue among themselves, but the presence of American soldiers seemed to eventually calm their nerves.

On the morning of May 10, only two of Anderson's guerrilla units remained at the Umiray—one assigned to the Scouts and the other to a listening post at a nearby "low-water" ford.

At 10:00 A.M., Alamo Scout Sergeant James Farrow issued orders to break camp. Their mission was complete.

Accompanied by their guerrillas, they journeyed to the bay, boarded the captured Japanese launch, and headed south.[3]

The guerrillas returned to the ford to join their comrades guarding that area.

Once again, a dispute developed among the Filipinos. Some wanted to follow orders and remain at their post. Others thought it wise to withdraw eighteen miles across rugged country to the Task Force Headquarters, the sawmill.

Just how much of a part superstitions played in the decision remains a mystery. Guerrilla NCOs reported to Major Connolly that Huks visiting the listening post used both the fear of Aswangs and the Japanese to frighten the men, who were already concerned about the Alamo Scouts' departure. Without the presence of the Scouts, they believed the Japanese might attack using numerical superiority. Huk leaders reported to Connolly that Anderson's men were simple, superstitious, inexperienced troops, and suggested that the responsibility should have been given to the Huks in the beginning.

Perhaps some of those factors were involved. In the early afternoon of May 10, 1945, the combined force of almost fifty guerrillas (plus some eight or ten Huks) pulled out of the Umiray area and marched north toward the sawmill.

Had they remained on duty at the ford or moved to the outpost and reinforced the compound there, the events that unfolded fifteen hours later might never have occurred.

The Connolly Task Force mission was now in more danger than anyone realized.

The Rangers had left the headquarters area and by mid-afternoon, their replacements, delayed for unknown reasons, had not yet arrived.

Lieutenant Reardon's death a few days earlier had left the Intelligence Section temporarily demoralized. No one in the section developed a plan for surveillance any different from the past: "increase patrols and report."

And now, the Alamo Scouts were gone, leaving the Task Force Headquarters with no information on enemy movements along the river. Intelligence data had to come from patrols and the information given to them by guerrilla listening posts on the Umiray. During the afternoon and evening of the tenth, Major Connolly was unaware that the guerrillas had abandoned the river. There were no listening posts and no one was guarding the low-water fords.

The tiny outpost at the mouth of the river was totally isolated, and

Connolly and Ice had no idea just how critical the situation could become.

Because of its location at the tip of a sandbar peninsula, the outpost had no outer perimeter of defense, only the protection of water on two sides. There was no one up the river to give advance warning if an enemy approached, and no way to escape the triangular-shaped compound.

The future of the seventy-five men defending the outpost seemed to be in the hands of the enemy. If Major Connolly were a superstitious man (there is no record that he was), he would know that not all news from the Filipinos was bad. In fact, the riflemen of Company A had been enjoying their "wild stories" about superstitions, including one of a friendly mystical creature the Filipinos called a Dwende (dwarf).

The Dwende is about a foot tall, the Filipinos said, and to see him one must go out in the light of a full moon, sit very still in an open area, and make every effort not to startle the creature.

Some believed the Dwende actually speaks, others said he simply stares and then his thoughts become yours.

Unlike the Aswang and the Manananggal, the Dwende is a friendly fellow, offering advice on personal matters—love, wealth—and warnings of danger.

A Dwende reportedly warned one guerrilla that "many Japanese" were coming, and suggested the Filipinos lead their American friends away from Dingalan Bay. The story, true or not, spread rapidly. "That advice," Connolly told a guerrilla captain, "must have come weeks before."

"How does the major know," the guerrilla asked, "if you do not believe in the Dwende?"

"We have a new moon tonight. It's totally dark. The full moon was some days ago," Connolly replied.

* * *

Germany surrendered. The war in Europe was over. The surrender documents had been signed a few days earlier, but now it was official.

The men at Task Force Headquarters quickly relayed the news by radio to their outpost at the Umiray River. At both locations there was some "handshaking, cheers, and backslapping," but then the soldiers returned to their duties.

Surely personal thoughts drifted to the possibility that Japan might surrender and again they each could dream of going home.

But one had only to look around to face reality. The war on Luzon waged on, and the men at Dingalan Bay knew they still had more battles to fight before anyone could go anywhere.

* * *

German Admiral Doenitz aboard submarine U234 received the radio message that Germany had surrendered. He was ordered to turn his boat around and return to Germany or a base that would be named later.

On May 10, he elected instead to surrender to Allied Forces. He was in the mid-Atlantic and believed his fate might be better in the hands of the Americans. His ship's cargo of uranium destined for Japan might, indeed, be a good bargaining point during the surrender. He ordered his sub to stop, and then explained the situation to the two Japanese Naval officers on board.

The Imperial officers had no intention of surrendering to anyone. They committed suicide by taking sleeping pills and were promptly buried at sea.

The U.S. Navy personnel accepting Admiral Doenitz's surrender had no idea the uranium on board the U234 was enough to manufacture two atomic bombs—just the amount promised to Professor Bunsaku Arakatsu for their program, which now had no chance for success. Japan's A-bomb program was doomed.[4]

* * *

The Japanese Imperial soldiers in the Dingalan Bay area lacked two major elements necessary for successful movements: aircraft for reconnaissance and radio communication equipment (of which they had little or none). They were left with only a determined spirit and obedience to orders, blindly trusting their officers.

If motivated by their leaders, the Japanese fighting morale remained high. But with morale in general dipping, with empty stomachs and weakened muscles, it became difficult for other than the most fanatical to respond quickly to commands. Regardless of training, conditioning, customs, and history, all humans eventually have a cracking point, and then they break.[5]

Unlike the Filipinos, the Japanese soldier was not concerned with superstitions, at least not on Luzon. They had no flying, blood-sucking creatures locked in their subconscious to worry about. The average Japanese was no more superstitious than Americans. True, many Japanese feared spirits of the dead, ghosts and phantoms. They believed that such things existed, but that did not control their daily lives.

Desperation wrapped the Imperial soldiers along the Umiray River like a rain-soaked blanket. Yet they were about to demonstrate once again their reputation for bravery and the ability to continue on to a goal despite hardships.

The loosely organized Japanese force on the south side of the Umiray certainly had their problems. Most of the men wanted to bypass the American outpost and continue to live off the land during the journey north. But apparently a fanatical group, perhaps an original infantry unit still intact, formed the nucleus of their force and decided that the only chance for survival would be to wipe out the U.S. outpost and seize food stocks, weapons, and ammunition.

The cadre had over thirty days to increase their ranks recruiting stragglers from a variety of units. By May 10, the group numbered a little over 240.

Most of those men were well armed. They had no stockpiles of ammunition, but a sufficient amount for one major attack. The majority carried the standard Arisaka rifle with bayonet. They had at least two "woodpecker" machine guns and two later-model Nambus.

Many carried "knee mortar" grenade launchers, plus there was a small supply of hand grenades.

The officers (there were at least four) and NCOs were armed with samurai swords (sabers). Some had pistols.

In addition to that firepower, three soldiers carried American weapons, apparently picked up in an earlier battle. Two had M1 rifles and one a BAR, but the man lacked the knowledge of how to reload it (it is not known if he had extra magazines of ammunition or only the one in the weapon).[6]

A few had no modern weapons, and undoubtedly planned to pick one up during the attack from a fallen comrade or a dead American. These men armed themselves with the *take-yari,* or bamboo spear. This ancient weapon, once used by Japanese (and Chinese) warriors was nothing more than a bamboo pole, six to eight feet in length, sharpened at one end.

The spear appeared primitive and "silly" to the uneducated Americans. In fact, John McKinney called it "a long pole."[7]

But in the hands of the Japanese warrior, the *take-yari* could be lethal. Each soldier had received at least introductory training in the martial art *take-yari so do* (bamboo spear—fighting style), which emphasizes a variety of twists, twirls, and jabs to disarm and kill an opponent.

The Japanese attack group not only had a good plan, they also had a number of lucky breaks.

They were aware that the Americans lacked a way of receiving a warning of an attack from the river. When the Filipino guerrillas withdrew from the shallow areas of the river, the Japanese could not know where they went, but they must have known that the number of defenders at the outpost had not increased.

The enemy could cross the unguarded river where it was only a few inches deep anytime they wanted to.

A few other factors favored the enemy. Winds had remained calm during the day for the past week, but increased to seven to ten miles per hour in the early hours through dawn. Those winds were coming from the southeast, off the ocean and across the bay. Americans on duty at dawn would have difficulty hearing troop movements, as sounds of crashing waves smothered footsteps.[8]

The moon would be completely dark in its "new moon" phase, affording very little visibility at night.[9]

The plan of attack was very simple and to the enemy, no doubt, seemed perfect. Everything favored the Imperial Army at Dingalan Bay on May 10, 1945.

Half of their force would cross the Umiray at the unguarded fords and move in close during the night. They would travel around the north end of the backwater creek on the west side of the outpost, and surprise the Americans by doing the unexpected—crossing the creek and attacking through an open area between the water and the outpost's western perimeter.

The other half of the attack force would move along a sandbar, penetrate the lightly guarded ocean perimeter, and turn the machine gun on the Americans. Caught in the jaws of a two-prong attack, the Americans should be annihilated in a matter of minutes. The time for the attack was set—dawn, when the Americans should be asleep and the perimeter guards tired and groggy.

11:00 A.M., May 10

Two junior Japanese officers approached a perimeter bunker erected by Colonel Muto Masayuki and his men about two and a half miles south of the Umiray River.

To their surprise the officers found five geishas inside the bunker.

Colonel Muto's group, including the girls, had survived their journey, arriving at a fishing village near the bay two weeks before.

The villagers, either through fear or their usual hospitality, had provided food, and even assisted with the construction of two bunkers, one assigned to the geishas and the other, some fifty yards away, for the colonel and his staff.

The remainder of the colonel's group had bivouacked in a coconut tree grove fifty yards away, building shelters from bamboo, palm, and banana tree leaves.

The girls pointed to the other bunker, and watched as the young officers met with Colonel Muto, Sergeant Yamashita Yoshi, and Sergeant Morii Fukutaro.

Because of the distance, the girls did not hear any of the conversation during that short meeting.

Soon, Colonel Muto approached their bunker and simply said, "I must leave. The Filipinos will feed you. Good-bye!" Then he paused and handed one of the girls an Army jacket still bearing the infantry colonel's insignia. It was a welcome gift, for her kimono top had almost deteriorated during their weeks in the wilderness. She bowed with a "thank you."

The colonel bowed sharply and strutted off, followed by his two sergeants and the junior officers.

A few minutes later, the entire group disappeared into the woods, heading north in the direction of the Umiray River.

The colonel and his staff would never see the girls again.[10]

4:30 P.M., May 10

Filipinos in the little barrio of Umiray did not know if the river was named for their village or the village for the river.

The barrio sat peacefully in a grove of trees about one mile southeast of the American outpost and the river that separated them, and a half mile inland from the bay. Before the war came to Dingalan Bay, the villagers had experienced a wonderful life. There were fish in the river, wild pigs to hunt in the woods, and crabs and shellfish to gather along the sandbar, which began a little south of the village and stretched north past the river and about a quarter mile beyond the outpost.

American patrols passed the village almost daily, and noticed that the population had begun to diminish. The people obviously were evacuating to somewhere to escape something. The Americans guessed correctly that the Japanese were the cause.

GI riflemen asked the villagers the usual questions, "Where are the Japanese? Have they been here today?"

And the answer was always the same, in Tagalog. *"Bondoc"* (mountains), they would say, pointing to the hills across the river and beyond the outpost perimeters.

"What did he say?" someone, of course, would inquire.

"Boondocks" would be the reply. "They say the Japs are out in the boondocks."[11]

Early in the afternoon on May 10, another American patrol led by Staff Sergeant Gerry Rampy passed through the Umiray barrio and noticed something odd. Everyone was gone except for a family of four, a husband and wife, a child perhaps one and a half years old, and an infant.

Sergeant Rampy was normally in command of one of A Company's 60mm mortar teams. That day, however, he carried his M1 carbine and a .45-caliber automatic pistol, leading a patrol that was to comb the woods and swamp around the river.[12]

Captain Ice had wisely increased the frequency and size of patrols once he knew the Alamo Scouts were out of the area. The number of Japanese encountered by the patrols had dwindled to zero during the past twenty -four hours. Why? Where were the stragglers they normally found?

Staff Sergeant Rampy paused to smile at the family. He and his men knew there had to be reasons why the Japanese had vanished, and why most of the villagers had also disappeared.

Rampy led his men farther upstream and crossed at one of the fording points. Exhausted, they reached the outpost about 5:00 P.M., with time to visit with friends before the motor launch carried them back to Task Force Headquarters.

Gerry Rampy noted there was no unusual activity at the outpost. The Filipino guerrillas squatted in little groups talking and laughing. Some were on duty with their American companions, alert at the perimeter. GIs were smoking, nibbling from open cans of C rations, or chatting quietly with one another. Gerry guessed his friend PFC John McKinney was at his machine-gun position near the far southeast point of the perimeter. He started in that direction.

5:30 P.M., May 10

Shortly after Sergeant Rampy's patrol left the Umiray village, a group of Imperial Japanese soldiers entered, and were surprised to find that one family still remained.

The Japanese had just begun sending squads of men toward the sandbar at the bay. They expected the village to be deserted, and planned to use it as a staging area where their south attack force could gather and regroup before actually moving on to the sandbar at dawn.

They could not risk the chance that someone from the village might warn the Americans. One squad rushed the family's nipa (grass) hut and quickly bayoneted the husband, child, and infant. Sound travels far in the wilderness, especially in the evening when the winds have calmed. The bayonet was the best weapon for silent killing.

Somehow the assassins missed the mother, who broke through their ranks and raced toward the trees at the village's edge. If she escaped and reached the Americans—a possibility in the evening shadows—their plan would collapse. The element of surprise would be lost and American reinforcements from the sawmill might race to the outpost.

Imperial soldiers raised their rifles and fired at the fleeing woman. She fell dead before reaching the trees, only a few feet from safety in the darkness of the woods.[13]

5:30 P.M., May 10

"Hi, Mac," Staff Sergeant Gerry Rampy called out as he found John McKinney adjusting his pup tent flap.

"Hey, Ramp, good to see you all," McKinney answered. "Been reading anything up at headquarters?"

"Nah," replied Sergeant Rampy. "Haven't had time to read since we hit Luzon! I told you how much I love mystery stories. . . ."

"Yep," Mac said, turning to face his tall friend.

"Well," Rampy continued, "we just left—"

He was interrupted by the distant sound of rifle shots. Both he and McKinney stared across the river in the direction of the village.

"Some of your men?" McKinney asked.

"Nope," said the sergeant. "Must be the Japs. I don't think there are any patrols out this evening. All my men are here in the camp waiting for our boat ride back to the sawmill."

McKinney nodded.

"I was about to say," the sergeant continued, "we were at that village across the river. Seems like most everyone had scrammed. They must be expecting some kind of trouble soon. Now, *that's* a mystery."

McKinney listened, but did not reply.

Then the sergeant added, "I got a funny feeling we are being watched!"

John McKinney stared at Ramp, then nodded his head slowly. "Yep."

"Any idea where they may be hiding?" Gerry Rampy asked.

John McKinney faced the hills west of their perimeter, then looked at the sergeant and winked.

Staff Sergeant Rampy smiled and held out his hand. "Take care, Mac. Good luck," he said.

In a few minutes, the sergeant and his men had pushed off from the shore. The engine made a few funny putting sounds, then the boat turned north, leaving the Umiray outpost behind in the twilight.[14]

CHAPTER 19

"I believe in the accuracy of the M1 rifle,
in hitting before you get hit, and the men who would
go to hell and back to preserve what our country
thinks right and decent."

Lieutenant Audie Murphy, *To Hell and Back*
Awarded Congressional Medal of Honor, World War II

Darkness is fear's companion. As children, we feared things we could not see but imagined were there in the night. We told ghost stories in front of campfires or acted out scenes from some horror movie to frighten one another.

When the fire's light grew dim and silence replaced the giggling, sometimes fear tiptoed inside us. Perhaps we told no one. We had to prove we were brave. But suddenly there would be a noise from the dark. Our logical mind tried to comfort us. There was nothing to fear. That sound might be only a bird fluttering in a tree or a small animal scurrying about. We knew safety was always nearby. A loved one convinced us there were no creatures waiting in the dark to tear us apart. We learn fear's power early. We experienced it gripping through us trying to terrify, while our logical brain, using reason, battled for control. Our brain convinced us it was only our imagination.

Fear always moves with the infantryman. It works on the gut while he is awake and haunts the dreams if he sleeps. Fear can rush forth with a thousand sounds, or it can sit quietly with a soldier in a muddy, blood-soaked foxhole and look down his rifle barrel as if they were friends. Then maybe fear would disappear once the battle begins.

For the infantrymen, the darkness can always be terrifying. He knows there are no imaginary creatures lurking in the night. There will not be a ghost story told around a campfire, no monsters from the id. The soldier knows true terror. Men are out there who are going to try to kill you. The enemy is real. There is no scoutmaster, no big brother, no mother to run to for comfort.

Fear visited the Americans at their position along the line of defense at Dingalan Bay near the Umiray River the night of May 10, 1945.

Anyone who has been in combat will speak of how fear, like a lingering disease, never goes away completely. The soldier learns quickly that every battle is different. There may be similarities in weapons, terrain, or weather, but one battle can't completely prepare you for the next. Then there's the anticipation of battle, the anxiety and frustration tearing the soldier's resistance apart, allowing the fear disease to come in and attack the brain.

Fear found a home. The six guerrillas who shared foxholes with Private John R. McKinney and his buddies did not fear the Japanese soldiers. The guerrillas were all combat veterans, having fought their enemy in close quarters during several previous battles. But now they shared a different situation. Their battle tactics had always been hit and run, attacking the Japanese with surprise and then disappearing quickly after the assault. The guerrillas were not at all comfortable being on the defensive on an open sandbar protected by a few mortars and machine guns. And possibly being outnumbered did not set well with them either.

They favored what they had been trained to do, attack in ambush from good concealment, hit when and where the enemy least expected. Fear of the unknown and superstition played on them as the hours crept by. The Dwende had warned hours ago that the Japanese would attack. The Dwende had suggested they leave the open sandbar and take their GI friends with them before the attack came. But no one in Able Company showed interest in warnings given by a foot-tall imaginary creature living inside a tree.

The morning of May 10, PFC Morris Roberts asked in a teasing manner what John McKinney thought about the Dwende's warnings. McKinney answered with a smile and his usual "I ain't talking!"

"You believe it?" Roberts pushed.

"Nope."[1]

4:30 A.M., May 11, 1945

Private John R. McKinney stared over his M1 rifle barrel into the darkness that enveloped Dingalan Bay. He could not see the Umiray River or much of the beach in front of him.

The stars on that moonless night were unusually bright, but the light shone only for their glory. They did little to illuminate the outpost.

He rolled his eyes under heavy lids to relieve fatigue, and glanced at his watch, squinting to read the faint numerals. 4:30 A.M. He and his three companions had been on duty since 2:00 A.M. Their shift ended at five. The men of the relief should be rested and alert, ready at daybreak.

The watch or duty on the perimeter at 5:00 A.M., just before sunrise, had always been critical. Organized Japanese infantry units throughout the Pacific notoriously chose two night hours to launch assaults, midnight and dawn. Of course, attacks could and did come at different hours, but traditionally they favored dawn. Tactically, this made sense. The logic was to catch the enemy asleep, or at least frustrated and tired. Tradition and symbolism also played a key role. Many important struggles in Japanese history had occurred at midnight. But the word "Nippon" (Japan), expressed in the ancient symbols of *kanji*, means "land of the morning sun." Dawn marked the beginning of a new day, a new life. That symbol depicted on Imperial Army and Navy flags stirred patriotic spirit with the Japanese just as the stars and stripes did for Americans.[2]

The Japanese around the southern sector of Dingalan Bay in May 1945 were not formed into a typical unit. They had been everything but organized until late April.

The Connolly Task Force knew this from captured enemy soldiers.

Captain Ice had sent messages to his outpost at the Umiray River. "Attack your position could come any night. Don't expect the usual. Expect the unexpected!"

Able Company had been fighting the clever enemy long enough. They did not need to be reminded.

* * *

The metal skin of the .30-caliber machine gun was cool and moist from Dingalan Bay's night air. It sat, a sleeping instrument of death waiting for someone to command it to sing.

McKinney tried to focus his eyes on the outline of the machine gun just a few feet away in the pit. It was almost impossible to see in the dark shadows. It was sitting there covered with brush and long blades of lilies cut earlier that evening. From the beach in daylight, the entire position could be mistaken as part of the natural terrain.

At the gun, Adolph "Red" Barrette leaned forward, his left forearm across the breech of the gun, his right hand cupped directly above the handle in easy reach of the trigger. His chin rested on his knuckles.

Was Red asleep?

McKinney, cradling his M1, with his head safely below the crest of their pit, crawled next to his friend.

"Mac?" Red whispered.

"Yep."

"See anything?" Their voices were hushed.

"Nope," McKinney replied.

"You feel anything? They out there?"

McKinney drew in a deep breath, inhaling the salty air.

"Don't feel nothing," he said. "They ain't out there, least not yet."

Red moved his head, twisting it to release a stiff neck. "Maybe they ain't coming tonight."

"Seems like," John McKinney replied.

Then his mind began to drift to another time. "Don't feel nothing," he repeated to himself. His thoughts moved back a few years to Georgia, and a night when he had watched the bobcat hunting in the swamp. He'd thought of that night often while sitting in the foxholes.

The bobcat moved silently that night on fur-padded paws through the darkness near Cannon Creek. He'd frozen statuelike for a moment where the cypress trees gave way to a grassy clearing. His short tail had twitched once and erect ears had turned slowly back, then to the front again.

Blending with shadows from the moonlight that bathed the tall trees, the cat lowered his body, belly touching the moist sandy soil. Then he sniffed the raccoon tracks left the night before. The tracks led to the muddy riverbank. A mother and three young coons would be coming again to the water's edge to feast on crawdads. The cat waited. Patience was one of its great virtues.

Through the crickets' rhythmic sound, the occasional splash of a fish breaking calm misty waters, over the night bird's call and beyond human understanding, the bobcat felt danger. He slowly raised his body and took one step, remaining as always in the shadows out of the moon glow. His head tilted, revealing an old battle scar above one eye. He breathed in through the nose, then opened his mouth to smell again. The cat had turned his attention from a juicy raccoon dinner.

Danger lurked nearby. In all the swamps and pine tree forests of southern Georgia, there was only one predator as clever as the bobcat. Man! Man brought death. Man was in the swamp. The cat could not see the man. And there was no scent. This told the cat where man was, somewhere to the front in the direction the breeze was blowing.

The bobcat contemplated the next move. He pretended he did not know man was there. He would trick man into believing that a cat can be taken by surprise, then escape with the shadows.

John McKinney watched as the bobcat vanished into the darkness. He had learned so many tricks from the cat during those early years in the swamps, especially the art of using night shadows for concealment and the magic of stealth, moving swiftly on soft soil without a sound. But he had never mastered the ability to *feel* the presence of another creature in the darkness. Only the cat could do that.[3]

Private McKinney moved up the forty-degree slope of the three-foot-high embankment, and peered in the darkness toward the beach once more. A thought remained in his mind. Could his enemy, like the bobcat, feel the presence of another warrior?

It had been a quiet night around the perimeter. Peacefulness seemed to be testing the nerves of tough men. Shifts changed every three hours, but few slept. They would take turns napping during the day. Now ears strained for that first sound, a shot, a scream, or a shout from the Japanese.

But that night nothing indicated anyone was about to do anything.

Less than an hour remained until the first light of dawn. At 4:40 A.M. McKinney slipped over the back rim of their twelve-foot pit and crawled north about twenty-five yards. There he found PFC Morris Roberts awake, sitting up in his pup tent shelter, M1 rifle in his lap.

"Ready?" McKinney whispered.

"Yeah. Ready. Got to wake up Homan and his Filipino buddies. See you in a few minutes."

Roberts had been a Michigan farm boy, but now his once-youthful face, like all the others, had changed. He was three years older than McKinney, but now looked even older. The stress, pain, and fatigue from war, sleepless nights, dirt, illness, and wounds had aged all of their suntanned faces. It was, at times, impossible to distinguish one from another with only a quick glance.

McKinney crawled back to the pit. The stars were losing their brilliance, becoming pale as dawn slowly approached.

*　*　*

At 4:30 A.M., only a few minutes before John McKinney alerted his relief guard, one hundred Japanese Imperial soldiers concealed by darkness moved toward the long sandbar at the south end of Dingalan Bay.

This group, compiled of men from a variety of units, would become the beach assault force. Their mission—penetrate the American perimeter at the south, fight 150 yards through the outpost, and attack the backs of the defenders at the north perimeter.

This plan appeared to be a relatively easy one to accomplish except for one obstacle, the American machine gun facing the beach. If the machine gun went into action, it could bring total failure to the mission.

The waters of the Umiray River blocked one side of the American triangular outpost. Dingalan Bay blocked the other side. This prevented the Japanese from attacking at either of those perimeters with any sizable force. But at the same time, the Americans had nowhere to retreat. The north would be blocked by the Japanese northern force, the south sealed by the beach attacking group.

The only route for the Japanese in the south would be up the sandbar to the beach to attack that one point protected by the machine gun. To overcome the threat of the machine gun, the Japanese had formed a special infiltration squad. They were to liquidate the American crew at the machine gun and a few others at that point, capture the gun, and turn it toward the American defenders inside.

With the machine gun in their possession, the infiltration squad was to move quickly to the center of the outpost and prevent the mortars located there from going into action. Shots fired in this effort would signal the beach assault force to overrun the American southern perimeter.

The Japanese northern attack force, consisting of about 148 men, crossed the Umiray River three miles upstream where the water flows swiftly at a depth of only about four to five inches.

These men were to be in the woods two hundred yards away from the northern perimeter by dawn. Their attack had to be launched when they heard the first shots inside the outpost. The Americans under attack from front and rear would be trapped in a vise.

The southern infiltration squad had a difficult task. To sneak through the American beach defense without detection, capture the machine gun, and move another fifty yards to the mortar positions would require the best of soldiers. The most experienced combat veterans were selected for this assignment, including the two sergeants who had accompanied Colonel Muto Masayuki and the geishas to Dingalan Bay.

These sergeants, carrying traditional swords, led the infiltration squads. Sergeant Morii Fukutaro, the smaller and younger of the two, had five men, all armed with Type 99 Arisaka bolt-action rifles fixed with bayonets. That machine gun, its operators, and the riflemen protecting it must be liquidated quickly.

The other squad was under the aging noncommissioned officer Sergeant Yamashita Yoshi. He also commanded five soldiers armed with Arisakas, bayonets fixed.

In daylight, Sergeant Yamashita was easy for his men to see. A large, husky man, five feet ten inches tall, he was much larger than the average Imperial soldier of the 1940s.

While Sergeant Morii's men went about their deadly work at the perimeter, Sergeant Yamashita would take his men undetected in the early morning light to the mortars at the outpost center.

* * *

At 4:35 A.M., as John McKinney crawled toward Eldon Homan, the Japanese NCOs led their infiltration teams onto the sandbar five hundred yards to the south. Trotting in a crouch, they moved north to the mouth of the Umiray River. There they regrouped, squatted down, and waited. Perhaps the sergeants assumed that the other squads were one hundred yards or so behind. That was the plan. Those men would have to launch a massive attack after the infiltration teams accomplished their mission.

The beach attack force from the south had been divided into groups of twenty men each led by an NCO. These would attack one after another, wave upon wave, along a fifty-yard front. This action, so typical of Japanese battle strategy, should overwhelm the American defenders of the outpost.[4]

Then things began to go wrong. For some reason, the attack groups were not moving onto the sandbar at the designated intervals.

Dawn was rapidly approaching and a dangerous distance separated the groups. Sergeant Morii and Sergeant Yamashita had no way of knowing that their infiltration might become, at least for a few minutes, an isolated effort. They lacked communication with the other groups, and visibility was no more than a few yards. The dark moon that concealed their advance now had a negative effect on the plan. Each group knew to move north on the sand, but spacing became a matter of guess.

Perhaps assuming their plan was perfect and no contingencies were necessary (an assumption often mistakenly taken by Japanese), Sergeant Morii's team began their twenty-five-yard crawl up the beach toward the outpost point.[5]

It was still dark. The sand and crashing waves covered their sounds.

Sergeant Yamashita and his five men moved in a left oblique, separating from Morii's group by some twenty yards. Then they turned toward the perimeter. Both squads now advanced slowly to a three-foot ridge at the perimeter's edge.

At the crest of the ridge and throughout the entire outpost, hyacinth bushes covered the sandy soil. Their green and purple leaves were thick, the plants in some places so high that a man hugging the ground could easily crawl within a few feet of another and not be seen.

Beyond the crest, the terrain looked almost flat, but rose at a ten degree angle until reaching the wooded hills some six hundred yards to the north, four hundred yards from the outpost's northern perimeter.

At the beach about eighteen yards up from the crest of the ridge, hidden in a pit and covered by cut lilies and grass, the American machine gun waited. Thanks to observation men placed in the hills at the north of the outpost the day before, the Japanese knew the approximate location of the machine gun. But they could not see it in the dark. The Morii and Yamashita squads suddenly froze. They heard movement at the American perimeter.

At 5:05 A.M., PFC Morris Roberts and his small handsome friend PFC Eldon M. Homan, along with two Filipino guerrillas, arrived at the machine-gun pit to relieve its sleepy crew. Crouching near the ground, one by one, they slid into the pit as the others climbed out.

Red Barrette had the farthest to go to reach his foxhole, located about twenty-five yards along the Umiray River edge of their perimeter. Halfway there, he passed PFC Edward S. Colwell's position. Colwell's home was similar to the others, a slit narrow trench two feet deep, dirt and sand packed about one-and-a-half feet high along the outer edge of the hole for protection. His pup tent served as the roof.

Located near the machine-gun pit, John McKinney's trench was much larger, two feet deep and twelve feet long and covered by two pup tents. McKinney shared his home with two Filipino guerrillas. Their position faced in the direction of the beach, but was twenty paces north of the machine gun toward the center of the camp.

At 5:20 A.M., John McKinney pulled the flaps of his end of the pup tent together to block the morning sun rays. His tent mates muttered something in Tagalog and fell asleep almost instantly.

McKinney unbuckled his web belt, rolled it around the bayonet and canteen, and placed it next to his helmet. He opened his shirt and collapsed upon a canvas ground cloth, the M1 rifle, as always, cradled between his body and right arm.

Meanwhile, at the center of the outpost, fifty yards north of the perimeter where McKinney, Barrette, and Colwell prepared to get a little sleep, First Lieutenant Max Ladin stretched out on his pup tent shelter half, pulling part of the canvas over his body.

He gently lowered a steel helmet to cover his face from the sun, which would soon be peeking above Dingalan Bay's horizon. Instinctively, Lieutenant Ladin reached under the canvas and grasped his carbine, pulling it close to his side.

Ten feet away, Technical Sergeant Victor J. Wendling covered some of his six-seven frame with a canvas, rolled over on his side, and faced the lieutenant. The sergeant closed his eyes, but for some reason had difficulty falling asleep.

The field telephone operator and the runner who had been at their post at the command tent with Sergeant Wendling and the lieutenant all night were relieved to return to their foxholes. Their replacements plus a clerk would be on duty at 6:00 A.M.

During those few minutes while men shifted responsibility, no one occupied the tent. The precious supplies of food and ammunition, the field phone, and the radio were guarded only by sleeping or half-asleep men.

A few feet beyond Lieutenant Ladin, the mortars sat like small stovepipes pointing to the north. Their teams sleeping nearby could leap into action, load the tubes, and fire within seconds after the order was issued by either Ladin or Wendling.

An uneventful night for all. Most of the men rested with the thought that they were within a well-guarded perimeter and that it was unlikely the Japanese would risk an attack after dawn.

Along the perimeter, shifts changed as they had each morning for the past few weeks. New men on duty checked their weapons in the darkness, while those they replaced settled like nesting animals attempting to find a comfortable position in their shallow foxholes. For a few minutes, all was quiet in the outpost along the Umiray River.

* * *

Sergeant Yamashita drew his sword, crawled over the small sandy ridge and onto the flatland. In his jacket pocket was his *inkan,* his personal seal with a family name carved on a clear quartz cylinder three inches long. No doubt he felt content knowing that if he was killed in battle, someone could identify his remains by the *inkan.* To a Japanese soldier the *inkan* was as important as the GI's metal "dog tag." In his pants pocket was another personal treasure, a wristwatch, the band long since rotted away, the crystal and hands gone. Even the dial face had faded, leaving the numerals barely distinguishable. It accompanied him into combat even though it had no practical use.

Yamashita started his long crawl through the hyacinth bushes toward the center of the outpost. Separated by only a few feet, his five men followed, silently making their way in a formation resembling a triangle with Yamashita at the point. They passed unnoticed in the darkness between the machine-gun pit and PFC Edward Colwell's foxhole. Once safely inside the perimeter, they crawled faster.

Shadows faded as light of a new day began to streak the sky. Time was running out for Sergeant Yamashita and his squad.

Sergeant Morii Fukutaro, his battle flag tucked inside his shirt, crawled with one soldier to the right of the machine gun and directly toward the large foxhole where PFC John McKinney was attempting to fall asleep. As planned, two soldiers inched their way toward the machine gun, while the last two crawled to the left. Their orders were to attack the machine-gun crew if their comrades failed in the attempt to take it. If this was not necessary, they were to rush the center, reinforcing Yamashita's squad.

At 5:30 A.M., the machine gun, camouflaged by its green blanket, pointed silently at the spot where the long sandbar connected with the beach.

The tide was still at its high phase, but had not covered the sandbar.

The southern Japanese attack group moved from land toward the bay. Even though they were behind schedule, they did have some luck. In May the tide was lower than in other months, and a "new moon" meant an even lower tide. So, at a time of the morning when the tide might normally have covered their path, the Japanese Imperial soldiers found the sandbar above water, ready for them to move easily into their attack positions.

Private John McKinney almost drifted off to sleep, but in those moments before the conscious brain surrenders, he heard a noise outside the tent. It sounded as if someone was attempting to open the canvas flaps.

"What the hell you all doing?" McKinney shouted with a smile, thinking the disturbance was one of his buddies being playful. He stood up.

No one answered. McKinney waited for another sound. Suddenly the flaps flew open.

Imperial Army Sergeant Morii Fukutaro and U.S. Army PFC John R. McKinney, two farmers the same size and age, but now enemy warriors, stood facing each other four feet apart. Sergeant Morii held his sword high, but raised it above his head, both hands firmly gripping the hilt in a classic *jodan no kamae* position. He swung the sword downward, intending to split McKinney's skull.[6]

But in the dim light, Sergeant Morii's aim was poor. The blade missed the skull, but its razor-sharp tip sliced through part of McKinney's right ear, taking a small piece of scalp with it. The blade continued downward toward the earth, ripping McKinney's shirt as it traveled.

Dazed, McKinney managed to seize his M1 and brought it up, stock first, in a perfect "vertical stroke" catching Morii under his chin. The sword fell from his hand as the head snapped backward. McKinney followed through with a downward vertical stroke, smashing his enemy's head with the butt.

Sergeant Morii's battle was over.[7]

John McKinney's personal struggle for survival had just begun.

The Japanese soldier who had accompanied Sergeant Morii jumped from behind the tent, screamed a war cry, and rushed at McKinney with his rifle lowered, bayonet ready.

With no time to aim, McKinney shot from the hip, firing his M1 twice. The Japanese reeled and fell, his chest oozing blood through his shirt. The soldier's body struck the ground. At that moment, the two Filipino guerrillas scampered from the foxhole. Rifles and bandoliers of ammunition scattering, they stumbled, regained their balance, and began a dash toward the north shouting, "Hapon! Hapon! (Japanese! Japanese!)" They would not stop until they reached the north perimeter a few minutes later. Complete panic had seized the guerrillas during the opening moments of the battle. Many dropped their weapons as they ran. Others, weapons in hand, darted about in the semidarkness screaming and shouting. The suddenness of the Japanese attack and the fact that the perimeter had been penetrated gave the enemy the advantage of surprise they'd expected. The Filipino soldiers desperately needed to form as a group and they lacked a leader.

McKinney paid little attention to his fleeing companions. His bleeding head wound and the shock of the Japanese attack left him stunned for the first few moments.

The crack of other rifle shots struck his senses like a lightning bolt. Suddenly, the sounds in the distance grew into a furious churning rhythm like heated popcorn. Unlike popcorn, the crackling sounds did not subside, but developed into a constant rattle. The shooting came from the northern perimeter more than a hundred yards away.

McKinney, blood flowing from the head wound and soaking his ripped shirt, turned to face the machine gun. Strange it had not yet fired. Perhaps Roberts and Homan were waiting for clear targets on the beach.

Then the silhouettes of two men appeared on the edge of the machine-gun pit. They were struggling with the cover over the machine gun, attempting to remove the camouflage. McKinney began to trot in their direction to help. A thought flashed in his mind. The machine gun would easily fire with the brush on top of it. Why would his friends remove the cover unless they planned to turn the weapon and point it in the opposite direction?

Sweat and the glow of dawn blurred his vision. McKinney stopped and wiped his eyes with a ragged shirt sleeve. Then he could clearly see the men standing on the mound. They were Japanese!

Without hesitation, McKinney reacted as he had been trained. He raised his M1 and fired. Both men fell backward off the mound.

McKinney turned. A cloudy brain began to direct his actions. Ammunition! He had no idea if there were bandoliers with clips of M1 bullets in his foxhole. Did the Filipinos take it all? It would still be dark in his tent. A quick decision. Run to the command tent fifty yards away. There would be plenty of ammunition there.

He moved a few paces trying to maintain his balance, then stopped. He saw two Japanese moving parallel to him only twelve yards away. Their rifles were lowered, bayonets pointing toward the command tent. The two soldiers were the last of Sergeant Morii's group racing to reinforce Sergeant Yamashita's squad. Of course, McKinney did not know that. The men saw each other at the same instant. The Japanese turned to point their rifles at McKinney, but they moved too slowly. McKinney, his rifle already at the shoulder, both eyes open to see over the barrel in the dim light, fired twice. His shots struck the men in the head. They fell as if jerked back by an invisible rope. McKinney had killed the entire six-man squad of Morii Fukutaro within the first two minutes of the battle.

At 5:33 A.M., near the command tent, while John McKinney faced Sergeant Morii and before the first shots were fired, Sergeant Yamashita and his squad had succeeded in reaching the American mortar position. Incredibly, they had penetrated the perimeter and avoided detection as they crawled fifty yards in the darkness through the undergrowth. The glow of dawn now gave the squad clear targets. Sleeping Americans lay scattered on the ground about the command tent.

Sergeant Yamashita stood up slowly and raised his sword. He had selected his first American to kill. A man sleeping directly to his front. The face was covered by a steel helmet, but the exposed neck presented a perfect target.

Yamashita leaped forward, bringing the sword down with a force that would easily decapitate Lieutenant Max Ladin. The shiny blade sliced through the air, missing the neck, and glanced off Ladin's helmet with a loud, dull *klunk*. The noise brought half-asleep Technical Sergeant Victor Wendling fully alert. He fired his M1 at the precise moment Sergeant Yamashita raised his sword to deliver a second blow. Yamashita spun around from the impact of the .30-caliber bullet and fell, his sword toppling from his hand.

Yamashita lay on his back gasping for breath. His right hand moved to his shirt pocket searching for the *inkan,* his personal seal. Then the fingers froze in death holding the little leather case containing the crystal cylinder.[8]

Lieutenant Ladin was up, carbine in hand, ready for another attack. His dented helmet lay at his feet.

Pandemonium engulfed the command tent area as Yamashita's five-man squad, still close together, began firing wildly. Their leader was down, but they had their assignment. The huge Sergeant Wendling, M1 at the shoulder, quickly positioned himself between his lieutenant and the Japanese fifteen feet away. Wendling fired rapidly, and the lieutenant emptied his carbine in seconds. Four minutes into the battle, the bold Japanese plan to infiltrate the outpost had failed. Sergeant Morii and Sergeant Yamashita along with every member of their squads, had been killed.[9]

Shots fired from Private John McKinney and Sergeant Wendling occurred almost at the same moment fifty yards apart, but served as a signal to the Imperial Army waiting in the woods north of the perimeter. They knew the infiltration squads had engaged the Americans inside the camp. They could not know the fate of their buddies. The first wave of Japanese charged across the open land in the dark and smashed into the American lines along a hundred-yard front.

Private McKinney paused after shooting the two Japanese soldiers who were rushing along with him toward the command tent.

He turned to look at the machine gun, clearly visible without its camouflage. It remained silent. The first three minutes of battle seemed like an eternity. From where McKinney stood, he could not see in the pit, even though it was only twenty yards away. Were Roberts and Homan still there hidden by the shadows?

John McKinney faced another decision, one of many he would need to make over the next twenty-five minutes. He had been trained as a rifleman. The M1 was his weapon. Hunting with a rifle had been etched in his soul since his early years in Georgia. But as with the other men at the outpost, he had also been cross-trained with a .30-caliber light machine gun. He knew its devastating capabilities, and understood that whoever commanded the gun would control their area and perhaps the battle.

"Mac! Mac!"

McKinney turned in the direction of the shouts. Private Edward Colwell had left his foxhole near the machine gun and, seeing McKinney, rushed toward him.

"Japs! Everywhere!" Colwell panted.

McKinney made his decision. "I'm going to the machine gun," he told Colwell. "Get to the supply tent. Fetch some bandoliers. I'm completely out of ammo!"

Colwell started jogging the forty-yard journey to the command tent.

Edward Colwell may never outlive his reputation as a "sad sack," an uncoordinated soldier, but McKinney knew that it had nothing to do with bravery. He had seen Colwell in battle before. Colwell had nerves of steel and never flinched in the face of enemy attacks.

Gunfire at the northern perimeter had become deafening. Screams, battle cries, and the popping sound of the Japanese rifles were almost drowned out by the sharp cracking of M1s, the rhythmic pounding of BARs, and the distant chattering of machine guns.[10]

Then explosion flashes in the woods beyond the perimeter. The American mortars had gone into action.

Private Colwell had taken about ten steps when he turned and fell without a sound. His rifle hit the ground, disappearing in the brush. He struggled to get up, then collapsed.

"Mac!" he managed to shout. "I am hit! Look at the blood!"

Blood was seeping through Colwell's shirt at the elbow and running down his arm, which dangled as if it was pulled from the base of a marionette. A Japanese bullet had struck him in the arm, ripping flesh and bone into a pink mess. A few steps brought McKinney to his side.

"You're going to be okay," he said, pulling Colwell's good arm to his chest. "Keep your hand pressed on the wound till we get help."

"All that shooting, Mac. No help's coming. Fighting for their life up there. We're going to die down here by this river!"

"Ain't dead yet," McKinney responded.

Colwell nodded toward a clump of hyacinth. "There's a full clip in my rifle. You take it."

"Any extra ammo?" McKinney asked as he exchanged rifles.

Colwell slowly shook his head. "No."

McKinney, on his feet, turned his attention once again to the machine gun. Still silent. Why? The sun was struggling to pull above the bay, but its light was washing away the night and painting high streamer clouds a mellow gray-orange.

He started toward the machine gun, pausing only to pick up another M1 apparently dropped by one of the guerrillas.

Four and a half minutes into the battle. McKinney reached the pit and froze in disbelief. The bodies of the two Japanese he'd killed minutes before lay sprawled in front of the machine gun. But the pit was empty!

Ten yards to the left, not far from his foxhole, PFC Morris Roberts sat, legs outstretched, at the edge of a clump of tall bushes. His face and shirt were smeared with blood. Cradled in his arms was the lifeless form of PFC Eldon Homan.

Apparently, the two men had instinctively turned toward McKinney's foxhole when they heard the first shots moments before. Homan had been struck in the back of the head by a Japanese bullet. Killed instantly, he'd toppled over onto Roberts's feet.

Roberts had attempted to drag his friend and hide him in the closest cover he could find in the dim light. PFC Morris Roberts had been a tough soldier. He'd always demonstrated plenty of courage. But at this point, his body and nerves could take no more. Maybe he had heard one too many explosions. Too many dying men screaming and moaning around him. He had seen too much blood and too many bodies torn apart. This time, when his buddy's skull was shattered by the impact of a bullet, something in Roberts snapped. It was not fear. Fear never influenced Morris Roberts. Battle shock had conquered his mind and spirit.

Morris Roberts knew McKinney was standing there. He witnessed the events that were about to unfold, but for a while he could not move or speak or even cry. He began to rock Homan slowly back and forth. His eyes locked on McKinney, but betrayed nothing.

"Morris! I think he's dead," John McKinney spoke softly. "I'm gonna need help with the gun!"

Roberts did not answer. He had lost all combat value. John McKinney peered over the edge of the pit toward the beach. His flesh began to crawl.[11]

The Imperial Army assault group was trotting up the sandbar, appearing as small toy soldiers moving on the sand a hundred yards away. The inability of the southern forces to follow closely behind Yamashita and Morii had disrupted the effectiveness of the Japanese attack.

He watched the first wave of Japanese leave the sandbar. They turned toward his position and began to jog at port arms, rifles pointed upward in front of their chests. The NCOs had drawn their swords and led the way shouting something. The crashing waves smothered their voices.

One hundred yards away. John McKinney placed his two rifles carefully next to the machine gun. He grasped a handle of the Browning and sighted down the barrel.

Seventy-five yards. The Japanese began their charge. McKinney turned around for a quick glance behind him. He hoped to see a few of his pals rushing to his aid. Even one squad of riflemen. Maybe two men with powerful BARs. A fantasy. He knew no one was coming. The others were busy with the defense of the northern perimeter where a battle was raging.

The guerrillas who had been with McKinney and Morris Roberts had vanished.

Private Edward Colwell lay helpless twenty yards away, drifting in and out of consciousness from shock and loss of blood. He also became a witness to the battle, but that was all.

Ten yards in the other direction, Eldon Homan lay dead in the arms of Morris Roberts. And Roberts was in shock, unable to move.

Private John McKinney accepted his fate. He must face the Japanese alone. For this he had no plan. He thought briefly about how he had already killed six men in a few short minutes. No time to analyze anything about that. Feelings must come later if there was to be a later.

Again he sighted down the machine-gun barrel.

Sixty yards. The Japanese lowered their rifles, bayonets pointing directly at him. A quick count. Thirty in the first wave followed by thirty in the second group fifty yards behind the first. And at least forty still on the sandbar.

McKinney expected to die at any moment. He hoped he could take a few of the enemy with him. And he knew that when he died, Colwell's and Roberts's deaths would follow quickly. Even worse was the thought that the Japanese might have an easy path to the inside of the outpost.[12]

His wound had stopped bleeding, the pain gone. He became conscious of only what was in front, death charging at him in Japanese uniforms.

His mouth went dry, his muscles tightened, his heart beat slow and steady. A man who had never boasted suddenly felt the need to reassure himself.[13]

"You boys are running right into a Georgia cyclone!" he muttered. Then his finger reached for the machine-gun trigger and began a slow, steady pull, five-pounds pull, six-pounds. . . .[14]

The first wave of enemy had broken into squads of six, now more difficult to hit.

McKinney turned the gun to the left thirty degrees, planning to move it to the right as he fired. Fifty yards. One half the length of a football field. The Japanese were running as fast as one could in the brown sand, some tripping but regaining their pace.

Forty-five yards. He could hear someone screaming, *"Totsugeki!"* ("Charge!") Then they were shouting their battle cry, *"Banzai! Banzai!"*[15]

McKinney continued the trigger squeeze. Seven-pounds pressure, eight-pounds . . . Suddenly, the machine gun erupted in a burst of loud, rapid explosions. A rain of metal bullets traveling at 2,800 feet per second ripped into the charging Japanese.

CHAPTER 20

*"All at once that foxhole got
awfully crowded!"*

PFC John McKinney

Umiray Outpost

May 11, 1945
Six and a half minutes into the battle

The Umiray River, like the Ogeechee, flowed dark and slow just before dawn. The forest in the hills, even the sandbar where he knelt waiting for the enemy, reminded him of the peaceful surroundings of his home in Georgia.

That was yesterday. Or was it the day before?

At first, the screaming and shots seemed far away. Then he could distinguish individual rifle "cracks" from all the rattling gunfire and almost count the popping of bullets as they passed above him. Suddenly, the fury of combat closed in like a violent storm.

With the first squeeze of the machine-gun trigger, he knew he had judged the distance correctly. The gun's elevation was perfect. A stream of hot metal ripped into men who were trying to move on the beach. Some fell quietly, others screamed as bullets burned through flesh.

He released the trigger and squeezed again, turning the machine gun slowly to the right.

Even with dim light, he could see them fall. Some had toppled into the river, their bodies disappearing in the darkness.

Release and squeeze, pause a moment and squeeze. The machine gun wasn't singing; it was laughing, happy to finally go to work.

Ten Imperial soldiers were at the center of the beach. Their bodies jerked when he moved the gun toward them and raked their forms with lead.

On the right, twelve more had fallen. He could not see the bodies because once more the river swallowed them. He was sure of the count.

He moved the killing machine to the left toward the ocean. Fourteen were prone on the beach. He squeezed the trigger. Some tried to crawl to the water, but they fell flat, arms stretching out as waves covered their hands and lapped about their heads.

The gun's skin was hot now. Even the ventilated barrel cover was hot.

John McKinney felt a moment of comfort, not for killing—he hated that part of it all—but with the knowledge that the gun belonged to him. It was his protection, his security; like that feeling a boy experiences while walking a dark street with his big brother—security.

So many were dying in the first wave of attack, but that did not stop the Japanese. More raced forward, replacing their fallen comrades. But fewer now, and scattered, some diving into the sand in a vain search for safety.

Some were too close for the machine gun's elevation. He had to stop them quickly or they would run right over him.

Seizing his M1, he fell against the mound of dirt separating him from the enemy. With the rifle at his shoulder, he raised up just high enough to take good aim.

Twenty feet! The men determined to kill him were only twenty feet away.

Something caught his eye in the foxhole. A trench knife next to the other M1, only a few feet away. It apparently had been left behind by Roberts or Homan.

Two charging Japanese paused long enough to lob hand grenades. One sailed over McKinney's head and exploded behind him. The concussion pushed him forward and red-hot slivers of metal burned through his trousers and shirt.

The second grenade exploded directly in front of the pit, the sand absorbing some of the blast, but the concussion caught his body, twisting him around. Again, metal fragments pierced clothing, but none touched skin.

Nearby, PFC Morris Roberts, conscious but unable to move, saw his friend emerging from the smoke, apparently uninjured, rifle at his shoulder.

Fifteen feet! The Japanese were also shocked to see the American still standing. Screaming, they closed in from three sides.

McKinney fired point-blank into the face of the man in the center who had raised his rifle, preparing to lunge with the bayonet.

The Japanese next to him held a sword. He caught the second bullet just under his nose before he brought the blade down.

Ten feet! Less than a second elapsed between shots as McKinney pulled the trigger. He was killing them, but it seemed as if they could not harm him. Then the high-pitched sound: "ping!" The clip ejected. The M1 was empty.

He attempted to reach for the second rifle and trench knife.

Too late! Japanese soldiers were pulling at the machine gun, trying to drag it over the mound and out of the hole.

For the first few moments, they ignored him. They were after the machine gun. *His* machine gun!

McKinney stepped forward, smashing one enemy soldier in the head with the rifle butt. Then he seized the handle of the gun and tried to drag it back into the pit. He succeeded, but a Japanese came with it, dropping his Arisaka rifle and grasping the machine-gun barrel with both hands trying to pull it away from McKinney.

It was an odd scene as the two men, about the same size, pulled the machine gun in opposite directions, like boys playing tug-of-war.

McKinney dropped his empty M1 and grabbed the trench knife. With a short jump forward, he plunged it into his opponent's throat.

At the same moment, he was aware of a fast movement on his left. An Imperial soldier was twirling a *take-yari* bamboo spear, and struck McKinney on the side of the head an inch above the sword wound.

But the spearman had made a critical mistake. Rather than ramming the pointed end into the American's head, he'd used the *blunt* end.

McKinney dropped the knife as the blow sent him tumbling. The knife disappeared in the sand, but luckily, his fall placed him within easy reach of the other M1.

The spearman twirled the weapon once again, but this time the point was heading toward McKinney. He fired from the hip. The man fell, a .30-caliber slug in his chest.[1]

The sword wound was bleeding again, the blood mixing with sweat and running down onto his shoulder and in little thin streams over his chest.

McKinney now turned his rifle on the other Japanese who were scampering into the pit for the machine gun. He fired until the rifle was empty. His attention turned quickly to the machine gun. It pointed skyward, the result of the tug-of-war.

He was out of breath, but he had to push and then pull the gun back into position.

Sighting down the barrel, he could easily see more Japanese charging up the beach toward him. They were in his sights. He squeezed the trigger. Nothing! The machine gun did not fire. He worked the bolt, ejecting a shell. The bolt moved forward, but not far enough to feed the next round into the firing chamber.

Jammed!

Sand and dirt had fouled up the mechanism during the scuffle.

He could hear the screams. They were coming closer. No time to try and fix the machine gun.

But the gun was his! Something in his brain commanded him to protect it, to save the gun, deny its use to the enemy.

He tried to lift it. His strength was drained. Even a thirty-five-pound gun felt ten times that weight. The best he could do was to drag it from the pit.

A hand grenade exploded at the spot where the machine gun had sat a minute ago. The concussion sent him backward, metal fragments whistling harmlessly overhead.

In an instant, a Japanese soldier broke through the smoke and jabbed at McKinney with his bayonet. The blade passed through the trouser leg, ripping material but missing flesh. The rifle was cocked back, bayonet ready for another try.

McKinney swung his fist into the man's nose. At the same time, he forced the rifle up with his other hand and sank his teeth into the enemy's wrist.

Shocked, the Japanese released his grip on the Arisaka and McKinney wrestled it away, turning the weapon and ramming the blade into the chest of its owner.

Then, as McKinney reported later, "All at once that foxhole got awfully crowded!"

His energy seemed to return just in time. Japanese were in the hole with him, some even shoving each other as they fought over the machine gun. Oddly, during the next few moments, none tried to shoot at him.

The fanatical fascination with the machine gun gave McKinney the seconds he needed to pick up an M1. Seizing it by the barrel, he began to swing it wildly, but he could feel the jolt as the butt smashed against heads.

Then, for a battle already filled with unusual happenings, one more "impossible" was to add to the list. His M1 stock snapped and broke just behind the trigger guard!

He stumbled over bodies, using his fists to fight off two more men, then picked up the other M1, again by the barrel, swinging it like a club.

A few more moments, a few more swings, then he realized . . . the stock was hitting nothing. There were no more Japanese alive in his foxhole.

He sank to his knees, struggling to calm his breathing. Then he looked up and began to count. Eight! Eight Imperial soldiers lay dead in the foxhole or sprawled over its banks.

The machine gun again lay on its side like a broken toy.

McKinney crawled up the bank.

Ten minutes into the battle

He raised his head for a better view of his surroundings. Not far from the foxhole, eleven more Japanese lay dead, but he could not make an accurate count. The light was still dim and some of the bodies were on top of one another.

Then he saw them. *Thirty yards away.* Hell was coming once again. They were moving slowly, rifles lowered.

The sun had begun to peek above the ocean, but seemed to have frozen in place.

He was aware of the battle waging behind him at the north perimeter, but that was 150 yards away. A different war, another world.

His world lay before him. Bodies scattered across the sand and at his feet. Some of the bodies were moving, crying, moaning, squirming, and flopping about in pain. The machine gun did that to people. It had no conscience. It would wound with gaping holes, leaving men to suffer and die later. But with his rifle shots, men died instantly. No one suffered. There was no time to rationalize or excuse the killing, except . . . except if the enemy was not stopped, they would kill him and then his friends.

Twenty-five yards away. They moved faster. He counted ten, each armed with rifles.

He grabbed the one good M1 and decided it was time to abandon his machine gun. He needed ammunition!

He dashed back to his tent. There he found two bandoliers full of M1 clips. He quickly inserted one. The bolt flew forward locking in the first round.

Crouching low, he moved between bushes to Morris Roberts's foxhole. There he found two more rifles and several bandoliers of ammunition. He hid it all in a nearby bush.

For the first time, a plan developed in his mind. He had no idea of how he'd survived so far, but realistically he knew his luck could not hold out forever.

He wasn't the only one who briefly questioned his survival. Morris Roberts and Ed Colwell were astonished that their friend had crawled out of that foxhole alive.

McKinney decided it would be foolish to stay and guard a broken machine gun. But he could use it as bait. To do that successfully, instinct and early training told him he had to change positions quickly, be where the enemy did not expect. Shoot and move. That was the plan. That was how the bobcat fooled him long ago. Now, he felt confident. Maybe survive a little longer, kill a few more, and prevent them from crashing into the outpost, attacking his buddies from the rear.

The hidden rifles were safe. If he died, which he expected, it was unlikely the enemy would find them. If he survived, the weapons were there waiting and he could circle back and pick them up to use.

He knew how to move quickly, quietly, from bush to bush, from foxhole to foxhole, but he was not like the elusive bobcat. The Japanese warriors were also expert hunters of men. They would spot him eventually.

McKinney stood up slowly. Then he realized his pants legs were ripped and his shirt was draped over his shoulders in shredded, blood-soaked rags.

He watched as the enemy reached his machine gun. It was almost comical to see men desperately trying to work the mechanism, one shoving the other away so he could demonstrate his engineering expertise. The struggle continued unsuccessfully for a minute; then McKinney calmly aimed and fired. The dead warriors fell without a sound and rolled down on top of their comrades at the bottom of the pit.

He moved to his right several yards. Two more Japanese appeared on the mound. He fired, killing both. But before he moved again, two enemy soldiers came rushing around each side of the pit.

They saw McKinney, aimed and fired . . . and missed!

Frantically, they cranked the bolt actions, loading another round into the chambers.

One fell to his knees, still clutching the rifle. His chest had been torn apart by two .30-caliber slugs from Mac's M1.

The other man fired again. The Arisaka slug passed harmlessly by McKinney's ear with a sharp "pop." Then the man's head snapped as an M1 bullet pierced his left eye.

McKinney followed his plan. He began to walk fast in a zigzag fashion, bending low, moving toward the large bush where Morris Roberts and Eldon Homan were hidden.

* * *

Simultaneously with McKinney's foxhole melee at the south perimeter, the battle at the north developed quickly as the Japanese took advantage of the shock created by their sudden surprise attack.

Near the center of the outpost, fifty yards north of McKinney's war, Lieutenant Max Ladin was still shaken from his narrow escape of almost being decapitated. He and Technical Sergeant Victor J. Wendling liquidated the Japanese assault squad before any of the mortar men were injured.

Wendling quickly organized his men, and the 81mm tubes were ready to fire.

"For effect . . . FIRE!" Lieutenant Ladin shouted. "I'll get on the horn for adjustments."

Ladin had planned to use the field phone to learn enemy positions, calculate adjustments for his men, and relay the results of each explosion. They did not know that the Japanese attack had breached the north perimeter and the phone line had been severed.

Still dark. The outpost command tent was without communication with any point on the perimeter.

"Watch for their flashes!" Lieutenant Ladin yelled. "That's your target!"

In the faint morning light, the mortar section would try and locate the Japanese by their rifle flashes.

But pandemonium engulfed the perimeter one hundred yards north. The first wave of enemy foot soldiers had sliced through the perimeter. An intense firefight was under way; impossible to tell who was who. The heavy mortars could not be fired. The blast might kill some of their own men.

Communication was desperately needed with men on the front line. How far away was the next Japanese wave or reserve line? How much time did they have?

Staff Sergeant Neal A. Cowin of Sandwich, Illinois, a section leader under Ladin, crawled up next to Sergeant Wendling and the lieutenant. He reported that he had planned to send a man forward to search for the break in the field phone wire. But he believed it was much too dangerous to cross that hundred-yard section in the midst of the battle. So Sergeant Cowin volunteered for the job, preferring to attempt the mission himself rather than send one of his men.

Cowin turned his section command over to another sergeant, and began to crawl toward the northern perimeter and the place where he believed the wire to be severed. Every few yards he had to pause, holding his breath as knee-mortar rounds and enemy hand grenades exploded nearby. He turned once, and noticed a few of his men were crawling behind. He didn't request help, but they were coming along anyway.

There seemed to be no Americans in the sector where he was heading, only enemy troops firing in all directions. But they were pinned down by fire from American foxholes.

* * *

The section void of American defenders that Sergeant Cowin was trying to reach had been manned entirely by Filipino guerrillas.

The sudden attack there by the Japanese produced the same results as it did at John McKinney's foxhole. The Filipinos, seized by panic, broke from their position and ran, screaming and shouting, in the direction of the command tent. They left a twenty-five-yard gap undefended. The Japanese, recognizing their early success, charged for the hole in the line. But after penetrating some fifteen yards, they were pinned down by Americans blasting them with M1s and BARs from each flank.

Meanwhile, the Filipinos began to run in circles, only to crash into their buddies, who had rushed north after abandoning their foxholes near McKinney.

That panic was about to bring disaster to the northern section of the outpost, and it was costing the Filipinos dearly. Standing and running made them easy targets, even in the early dawn. In the first few minutes, one soldier fell dead from Japanese rifle shots and two others dropped with serious wounds.

The guerrilla commander, a small but tough captain, accompanied by four experienced NCOs, joined his men, trying to calm them and organize them into a fighting force. Threats, humiliation, prayers, and swearing—nothing seemed to have a positive effect. The mob simply refused to listen to its leaders. Two more men crumpled to the ground with serious wounds.

In this chaos, three things began to develop so rapidly that it is difficult to break them down into separate time frames.

As Sergeant Cowin continued his crawl toward the perimeter's edge and the band of panic-stricken Filipinos, nearby a twenty-five-year-old former paint sprayer from Leaf River, Illinois, realized the dangerous situation they were all in. He was Second Lieutenant Edwin F. Voss.

Ed Voss had risen from the rank of private to platoon sergeant, and had been recently commissioned a second lieutenant on another battlefield. He loved his men, who remembered him as "forceful and fearless." One of his soldiers stated, "He was the kind of natural leader who didn't look for a fight, but if one came, Voss was like a demon turned loose."[2]

Lieutenant Voss disregarded enemy fire and rushed into the group of guerrillas. Then he began to walk calmly among them, issuing stern commands but touching each Filipino on the arm, assuring them that he, an American, was willing to die for the Philippines. He would lead a counterattack if the Filipinos would follow.

Ed Voss had as much to lose as any of them, he said. As the captain quickly translated English into Tagalog, explaining that the lieutenant was ready to die if necessary, but that he "planned to kill the Japanese, then return home to the States and his wife and young daughter," Voss pointed his carbine at the gap in the perimeter and started toward the enemy.

Lieutenant Voss was the kind of leader the guerrillas needed. They began to move with him, some at his side, others close behind.

The Japanese, seeing Lieutenant Voss and the Filipinos advancing, directed their fire toward them.

One guerrilla next to Voss fell as an Arisaka bullet passed through his head. But they didn't stop. Their small unit turned slightly to the left, not knowing the exact positions of the Japanese.

* * *

Staff Sergeant Neal Cowin had moved to within thirty feet of the enemy and luckily found the break in the main communication line. He started to repair it, then looked up at a frightening scene. A lone Japanese soldier was crawling directly toward him, but had not spotted Cowin in the early morning shadows.

Then, to Cowin's surprise, shouts came from the Filipino guerrillas and Lieutenant Voss on his right. If they continued in that direction, they would soon be firing on Americans in Cowin's sector. But if Sergeant Cowin shouted a warning, the Japanese to his front would quickly kill him.

The enemy soldier was now only five feet away. The sergeant stated later that he could "almost reach out and touch him."

Sergeant Cowin leaped to his feet, and blasted the Japanese with his .45 automatic pistol, then began to wave at Lieutenant Voss pointing to the enemy.

Immediately, the Japanese at his front shifted their fire, directing it at him. Sergeant Cowin had saved the lives of the men in his sector.

Lieutenant Voss, now directed toward the enemy, led his guerrillas in a fierce counterattack, annihilating the entire Japanese group who had breached the perimeter in that section a few minutes earlier. Finally, the Filipinos were back in control of their area, and began to fire at the second wave of Japanese charging their lines. Inspired by Voss, this time they did not break and run.

Fifteen minutes into the battle

Twenty-four-year-old Leroy Nix was tall, handsome, and with dark, wavy hair looked like a 1930s Hollywood movie star. But during the outpost battle, Sergeant Nix led a 60mm mortar squad dug in some thirty yards behind the north perimeter.

Within two minutes of the initial Japanese attack, his squad began to fire prearranged mortar concentrations to the north. The shells landed in the ranks of the enemy's second wave as they prepared to charge across the open area.

Enemy knee mortars registered in on Sergeant Nix's position, but the exploding rounds caused no injuries to his men.

With enough daylight, the sergeant calculated counter-mortar fire, which silenced the knee mortars killing their crews.

Just as Nix's squad completed that mortar bombardment, a group of enemy soldiers, having broken through another breach in the northern perimeter, charged into his squad. A violent hand-to-hand battle followed. A few Filipino guerrillas joined in. They killed all the Japanese in the mortar sector without losing a man.

Sergeant Nix noticed his shirt was soaked with blood. He had been wounded by rifle fire. Still, he organized the men for a counterattack. As he led his squad, they charged toward the break in the perimeter, killing five more Japanese. The guerrillas with them now manned empty foxholes at the perimeter, and the Americans returned to the mortars. With systematic and continued mortar fire, they cut off any chance of an enemy escape to the north.

Later, while receiving medical aid, the lanky Sergeant Nix remarked, "I just wanna get home to my wife in Oklahoma!"

Twelve minutes into the battle

PFC John McKinney had circled back to the bush where Morris Roberts still cradled the body of Eldon Homan in his arms.

McKinney feared that in the new dawn light the Japanese might spot his buddy's hiding place.

Fear confirmed. Four enemy soldiers were moving cautiously toward Roberts. Apparently, they wanted to be sure the Americans were dead.

John McKinney jumped from behind a bush and stood directly between his friend and the advancing enemy. At thirty feet the Japanese fired at McKinney, and missed. They were answered by M1 shots. Three Japanese fell instantly. Then the familiar *ping*; the M1 was empty. He seized a fresh clip from the cotton bandolier slung over his shoulder. The bolt flew forward; the weapon was ready to fire. He raised it to his shoulder to take aim, but as he did he saw the white puff of smoke from the Arisaka. The Japanese had aimed carefully as he reloaded, but the shot missed.

Mac fired. The enemy's service cap with neck flaps flew into the air as the top of his skull exploded from the impact of the M1 slug.

McKinney knew he could not remain and guard Morris Roberts. He would only draw more attention to the position.

He pulled a large round bush from the sand and placed it in front of Roberts, hoping it would conceal him for a while.

Then he circled back to his original foxhole. Ed Colwell saw him and called out, "Mac! I'm bleeding bad! How we doing?"

John McKinney did not answer. His own private war was still under way in a twenty-square-yard area. His entire focus remained on that battle and . . . surviving.

He thought from time to time. How many had died? More than sixty. And not one shot had struck him. Why? How could the enemy continue to miss, especially at close range? He had no time to analyze all that. The thoughts of how many he killed crossed his mind, but he was alive. Maybe he could not be killed. Was that possible?[3]

Exhausted and confused, McKinney sat down on a mound of sand. A few moments passed and no Japanese charged over the ridge. Were they still on the beach?

His arms began to shake and his legs seemed to no longer be part of him. His entire body was trembling now. Then he started to laugh, but that quickly faded to sobs. He fought to control it.

Ed Colwell was watching McKinney, and at first thought his friend had been wounded. But then he heard John McKinney cry out in a shaky voice, "God! Make 'em stop! Tell 'em, God! They're all gonna die!"

He was quiet a moment, and the trembling disappeared. "Please, God! Tell 'em to stop!"

But the Japanese were not going to stop, at least not yet. The warrior voice in their minds had smothered any logic or reason with one order—attack!

Ed Colwell heard the screaming. They were coming up the beach again. In a minute, the Japanese would reach the machine gun.

Colwell forgot his pain. Now it was only the immediate terrifying situation. Would John McKinney still fight? Could he hold his rifle and stop them one more time? Or was death about to take them both?[4]

CHAPTER 21

"I am a witness to the fact that God
did help me out of that hard battle
for the bushes were shot up all around
me and I never got a scratch."

Sergeant Alvin C. York

Awarded Congressional Medal of Honor, World War I

May 11, 1945
Twenty-two minutes into the battle

The sun suddenly leapt from the ocean and hung in a clear blue sky just above the horizon.

PFC Red Barrette understood the importance of remaining at his foxhole until relieved. If he pulled out, the enemy might take advantage of the gap in the perimeter and rush through it.

Red's position faced the Umiray River. Everyone guessed that an attack there would be highly unlikely. Nonetheless, he obeyed orders, and watched for Japanese who might *swim* across the river.

His situation became increasingly frustrating. A violent battle continued for over twenty minutes 150 yards behind him at the north perimeter. Another fight had been under way in John McKinney's area. Red wanted desperately to be involved, but had to wait.

After twenty minutes, the storm at the north subsided; no more mortar explosions and only an occasional *crack* from an M1.

In McKinney's area, sounds of the battle seemed to be subsiding also.

Was it over?

The desire to investigate became overwhelming. Maybe someone needed help. Rifle in hand, Red crawled out of his hole and headed toward McKinney.

He paused to check Ed Colwell's foxhole. Empty! Where was Colwell?

Red picked up speed, trotting toward the machine-gun emplacement. He stopped a few yards from it. A nauseating feeling swept over him. There were bodies of dead Japanese stacked about the pit. A lone GI stood with them "looking like a dead man who had just crawled out of a grave. Then I realized it was McKinney, standing in that slaughter field," Red Barrette reported later.[1]

"Mac! What the hell happened here? You . . . okay?"

"Yep," answered John McKinney, who pointed toward their wounded friend lying in the tall grass.

"Colwell's hurt bad. Can you get a tourniquet on him?"

The two men met at Colwell's side. He was conscious.

"How we doing?" Colwell asked McKinney.

"We're still alive." McKinney grinned.

"I got a first-aid satchel in my tent," Red stated. "Cover me, Mac. I'll get it."

Red jogged toward his tent as Mac ran parallel to him.

Suddenly, McKinney stopped and backed up to a clump of bushes, his rifle pointing at the sandy ridge that separated them from the beach. Twelve Imperial soldiers had reached the ridge. They immediately shot at Red, but at first did not notice McKinney.

Mac held his fire, fearful of hitting Red, who had changed his pace. He was now using sharp, darting movements, making himself a more difficult target.

In a moment, McKinney was confident that he had clear targets. He pulled the trigger. The first Japanese toppled over. Then another and another.

Red had the aid satchel over his shoulder and started for Colwell.

McKinney now started directly toward the enemy, rifle at his shoulder, firing, reloading, crouching, firing, reloading, firing as he moved closer, step by step, like a geared machine.

Then, for the first time in the battle, a round became stuck in the chamber.

His rifle jammed.

Immediate action! Every rifleman had been drilled in the action necessary to correct a jammed rifle.

He pulled the bolt back, then let it fly forward. No results. The bolt would not slide all the way. He repeated the procedure. Still, the cartridge refused to eject.

Mac glanced at the ridge. The Japanese were gone—either dead or hiding.

Red had reached Colwell and was working on his wounded arm.

McKinney rushed a few yards to the bush where he had hidden two M1s a few minutes before. He grabbed one and a bandolier of ammunition. A quick check. The rifle had a round in the chamber ready to fire.

He glanced over at Red; still busy with Colwell's arm.

The sun struggled to pull farther away from the ocean, and with its warmth, it chased away the evening breeze. Now smoke and dust hung close to the earth, trapped in the humid morning air. But there was very little smoke on the beach—nothing to hide the scattered bodies lying in grotesque forms on the sand.

With the light, he could see the dead bobbing in the river and a few more bouncing against the shore, moved by waves crashing in from Dingalan Bay.

McKinney started to the rear of his machine-gun pit. The gun still lay on its side, tilted upward, surrounded by dead enemy.

Once again, Japanese soldiers were coming up the beach, moving slow this time, perhaps testing the American defense line.

They had no way of knowing the defense was only one exhausted soldier with an M1 rifle. They stepped over and around dead comrades and pressed cautiously forward. Perhaps they expected the machine gun to open up.

Twenty yards away. Imperial soldiers armed with Arisakas. He counted ten of them.

Eighteen yards. Still moving slow. Then he saw the reason. One man, about thirty yards behind the ten warriors, was squatting down, placing something in a short tube.

Knee mortar! The Japanese were waiting for a barrage of mortar rounds to blast a clear path. Then they'd attack.

McKinney fell back into the pit just as the first round exploded a few yards from the edge.

Before the smoke drifted, he scampered up the mound of earth. In a kneeling position, he took aim, then fired one shot. The mortar man fell on his side, a bullet in his head. But he had launched one more projectile before McKinney's bullet struck him.

The explosion directly in front of McKinney went up and out in a typical cone-shaped pattern. Because he was so close to the blast, the metal fragments missed, but the concussion knocked him backward and scorched a few more holes in the fragments of cloth still clinging to his skin.

His rifle flew from his hands landing nearby. He grabbed it and, using the weapon as a crutch, pushed himself erect.

Thirty minutes into the battle

McKinney did not hear the screams of the charging Japanese warriors. The mortar blast caused a temporary loss of hearing.

The enemy moved faster now, toward the smoke cloud. It would have been logical for them to assume that the man caught by the explosion was dead, blown to pieces. But to be sure, one Japanese tossed a hand grenade into the smoke. Orange flames ripped through the air.

In seconds, the smoke broke apart into a fog of black-gray streamers.

There were only four Japanese now, two not far behind the lead two. They halted less than eight yards away.

PFC John McKinney stood, waiting for them. The left side of his head was a bloody mess. Skin visible below his ripped and shredded clothing was covered with splattered blood, sand, and gray-black smudges of burnt gun powder.

"He did not seem to be breathing and his eyes were red and glaring. Smoke was all around his legs," PFC Barrette reported later.[2]

McKinney slowly raised his M1. His strength had returned again. His right cheek pressed against the rifle stock and he leaned slightly forward, index finger touching the trigger.

The first two Japanese soldiers, sweating and panting for breath, seemed frozen, shocked at the sight of the thing standing before them.

The enemy warriors were so close, McKinney remembered their sweat-drenched faces—young, maybe under twenty, and each face was etched with a look of fear.

Events unfolded in seconds, but flowed like a movie in slow motion.

The Japanese on the left fired, followed quickly by the soldier on the right. Both missed!

McKinney's first shot smacked into the forehead of the man on the left just below his cap brim. Then, quickly, he pointed the M1 at the next man, but paused. He never remembered why.

That soldier fired again, and missed again. His hands trembled as he tried to work the rifle bolt to load another round. He must have been puzzled why he missed a target at such close range. He paused, looking at McKinney as if staring into the face of death.

"*Mabaroshi?*" the Japanese muttered.

McKinney could not hear him.

Then the Japanese screamed loudly, "*MABAROSHI!*" (PHANTOM!)

McKinney heard part of the word, but had no idea of the meaning. He fired, and the young warrior dropped to his knees, then pitched forward.

Two more enemy soldiers now stood behind the bodies of their dead comrades. They held their rifles at waist level, staring at McKinney.

"*Mabaroshi?*" one repeated, as if questioning the possibility.

Red Barrette and Ed Colwell, only a few yards away, heard the shouts, but thought it may have been "men swearing before death." Red said later in an interview, "The scream was one of real terror!"[3]

The Japanese fired from the hip and missed.

In the same instant, McKinney pulled the trigger. The body of the enemy jerked backward, killed instantly.

Shock for the other soldier vanished quickly. He apparently had no fear of phantoms or enemy soldiers. He had planned to die, ready to meet the thing before him. Quickly, he raised the rifle above his head, bayonet pointing at McKinney.

"*Mabaroshi!*" he yelled, lunging forward to impale the American on his blade.

He fell on his face, blood gushing from his neck. McKinney's shot had ripped an artery in the man's throat.

Mac lowered his rifle, his eyes scanning the beach. Where were the other enemy soldiers?

Then he saw them, twenty yards to the right, attempting a flank attack. But in the same moment he noticed two more Imperial soldiers charging toward him. One carried a Nambu machine gun.

At thirty yards distance, the man with the automatic weapon pitched to the sand. The Nambu began to spit lead with its steady, sharp *tap, tap, tap*, the bullets kicking up dirt at McKinney's feet.

He could not hear the gun, but saw the muzzle flashes. He raised his M1 and fired. No more flashes!

The next man rushed to the machine gun, but before he could fire it, McKinney's rifle spoke. The body fell on top of the first gunner.

Now McKinney turned to the right. Six Japanese were shooting at Red Barrette, who was firing back. In less than fifteen seconds all of the enemy soldiers were dead.

"Nice shootin'!" McKinney yelled to his friend.

Red lifted his rifle high and waved it.

An eerie stillness fell on John McKinney's battlefield. Smoke hung in little patches, but there were no more rifle shots or explosions.

He staggered to his machine-gun pit and collapsed on his back at the mound.

The machine gun was still there. It belonged to the Americans. All those who tried to take it had died.

His body began to shake again, but no tears this time. He rolled over onto his side to see how Ed Colwell was doing. Red was at Ed's side releasing the tourniquet and cleaning the wound.

McKinney began to think of the sequence of enemy attacks. Why did the Japanese bring the Nambu up now? Perhaps it and the knee mortar were to support the enemy charges, only no one seemed to be in command. The last few Japanese had resorted to a reckless, unorganized effort to overrun the south perimeter.

The shaking suddenly stopped, replaced by a feeling of fatigue. He had survived so far. He could not believe it, and struggled to grasp the fact that he was alive.

Thirty-six minutes into the battle (approximately 6:07 A.M.)

Shouts and screaming on the beach!

Were they coming again? McKinney flipped over, rifle pointing in the direction of the noise.

A lone Japanese soldier was being chased by a Filipino guerrilla waving a samurai sword he'd found on the battlefield.

The sword came down on the enemy's arm near the shoulder. Blood spattered and the victim began to stagger.

The guerrilla chopped at the other arm.

One rifle shot from McKinney and the soldier fell. Mac had put the man out of his misery.

McKinney lay on the mound facing the beach, his rifle, as always, ready. There might be more Japanese out there on the sandbar somewhere.

He heard voices. His sense of hearing was returning. People were talking, *in English,* and behind him this time.

Sergeant Alfred W. Johnson and a squad of riflemen had broken from the northern perimeter where the battle had ended several minutes earlier. They rushed to the south perimeter to reinforce the defenders there.

Not far behind them, other men searched the outpost for American casualties.

The Japanese attack force at the north, in spite of their early success of penetrating the perimeter and causing the guerrillas to panic, had been annihilated. Mortar fire cut off their escape (not that many planned to retreat anyway) and killed a number of men waiting in reserve.

The medical aid men with Sergeant Johnson were already working on Ed Colwell's arm.

Johnson looked at PFC Red Barrette and down at Colwell. Then his eyes scanned the macabre scene around him. The bodies of dead Japanese littered the ground near the machine-gun emplacement. Some were on top of one another, practically hidden by smoke and fog, which still hung low as if it contained the spirits of those who had died.

"Who killed all those Japs?" Johnson finally inquired.

"Mac!" answered Red Barrette.

"McKinney?"

"McKinney . . . by himself."

"I seen him!" Ed Colwell managed to say. "He stopped 'em!"

"Where is McKinney? Dead?" Johnson questioned.

"He sure looks dead, but he ain't," said Barrette.

Then he pointed to the pit. "There!"

Sergeant Johnson, followed by four men, walked toward the pit, carefully stepping over bodies. They stopped a few feet away from the edge.

McKinney was in a prone position, facing the beach. The machine gun lay at his feet.

"We found McKinney in firing position, bleeding profusely from a head wound," Johnson reported later.[4]

"McKinney!" Johnson called out. "You okay?"

John McKinney recognized the voice. "Okay, Sergeant!" came the reply.

Sergeant Johnson walked around the pit. McKinney tilted his head slowly to look up at him.

"We'll get you some help, Mac," Johnson said in a comforting voice, somewhat out of character. "You're gonna be out of here and get some good treatment up at headquarters."

He surveyed the battle scene on the beach. Two of his men had found Morris Roberts and Eldon Homan and were attending to them.

Sergeant Johnson knelt down to be close to McKinney.

"How many?" the sergeant asked. "How many you think you killed?"

PFC McKinney did not answer. He had been crying, and used a moment to wipe at his cheeks with a bloody hand. Then he said, "About a hundred, Sergeant. I lost count 'cause, at first, some fell in the river and the ocean. It weren't light yet, so I lost count 'cause I couldn't see all them boys clear."

"About a hundred?" the sergeant repeated.

"Maybe twenty or thirty more," McKinney quickly added. "Red got six! All by himself. I seen him. Real brave, that Red is. Stood up and blasted 'em!"

John McKinney's effort to share credit with his friend did not register with Sergeant Johnson at the time.[5]

"A hundred, plus maybe twenty or thirty," Johnson repeated, shaking his head. "I've got to report this right away. May be some kind of record for one battle. Captain Ice will have the details by the time you get your wound patched up. Who knows, McKinney. You may have earned a medal—"

"Excuse me, Sergeant." McKinney sniffled. "You better get down. There may be more a-comin'."

Sergeant Johnson's laugh was short but healthy.

"There ain't no more Japs coming today, Mac. You've done killed them all!"

* * *

Shortly before the battle at the Umiray River outpost ended, Lieutenant Max Ladin's radioman finally got a message to headquarters. *"We're under attack!"*

Up to that time, the struggle had been so ferocious, no one even thought of the radio.

A few minutes before 6:00 A.M., the Task Force motor launch, towing two native boats, departed the sawmill heading south. On board were BAR men, several riflemen, and six guerrillas along with extra ammunition and first-aid gear. They would not arrive at the outpost until 7:30 A.M. By that time, the business of cleaning up after a battle was well under way.

The body of each Japanese soldier had to be searched for explosives and weapons. Other than a few hand grenades, nothing was found.

No maps were found. Documents consisted of personal letters and photographs. Nothing useful for Corps Intelligence.

Where to bury the Japanese presented a problem. The deepest one could dig was three feet. At that level, water seeped in and filled the hole.

Wide pits were dug at the tree line 150 yards north of the perimeter, about the same distance inland from the bay.

Bodies had to be dragged by hand that distance, placed in the three-and-half-foot-deep pit, and covered with earth and sand. More dirt, again carried by hand, was piled on top, forming large mounds. A total of 248 were buried. Most in the river and bay were not recovered.

Men had gathered about John McKinney's machine-gun emplacement to study the results of his "one-man stand" while Lieutenant Max Ladin pulled out his small Brownie camera and began taking pictures. It would be a long time before the film was developed. Many of the photos were blurred, the result of the camera and film being subjected to high humidity, dust, and heat.

He did not photograph John McKinney, who was receiving first-aid treatment for his sword wound, but he did take pictures of some of the Japanese dead and Sergeant Victor J. Wendling, who'd saved his life. Actually, Lieutenant Ladin took no pictures of the men who had defended the perimeter. He was angry with them for permitting the Japanese to slip through the line, regardless of the circumstances.[6]

Sergeant Al Johnson reviewed his report on McKinney's battle with Second Lieutenant Ed Voss and Sergeant Leroy Nix. His official report sent by radio to the Task Force Headquarters read as follows:

There were—by actual count—38 freshly slaughtered Japs stacked in piles of twos and threes around the emplacement within a 15-yard radius. Another few yards away were two more slumped over a machine gun and then 40 yards out, two more next to a knee mortar. Final tabulation of enemy casualties—95 killed on the sandbar beach plus 42 around the machine gun emplacement. Those Nips all belonged to Mac.[7]

Sergeant Johnson was presented a typed copy of his report, which he signed, upon his arrival at Task Force Headquarters. Testimonies were taken from PFC Ed Colwell, PFC Red Barrette, and PFC Morris Roberts in addition to Sergeant Johnson.

Roberts added this statement, "The place seemed to swarm with Japs. His [McKinney's] actions were split-second in duration, shooting some, bashing others with his rifle butt, kicking and trying to pull the machine gun back."[8]

American casualties from the battle were three dead (PFC Homan and two guerrillas) and seven wounded (four Americans, including John McKinney, and three guerrillas).[9]

John McKinney stayed close to his friend Ed Colwell while they waited for their boat ride to the sawmill. They were the first evacuated.

When they arrived at the sawmill, the medical team went to work sewing McKinney's ear back in place. They performed their work well; the scar was barely visible by the end of 1945.

McKinney was cleaned and given a new set of combat fatigues. On May 12, while he lay on a cot recuperating, Captain Harry Ice and Major Connolly came to visit. As usual, McKinney had little to say. He simply answered their questions without elaborating. Then Captain Ice informed the Georgia farm boy that he had been recommended for the Congressional Medal of Honor.

Both John McKinney and PFC Red Barrette were promoted one grade to the rank of buck sergeant.

* * *

Twenty-one-year-old Ensign Robert Colwell was at sea aboard U.S. Navy ship PCE 882, part of a fleet on weather patrol between Guam and the Philippines. His "floating weather station" had been ordered to track a large typhoon heading north toward the Philippines.

He was on duty as navigator when the communications officer handed him a radiogram. It read:

> Your brother, PFC Edward Colwell, has been wounded in combat on Luzon, Philippine Islands.

It would be near the end of the war before Ensign Colwell learned more details about his brother's condition.[10]

At the sawmill, Ed Colwell and John McKinney exchanged home addresses, promising to contact each other after the war. With a good-bye wish of "good luck," medics loaded Colwell aboard a truck bound for a field hospital.

For Ed Colwell, the war was over. John McKinney would never see his friend again.

* * *

Radio and written messages bounced between the Connolly Task Force and I Corps headquarters concerning the Umiray outpost battle and, indeed, the entire situation at Dingalan Bay.

Major Connolly had insisted for several days that one rifle company was not enough to contain the Japanese trying to escape north. The outpost battle only proved how vulnerable A Company was, in spite of guerrilla support.

But reinforcements were slow coming, and now with dead, wounded, and exhausted men, Connolly insisted on immediate help.

The Connolly Task Force had, in fact, accomplished its mission. The steady flow of Japanese troops northward had been disrupted, twenty-two prisoners had been taken, and since A Company had arrived at the sawmill, 368 Japanese had been killed.

By late afternoon on May 11, only nine hours after the outpost battle ended, reinforcements began to arrive at the sawmill. They brought with them new orders and instructions from I Corps. The Connolly

Task Force was to be disbanded as soon as all elements of the First Battalion, 136th Infantry were in position.

The new unit taking over the Dingalan Bay mission was known as the Ehrlich Task Force, named for the First Battalion commander, Lieutenant Colonel Milton Ehrlich.

With American successes around Manila and Baguio, higher headquarters believed they could now provide more men and equipment to Dingalan to finish the job Connolly and A Company of the 123rd Infantry had started.

Over the next six days, patrols continued as men of the 136th were introduced to trails and streams frequently traveled by A Company squads.

By May 14, it was obvious to everyone at the sawmill that the American Army intended to finish off the Japanese in the area. Tons of bazookas, rockets, machine guns, and mortars arrived by truck accompanied by several amphibious combat vehicles, all things Connolly had repeatedly requested but had been unable to obtain.

The entire B Company of the First Battalion under Lieutenant William S. "Bud" Harris was assigned the sandbar outpost at the Umiray River. It would now be defended by two and a half times the number of men who repelled the Japanese on May 11. In addition, Lieutenant Harris had twice the firepower in heavy weapons—more 81 and 60mm mortars, light and heavy (water-cooled) machine guns, and bazookas (rocket launchers).

Sawmill headquarters continued to furnish squads of riflemen for patrols in the river area, only now they were guaranteed safe, more rapid delivery in an LCM, a landing craft with metal armor sides, propelled by twin "screw" propellers.

Even more exciting for Lieutenant Harris was the arrival of four LVTs (landing vehicles, tracked) nicknamed "Alligators" by GIs. These strange-looking vehicles moved slowly through the water because propulsion came from their two tanklike tracks. But it was those tracks that permitted the vehicle to crawl up onto a beach and proceed inland with its awesome firepower while carrying a squad or more of riflemen.

Lieutenant Colonel Ehrlich employed his other companies in and around the sawmill headquarters for security.

On May 14, as Lieutenant Harris and B Company settled into the outpost, the Japanese apparently mustered enough men to launch a new attack.

This time they met stiff, deadly resistance at a heavily armed perimeter, and were cut down as soon as they appeared in the open.

The lifesaving stocks of rations inside the perimeter remained irresistible to starving Imperial soldiers. Over the next few days, again and again, they charged the outpost, only to be slaughtered before advancing a few yards.

Lieutenant Harris worried that the enemy might only be testing the defense lines, but two captured Japanese soldiers confessed that hunger had been the only motivation. It was more honorable to die trying to obtain food than to starve to death.

In seven days, 108 Japanese died, a few at a time, attempting to penetrate the outpost perimeter.[11]

Then the attacks became less frequent.

Lieutenant Harris now had time to develop a new strategy. First, he planned to leave limited supplies of food outside the perimeter with propaganda leaflets written in Japanese suggesting the enemy surrender. Food, medical attention, and good treatment were promised to any man who left his weapon on the beach and approached the perimeter with the surrender document.

Next, by employing the LVT Alligators, he planned to take the war to the Japanese rather than wait for them at the outpost.

May 16, 1945, Sawmill Headquarters, Dingalan Bay

All John McKinney's friends knew the Georgian had a healthy appetite and, as his sister Betty once said, "would eat anything you put before him on the table."

McKinney had spent most of his time during the past five days answering questions for military news reporters and representatives from the Thirty-third Division and I Corps Headquarters, and assisting Captain Ice's men with details of the battle.

Then, between interviews, he would be off to the chow hall to see what his old friends the mess sergeant and staff had set aside for him. To all the men in Company A, John McKinney was a hero, even if the U.S. Army had not yet officially declared it so.

At first, McKinney thought nothing of the fact that Sergeant Gerry Nutt and six other men were with him wherever he went. He guessed they were just being friendly. And since Mac always carried his M1 rifle, it did not appear strange that Nutt and his men were also armed.

It was 10:00 A.M. McKinney felt hungry. As Sergeant Nutt and company approached the chow hall, Sergeant Gerry Rampy saw them and called out.

"Hey, Mac! What happened down there after I left? We knew the Japs were going to hit soon!"

McKinney did not answer, but waved his friend over. Rampy noticed the bandaged ear.

"You hurt bad?" he asked.

"Nope," McKinney replied. "Just a little ole cut on the ear. That's as close as that Jap ever got. He couldn't touch me after that."

"Damn!" Sergeant Rampy exclaimed. "I've been out on patrol since I saw you last. Showing the new fellows some of our tricks. I heard what you done. They say Ice has put you in for a medal. Assigned you these bodyguards for protection."

Sergeant Rampy laughed, but McKinney stared at him with a puzzled look. Then he glanced at Sergeant Nutt and the men gathered around him. Rampy had to be joking.

"Bodyguards?" McKinney asked. "What for?"

"Why, didn't you know, you're the Thirty-third Division's pride and joy. They don't want nothing to happen to you!"

McKinney smiled. "Kind of silly, ain't it," he remarked.[12]

A few more paces and Sergeant Jesse Frazee of Peoria, Illinois, came up.

"Can I shake your hand, Mac?" he asked.

"Sure," McKinney answered as their hands met.

"What the hell happened down there?"

"I ain't talking," came the usual answer. "I'm kinda hungry right now."[13]

Sergeant Gerry Nutt had had no more disasters with his glasses since that one night so many weeks ago when the mortar tube put him out of commission for a while.

They sat down at a table, and Sergeant Nutt began to clean those glasses as they talked. "Good thing about guarding McKinney, he was a very likable fellow and he sure loved to eat," said Gerry Nutt in an interview later. "And when he ate, which seemed all the time—we ate! We sat there that day in the kitchen tent never dreaming a Jap sniper might try to kill McKinney."[14]

Suddenly, the sound of three shots rang out.

Nutt and his men dove to the floor, weapons pointing in different directions.

"Where's Mac?" Sergeant Nutt yelled.

Men glanced around. No McKinney in the tent.

"Don't know, Sarge," one man answered. "He was here just a moment ago!"

"Damn!" exclaimed another soldier. "If anything happens to Mac, we're dead!"

Then *crack, crack, crack*. Three more shots.

"Follow me!" Sergeant Nutt shouted as he started out the door holding his tommy gun in front, ready for action. "Fan out!"

Two men with M1s moved to the left. Two more, also carrying M1s, drifted to the right as they ran in the direction of the shots. Two with carbines followed a little behind their sergeant.

They jogged until reaching the crest of a small wooded hill about twenty-five yards from the mess hall.

Two more shots. The sounds were closer this time.

Nutt's squad slowed, ready for the enemy.

And then they saw a rifleman leaning against a tree, calmly injecting a fresh clip of ammunition into an M1. It was John McKinney!

"Mac! What you doing? You scared the hell out of us! We thought the Japs got ya!" a relieved Sergeant Nutt said all in one breath.

"You boys were a-busy talking, so I came out here to do a little target shooting. Didn't mean to scare you all," McKinney answered.

Then he added, fearing he might be in trouble, "The captain said it was okay to go shooting every day if nobody gives me nothing to do."

Sergeant Nutt glanced at the bullet-pierced cans Mac had been using as targets. "I've always said, you're a hell of a shot!"

John McKinney looked at his bodyguards and smiled.

"Hell," he said, "everybody should know how to shoot this good ole rifle by now. It's *practice* what counts!"[15]

CHAPTER 22

"Watashi tachi tasukatta!"
(We are saved!)
The Umiray Outpost

May 1945

"What the hell's going on down there?! You under attack? Repeat. Are you under attack?"

It was a clear, windless morning at the outpost. The sounds of huge explosions carried across the bay and echoed off the surrounding mountains.

The Ehrlich Task Force Headquarters at the sawmill reacted quickly to the noise. To them, the sounds could be coming from artillery. Were the Japanese attacking the outpost with mountain cannons?

Lieutenant Donald Murphy was standing near the command post at the camp's center when the frantic radio call came in. The operator stared at him and asked with a smile, "What do I tell them, sir?"

"Tell the truth," Murphy answered. "Tell them, 'Negative! We are not under attack. The men are fishing with dynamite. That is all!'"

Headquarters did not reply.

Company B had enjoyed a few days of peace; no Japanese attacks for more than forty-eight hours.

Some of the men, tiring of canned food rations, began to talk about fresh fish. Here they were on a bay that must have plenty of fish. But no one had anything that remotely resembled fishing equipment.

The troops persuaded Lieutenant Murphy to talk with their company commander, Lieutenant William S. Harris, about their theory. Harris agreed. The men were given permission to test their idea.

A few soldiers waded into the water armed with sticks of dynamite tied together. The concussion from the blast immediately killed a quantity of fish, and in a minute they began to wash ashore.

Don Murphy had been close to William "Bud" Harris through most of the war. Lieutenant Murphy described his friend as a "handsome, likable fellow with a great personality . . . an eager beaver who seemed to thrive on combat. He would rather go out on patrol, itching for a fight, than be stuck at the outpost. Overall, Bud Harris was a good officer."[1]

Lieutenant Harris was creative with his "little army" at the outpost, especially when it came to modifying the LVT Alligators for special missions. Company B was known around the battalion as the "Butchers of the Bay" for their highly successful program of taking the war to the Japanese. Mostly, it was the Alligators delivering them.[2]

Harris first had sandbags stacked along the sides of the LVTs to add more protection from snipers. Then, for armament, he added two bazookas (rocket launchers) and four light machine guns to each amphibious vehicle. This, plus the firepower of twelve to fourteen men per Alligator armed with their M1 rifles, BARs, and tommy guns, resulted in a serious little invasion force.

Usually two Alligators traveled together up the Umiray River and south along the coast. If Japanese were spotted, they were first blasted with rockets and machine-gun fire as the Alligator crawled onto the beach. The riflemen, covered by the machine gunners, chased down and killed whatever was left of the enemy.

On May 19, 1945, a little more than a week after John McKinney's "one-man battle," two fully armed Alligators left the outpost sandbar on a special patrol. The results were to give the survivors something to remember for many years.

Lieutenant Bud Harris, as usual, led the raiding party from the first Alligator.

They headed south along the coast to a section of land where the Filipino guerrillas reported seeing a sizable Japanese group.

The trip down was uneventful, but the anxiety of encountering the enemy naturally had all thirty-six men a little jittery.

In an hour they reached the spot marked on the map by the guerrillas. The Alligators lumbered onto the sloping sand beach and rolled to a stop. The men went over the sides and deployed into a wide skirmish line as they sprinted to the cover of nearby palm trees. The machine gunners covered them from the Alligators, ready to fire once the enemy was located. But at first, no one was in sight. The Japanese had concealed themselves well.

Suddenly, a squad of five Japanese emerged from the brush, trotting in an odd fashion toward the Butchers of the Bay.

Then they slowed, raising their hands, indicating a desire to surrender, but their arms were waving back and forth, not in the usual "reach for the sky" position.

Each man in the patrol remained alert, safeties released, ready for a trick. Most had either witnessed or heard of Japanese pretending to surrender, only to set off a hand grenade as an American came close, killing himself and at least one GI.

"Careful!" Lieutenant Harris warned. "Watch the flanks!"

Bud Harris, his carbine pointing toward the enemy, and four men with M1 rifles advanced cautiously, spreading apart a few paces. Harris motioned to the Japanese to come closer. He could then see that one of the enemy was wearing an officer's shirt with the insignia of a colonel.

Lieutenant Harris's first thought, although a brief one, was of how proud he would be to return to headquarters with a captured colonel. That would truly be a valuable accomplishment.

But then the Butchers noticed something very unusual about the colonel and the rest of his squad. All the soldiers had long dark hair that reached their waists! And the colonel's shirttails were hanging out, loosely covering a tattered . . . skirt!

In fact, all five were wearing skirts.

These were obviously not Japanese warriors led by a real colonel.

The Butchers of the Bay now had the distinction of being the first unit in the Thirty-third Golden Cross Infantry Division to capture five young Japanese women.

As the Americans stared at their conquest, almost in shock, the girls all fell to their knees in the sand and pitched forward, heads bowed, arms outstretched.

"*Watashi tachi tasukatta!*" they repeated two or three times.

"*Arigato gozaimasu!*"

"What are they saying?" Bud Harris asked the rifleman on his right who understood a little of the Japanese language.

"They are telling us, 'We are saved. Thank you very much.' They look starved!" the soldier added.

The incredible five-month odyssey of Colonel Muto Masayuki's geishas was over. They had, indeed, been saved.[3]

And then, another surprise. One of the girls spoke limited English and began to relate a little of their story—how they had been marched by the colonel and his men from Manila to Dingalan Bay, how their friends had died at the hands of the colonel, and how they had been deserted over a week before, left with only a few scraps of food.

The girl had no knowledge of the attack at the outpost on May 11, but upon learning of the battle, assumed that was the destination of Colonel Muto and his men.

Then she guided Lieutenant Harris to a large pit sheltered from the sun by a grass thatched roof. It had been their sleeping quarters for the past several weeks and was "cluttered with ladies' unmentionables, kimonos, face powder, hair brushes, and most everything else needed to round out a lady's boudoir."

The girls were lifted aboard the lead LVT Alligator, and the raiding party returned to their outpost with their prisoners.

The men of B Company had a lot to joke about when the Butchers returned.

Lieutenant Don Murphy remembered all the laughter as Harris's men unloaded the geishas.

"Those poor girls were ragged, thin, and hungry. Of course, they seemed to be happy as our prisoners. They may have been pretty at one time, but not when I saw them. The one who spoke a little English said she was a nurse. Of course that brought more comments from the fellows."[4]

"So, how was the ride back?" Murphy teased Bud Harris.

"Those girls were willing to seduce the whole boatload of GIs for one can of C rations!" Harris replied.[5]

The geishas were given a full meal, including C rations and fresh-broiled fish, their first in a long time.

Within a few hours, Lieutenant Harris, accompanied by a rifle squad and the geishas, was at the sawmill headquarters.

The Intelligence section, S2, listened to Bud Harris's report on his successful mission. "Looking in their bunker," Harris stated, "I thought for a moment I was standing next to the cosmetic counter in the Evansville, Indiana, five-and-dime store."

One of the S2 officers laughed. "Really! Did you see any nylons in there?"

"Nylons?" replied Harris with a puzzled look. "No. That was one thing they didn't have. Japanese girls don't wear nylons, do they?"

"How would I know?" the officer answered. "I've never been to Japan. Guess we'll find out soon!"[6]

The girls were fed again and moved to I Corps Headquarters for questioning. I Corps was especially curious about the missing colonel. It was logical to assume he'd perished in the May 11 battle. But there'd been no colonel found among the Japanese dead.

A field hospital was the next stop for the girls, and then on to a Red Cross station. For these geishas, the war was finally over.

A few days later, on May 30, 1945, the Ehrlich Task Force was disbanded. Its members, the First Battalion, 136th Infantry, rejoined the Thirty-third Division at their new base at Baguio where they could get a little rest in the cool climate of the mountains. During their three-week mission at Dingalan Bay, they had killed 276 of the enemy and captured thirty-two Imperial soldiers (plus five young geishas).

* * *

A Western Union telegram arrived in Hull, Illinois, on June 8, 1945, addressed to PFC Ed Colwell's mother, Mabel. It read, "The Secretary of War desires to express his deep regret that your son, Pvt. Colwell,

Edward, was slightly wounded on Luzon 11 May '45." It was signed "The Adjutant General."[7]

On May 15, four days after the outpost battle and three weeks before Mrs. Mabel Colwell, Ed's mother, was officially notified by the Army, PFC Ed Colwell was in a Luzon field hospital dictating a letter to an American Red Cross nurse.

Ed's letter read, in part:

Dearest Mom:

I'm not able to do my own writing so another party is helping me . . . my forearm on the right arm is injured. I was hit early in the morning of the 11th. There is a fractured bone too. . . . I will move back to a larger hospital of some kind in the next few days. . . . Don't think I'm having a hard time because of pain because I'm not having any. . . .

The war was not over for Ed Colwell.

On October 2, 1945, a Red Cross "Gray Lady" at Nichols General Hospital in Louisville, Kentucky, wrote a letter to Ed's mother as he dictated. "I am getting along all right. They operated on me last Friday."

Then, from Beaumont General Hospital in El Paso, Texas, Ed wrote a letter to his mother using his left hand. "I got the bandages off and the wire pulled out of my thumb. . . . It's beginning to look like spring, the leaves are coming out. . . . I noticed some tulips blooming."

The letter was dated April 18, 1947. Colwell had been in military hospitals just a little less than two years. It would be almost three years before he was permitted to return home to Illinois. He never regained the use of his right arm, in spite of all the efforts of surgeons over those years.

* * *

The fall of Baguio did not end it. No one from General MacArthur on down to the lowest private really expected it to.

The Japanese Army left Baguio in a big hurry. Stockpiles of ammunition and supplies were left behind. Their wounded, as usual, were either murdered in their hospital beds by doctors and the medical staff or, in some cases, simply left without medicines, food, or water. Those critical items were needed by Imperial warriors who could still fight.[8]

General Yamashita's five-year defense plan had practically been reduced to four months by the U.S. Sixth Army. Yamashita and his survivors were now waiting in the mountains lining the fertile Cagayan Valley in the northern part of Luzon. The Japanese realized they must hold these mountains or eventually perish as an organized force.

New battle areas developed at places like Skyline Ridge, Mountain Trail, and Horizon Ridge. And more American blood was shed as the Japanese fought to the last man on some hillsides, and fell back on others, dynamiting cliffs to cause huge landslides as they withdrew; trying anything to delay the advancing Thirty-third Division.

Another member of the Golden Cross, Staff Sergeant Howard E. Woodford from Barberton, Ohio, stopped a Japanese attack, organized a unit of Filipino guerrillas, and led them in a defense of their small perimeter. Alone with his M1 rifle, he killed thirty-seven enemy soldiers. Sergeant Woodford was, himself, finally killed as they repelled the last enemy attack. He was nominated for the Congressional Medal of Honor. Seven months later, the award was presented to the sergeant's father, Mr. Dwight D. Woodford.

The Thirty-third Division now had three soldiers nominated for the Medal of Honor, the third being Sergeant Dexter J. Kerstetter, a cook's helper, who, sickened by seeing his buddies chopped to pieces by an enemy machine gun, had seized his rifle and a few grenades and charged the Japanese alone. He'd succeeded in destroying the enemy position and been nominated for the medal. Sergeant Kerstetter would survive to receive the medal shortly after the war.

Now it was June 1945, and the war on Luzon dragged on each day as if it would continue through eternity.

John McKinney's A Company was back in combat with their First Battalion, but without McKinney. He had been temporarily assigned to Battalion Headquarters, where interviews continued regarding his unbelievable "one-man stand." The battalion began to refer to the Outpost attack on May 11 as "the war against McKinney."

Although Captain Ice, McKinney's Able Company commander, recommended the Georgian for the Medal of Honor within a day or two after the battle, Battalion Headquarters did not officially notify their 123rd Infantry Regiment commanding officer until May 21. Then the long, slow process some called "Army red tape" began.

Meanwhile, what to do with PFC John McKinney? (Soon to be Sergeant McKinney.)

Of the three nominees for the Medal of Honor, one had been killed in the process of earning it. Though the story of his action was dramatic and inspirational, the Army needed *live* heroes—men the other troops, indeed the American public, could see and hear. Heroes whose photographs and story could appear in newspapers and magazines back home.

Nothing was unusual about that belief. Since the beginning of recorded history, each civilization has idolized military heroes. Statues were erected by the ancient Egyptians, Romans, Greeks, and Babylonians honoring those who had saved them from their enemies.

So, the concern for John McKinney's safety shifted from A Company to First Battalion. Generally, the plan was to keep him around the Battalion Headquarters area, where he would be somewhat safe from the enemy, and give him light duty while the paperwork continued through different levels of military command.

From the beginning, a problem existed regarding the exact number of "kills" credited to McKinney. He knew, and Sergeant Johnson originally reported, that the number was way over one hundred, maybe as high as 140.

Even the Army had a difficult time believing those numbers. Staff officers *wanted* to believe. A little man standing alone with the aid of a knife, rifle, and his bare hands killing over one hundred attacking enemy soldiers—that was the kind of story members of the military love to relate in the barracks, in bars, and to historians who will listen.

Of course, many of the Japanese killed by McKinney were in the first wave devastated by his machine gun; until he was overrun and the gun jammed.

But what number would sound believable and how should they arrive at that figure?

There is nothing in the National Archives describing the process in which they derived the final number. However, it is logical to assume that most of those killed on the beach would not be credited as "kills."

The witnesses to John McKinney's fight could not see what was happening on the beach. They could only testify to what they *did* see—the enemy soldiers killed by McKinney in or near the foxhole. The dead Japanese soldiers on the beach, in the river, and the surf of Dingalan Bay would not be credited to McKinney, or anyone.

Then there was a disagreement about the "witnessed killed" number. The total mentioned in one report was thirty-eight, another forty, yet another forty-two.[9]

* * *

Sergeant Henry Van Westrop's interest in photography led him into a rather unusual position with the Thirty-third Division.

Major General P.W. Clarkson, the division's commander, discovered Van Westrop's talents and appointed him "Division Photographer." It would become his duty to move with the division and make a photographic history of everything from decoration award ceremonies to combat action.

At first, the assignment seemed like a "photographer's dream," but once he was on Luzon, the demands and dangers of the job became apparent.

Long periods of time without rest and the stress of combat might have destroyed an average man. But Sergeant Van Westrop proved his value time after time, and was awarded the Bronze Star Medal for bravery.

The Golden Cross had no darkroom equipment, so the sergeant had to design his own using ingenuity, imagination, and some good old Army wheeling-dealing to build a compact semimobile unit. From this darkroom he produced hundreds of high-quality photographs. Understandably, he and General Clarkson became close friends.

On June 7, 1945, Henry Van Westrop visited the command post north of hill KP21 in the area of Luzon the Army called Mountain Trail.

Bitter fighting had temporarily ceased due to a heavy fog that drifted in about 1:00 A.M. Even in the early morning hours, the fog was so thick that it blanketed all the Golden Cross objectives. All howitzers, tanks, mortars, and machine guns went to an inactive role.[10]

Men on the perimeter were cautioned to remain especially alert for snipers and suicide bombers who might take advantage of the foul weather and try to slip through the lines.

Sergeant Van Westrop was in a foxhole talking with an infantry sergeant when they were visited by a lieutenant colonel. He would learn later that the colonel was Thomas Truxtun, a popular commander of the 210th Field Artillery Battalion who had come to the command post to personally direct artillery fire once the fog lifted.

Suddenly someone shouted, "Jap sniper!"

The sergeant next to Van Westrop yelled at the colonel, "Get down, sir! Sniper!"

But instead, the colonel stood up as if impulse guided him to look for the sniper.

Then there was the sound of a shot. Lieutenant Colonel Truxtun fell dead, a bullet in his brain.[11]

A few moments passed, and then another shot was fired from somewhere in the fog beyond the perimeter.

Major Balch, executive officer for the Third Battalion, was also hit in the head by a sniper's bullet. Medics administered first aid and evacuated the major to a field hospital where he held onto life for several days. Then he died from his wound.

Members of the 210th Field Artillery Battalion held a special ceremony to pay final respects for Lieutenant Colonel Truxtun. The weather had begun to change, but clouds still hung about the hilltops and fog clung close to the ground, producing an eerie scene as the men gathered in formation.

Sergeant Henry Van Westrop climbed a small hill with camera in hand and recorded the solemn ceremony on film.

Word of Colonel Truxtun's death by sniper fire reached the First Battalion Headquarters within twenty-four hours. The decision was quickly made to send Sergeant John McKinney to the 123rd Regiment headquarters area where he would be even farther from the front lines and the enemy.

There, McKinney met his new "bodyguards," four riflemen who accompanied him everywhere. He only knew that he had been recommended for a "high award" and as he wrote his mother during the first week of July, "Food sure is a whole lot better where I'm at now. And there's lots of it."[12]

CHAPTER 23

*"It is believed this action merits the
Medal of Honor."*

General Walter Krueger to General Douglas MacArthur

(Recommendation for PFC John McKinney)

The Thirty-third Division combat missions continued until June 25, 1945. Then units were ordered back to their headquarters. By June 30, the entire division was at Baguio for a rest. They had been removed from "operational status," but that did not mean the war was over for the Golden Cross. To the contrary, the Army had something "big" planned for them.

Before anyone could relax, the Thirty-third was on the move again, this time to the west coast of Luzon and the beaches along the South China Sea from Bauang south to Aringay. By July 11, two months after the Umiray outpost battle, the division had settled in and was waiting for their next assignment.

But first, some entertainment for the battle-weary troops. Kay Kyser and Gracie Fields gave an enjoyable performance in a tropical rainstorm before five thousand men.

The next day the division got down to serious work. The first priority was more amphibious training.

Then the men were told the mission: JAPAN! The Thirty-third Division would be going in first. The date, "sometime in the fall," was all they were permitted to know. The *where* also remained a secret.

The division trained by regiment, not battalion, indicating a landing would be made over a wide area. And now, unlike the training in Hawaii and New Guinea, there was no shortage of transport ships and landing craft.

Combined with amphibious landing training was more emphasis on patrols and attacks on pillboxes and other types of enemy fortifications.

Sergeant John McKinney was spared from most of the training, often becoming an "observer," reporting his ideas and suggestions to the staff, which gave him that detail each day.

Near the end of July, McKinney became sick and was sent to a field hospital, where the doctors diagnosed his illness as malaria. He apparently had had the disease for some months but, like many soldiers in the Pacific, had performed his duties until finally becoming too sick to carry on.

With some modern (1945) medicines and seven days rest, he was back at the 123rd Headquarters on "limited duty" (which described his status for the past several weeks).

Meanwhile, the Army continued with their war plan for the invasion of Japan, now called "Operation Olympic Coronet."

In this plan, I Corps, composed of the Thirty-third, Twenty-fifth, and Forty-first Divisions, would attack at Miyazaki on the southern island of Kyushu.

The date for the invasion was set for November 1, 1945.

Strategy called for the Thirty-third Golden Cross and the Twenty-fifth Division to go in first, abreast, while the Forty-first waited in reserve. The Golden Cross would commit the 130th and 136th Infantry Regiments, while McKinney's 123rd floated in reserve.

A few minutes after the invasion landing, the Ninth Corps and the Fifth Marine Amphibious Corps were due to assault the beaches at Ariaka Wan and Kagoshima.

The Eleventh Corps was to make a feint at Shikoku to attempt to draw the enemy air and Naval forces away from Kysuhu.

General MacArthur announced that his Headquarters estimated that two out of every three GIs who hit the beach on November 1st would be a casualty. For the final and total conquest of Japan, MacArthur reported he expected more than one million U.S. servicemen to be killed.

* * *

"In obedience to the gracious command of His Majesty, the Emperor, who, ever anxious to enhance the cause of world peace, desires earnestly to bring about an early termination of hostilities with a view to saving mankind from the calamities . . ."

Thus began the message delivered to the United States government through the neutral Swiss government at 7:45 A.M., "Eastern War Time," on August 10 by the Japanese.

On August 6, an American B-29 Superfortress had dropped an atomic bomb on Hisoshima, followed by Russia formally declaring war on Japan. Then Nagasaki was wiped out by a second A-bomb.

There was excitement among the men of the Thirty-third on Luzon, but training continued as usual.

On August 11, Secretary of State James F. Byrnes, speaking for all Allied nations, responded to the first message from Japan. The surrender of Japan must be *unconditional*. At 7:00 P.M., August 14, the Japanese accepted Allied terms.

The war was officially over.

V-J Day (Victory over Japan Day) fell on September 2, 1945, when the surrender documents were signed aboard the Battleship *Missouri* in Tokyo Bay with General MacArthur presiding.

A day later, in Baguio, General Yamashita surrendered all Imperial Japanese land, sea, and air forces in the Philippines.

"I sure would like to have a picture of that ceremony!" General Clarkson mentioned to his photographer, Sergeant Henry Van Westrop.

Sergeant Van Westrop somehow managed to bluff his way into the room where the surrender documents were being signed and take some candid shots for his general.[1]

* * *

Shortly before the war ended, the Army paper mill continued to operate on Luzon, thriving on an abundance of red tape and the "Army way."

Colonel George S. Price, assistant chief of staff at Sixth Army

Headquarters, had reviewed the report on John McKinney and the nomination for the Medal of Honor. The original summary of McKinney's action covered two typewritten pages and was fairly accurate. There were no exaggerations. Only the sequences were somewhat off.

The document from Colonel Price was a follow-up on a letter sent to the "Commanding General, 33rd Infantry Division, Thru: Commanding General I Corps," dated June 27, 1945.

That letter stated:

1. . . . incontestable proof of the performance of service will be exacted.
2. . . . the attached affidavits do not support, as eyewitness accounts, many of the statements made in the basic recommendation.
3. It is requested that, if possible, additional testimony of eyewitnesses be secured. . . .
BY COMMAND OF GENERAL KRUEGER[2]

General Walter Krueger, the Sixth Army commander, did not wish to block a Medal of Honor recommendation like the one for John McKinney. But the summary did offer facts that Krueger knew would be hard for even the news media to believe.

He also understood General MacArthur's thinking completely. Everything must be accurate and documented by as many witnesses as possible. General Krueger was not about to forward the recommendation to General MacArthur until all possible questions were answered.

But the Army in the Pacific needed heroes Americans could relate to as the date for the invasion of Japan drew closer. Everyone involved with the award process was requested to give the John McKinney affair full and fast attention. But "keep it accurate, documented, and believable!" ordered Krueger.

So the Thirty-third Division applied pressure to the 123rd Regiment, which pressured the First Battalion, and it ended up in Captain Ice's lap again. He quickly gathered signed statements, and more details, from those few who had witnessed John McKinney in combat on May 11.

On the seventeenth of July, a new recommendation with more affidavits was submitted by the Thirty-third Division. Again, Colonel Price had a few questions. In a section of his letter entitled "Analysis," the following was recorded, with the Golden Cross's answers:

Was the act of gallantry:

Far above and beyond the call of duty?—Yes.
Self-sacrifice?—No.
In face of almost certain death?—Yes.
Did it markedly affect the success of the operation?—Yes.

The regimental commanding general signed it, along with General Clarkson of the Thirty-third Division and General Swift, commander of I Corps.

That was enough for General Krueger. He added, "Remarks: It is believed this action merits the Medal of Honor," and signed the recommendation.

On August 16, 1945, General Douglas MacArthur ordered his staff to send a radiogram to the commanding general, Thirty-third Division. It read, in part:

To: Commanding Gen. Three-three Inf. Div.
Thru: Commanding Gen. Sixth Army
PFC John McKinney, Company Able One-two-three Inf. Regt.—
Recommendation for Medal of Honor APPROVED. Please radio this
HQ immediately whether EM [enlisted man] desires theater presentation or return to U.S. for White House presentation. . . .

MacArthur's approval was now off to Washington.

When the details were explained to John McKinney, a celebrity in the Thirty-third Division, he, naturally requested to return home, since the opportunity was offered.

But that presented a problem. The 123rd Regiment was to embark for Japan on September 20 for occupation duty. John McKinney, now actually a sergeant, had been scheduled to be a member of that occupation force. He departed for Japan one day after receiving the news of his award's approval. Georgia had to wait.

Some units of the 123rd Regiment made a "wet landing" at Wakayama on September 25, and boarded trains for a six-hour ride to Takarazuka, where their headquarters were established. The movement was uneventful.

The First Battalion was quartered in a huge opera house adjacent to the headquarters. The remainder of the regiment was scattered out over a six-mile area.

The Japanese throughout the prefecture cooperated with American authorities. Their respect for authority made the occupation mission a far easier matter than anyone imagined.[3]

October brought something new for the occupation forces. Cold weather! For men who had survived the many months of steamy jungles and swamps, the change in climate was, at first, a shock.

But there was time off for fall sports as football teams were organized and competition started between units.

The 123rd, as most regiments stationed in Japan, had, in the beginning, an important responsibility in patrolling their sectors. All Japanese Army and Navy installations were seized and searched. War equipment was destroyed, but anything that could be used by civilians—blankets, food stocks, medicines, etc.—was turned over to local authorities for distribution.

Civilian firearms and other weapons were also seized.

In most areas, the troops entering a small town were the first Americans the population had ever seen. The women and children generally responded with gladness. Many of the men were resentful.[4]

John McKinney did not write to his mother during his assignment to Japan. His friends from Company A seldom saw him and when they did, he "seemed to be just wandering around the Headquarters area."

McKinney reported some time later while talking with his sister Betty that he felt extremely low while in Japan. "It was hard for me to look them people in the face after killing so many of 'em," he told her.[5]

When the 123rd Regiment arrived at Takarazuka, their strength was 140 officers and 3,311 enlisted men. By November 2, the numbers dropped to forty-four officers and 1,675 enlisted men. In keeping with the War Department's policy of demobilizing men with a high number of "points" and with extended periods of overseas duty, those "missing" men had earned the right to return home to the States.

Replacements arrived, men who had never experienced combat, and the strength of the 123rd increased.[6]

On December 6, Mac's friend Adolph "Red" Barrette, now a staff sergeant, received instructions to transfer to the Eleventh General Replacement Center and to "await further orders to proceed to U.S."

The next day, December 7, exactly four years after the Japanese attack on Pearl Harbor, the Morning Report listed Sergeant John R. McKinney receiving the same orders as Red.[7]

At last, J.R. was going home.

It took almost a month for John McKinney to cross the ocean and reach the processing center at Fort McPherson near Atlanta. There he was presented his Honorable Discharge paper and instructed to keep his uniform handy. The Army would contact him soon regarding plans for his trip to Washington to meet the president.

J.R. arrived in Sylvania the same day as his brother D.H. "Tink." Ironically, D.H. had been processed for discharge at Camp Gordon near Augusta. Nothing can completely describe the thrill and joy felt by the McKinney family, especially Betty.

To Betty, her hero and best friend, J.R., had returned from a hell she never completely understood. But he was alive and home.

CHAPTER 24

"All I want is just a little ole farm
back home in Sylvania."
John McKinney
Augusta Chronicle, January 22, 1946

Betty McKinney, an attractive teenager in January 1946, watched with fascination as excitement mounted about their home "like it was the week before Christmas."

Jack was still in the Navy and based in Japan. His letters arrived frequently now that the war was over.

Twenty-three-year-old D.H. had received the Bronze Star for bravery while fighting in Normandy, but he and J.R. seldom discussed the war. Most of their time was spent listening to Ralph, who'd returned from the Navy Seabees some months earlier. It seemed Ralph already knew all the news and recent events in and around their new hometown of Sylvania.

Mr. McKinney had taken a job at a veneer factory in Sylvania. With all his sons "off to war," there was no one in the family to work even a one-horse farm at Woodcliff. But this new job had produced a steady income, and with it he rented and furnished a house in town.

Their days of sharecropping were over. In fact, the county was experiencing an exodus of farmers, as men, returning from military service, moved to cities to secure their future. Most would never return to work the fields. Mechanical farm equipment quickly replaced manual laborers as the postwar industrial revolution joined the building boom, drawing America into prosperous times.

Though Woodcliff was less than an hour from Sylvania, the old farm seemed to be of a different world, and it would take some time for the McKinneys to adjust to the change.

But now they enjoyed a home with running water, electricity, and a radio, luxuries they'd only dreamed of a few years earlier.

Not every GI deserted the farms. With all the homecoming celebration and his celebrity status, J.R. made it clear to everyone that he had his own plans for the future and those surely would include farming, fishing, and hunting.

Reporters from Georgia newspapers descended on the McKinney home trying to get J.R. to grant interviews before he was off to Washington to meet the president.

Since the week after the Dingalan Bay battle, J.R. had floated on a wave of attention and publicity. He confessed to Betty, "I enjoyed it for a while. It never happened before, and it ain't gonna happen again. I wish it would all go away."[1]

One might suspect that John McKinney, a man of so few words, would be a poor subject for interviews. Maybe he had nothing of interest to say to the public. The opposite was true. What J.R. said was exactly what Americans wanted to hear from a war hero.

J.R. exemplified the common man, a farm boy who proved he was willing to fight against impossible odds to protect his buddies and the country he loved; an unassuming GI who performed an unbelievable, almost superhuman, act of bravery while demonstrating that greatness must be measured in America by many different standards.

A reporter for the *Augusta Chronicle* said to J.R., "I suppose you'll be thinking of running for public office. You're a hero. You saved the lives of your pals and you'll be meeting President Truman. Is it true you told another reporter that you want to return to farming?"

An amused J.R. answered, "I ain't no politician. We got plenty of them already. All I want is just a little ole farm back home in Sylvania."[2]

A *Chicago Daily News* writer tossed a good question. "You and so many boys returning home now fought to preserve our freedom. What's your idea of freedom, Sergeant McKinney? What does freedom mean to you?"

J.R. answered without hesitation, "I want to catch a fish in a Georgia river and cook it on the riverbank. That there's one kind of freedom."[3]

The *Atlanta Journal* reported, "John McKinney of Sylvania says he is honored to meet the president and appreciates the decoration awarded him, but he doesn't seem very excited about the trip to Washington."[4]

An *Associated Press* article stated, "Sergeant John McKinney was shy and didn't want to brag about what he had done to be a celebrity. I asked, 'How does it feel to be a hero, Sergeant?' The Georgian said, 'I ain't no hero! I was trying to stay alive. I'll tell you about heroes. Them American boys lying dead on an island. Every one of them's a hero. I just wanted to stay alive and come home. The heroes didn't get to come home.' "[5]

J.R. put on his Army uniform one last time as he and the family prepared for the train trip to the nation's capital. Accompanying J.R. was his father and mother, uncle Lee McKinney, brother Tink, sister Betty, Mrs. Claude R. Mobley of Millen, Georgia (a family friend and correspondent for the *Augusta Chronicle*), and Democratic Representative Peterson.

Betty reported that everyone was nervous, but "Tink, the clown in the family, kept us at ease with his joking and kidding with J.R."

The presentation ceremony took place on the morning of January 23, 1946, in the White House Oval Office.

Sharing the spotlight was another Medal of Honor recipient from Alma, Georgia, First Lieutenant Daniel W. Lee, who had risked his life to silence two German mortars in September 1944.

The news media reported, and Betty remembered, some of the words spoken by the president to the young men. "This is a wonderful citation," he said, placing the blue ribbon and medal over the head of John McKinney. "There is no greater honor in the world!" he added a few moments later.

Then, as he held the medal up from J.R.'s chest for photographers, President Truman stated, "To tell you the truth, I'd rather have earned one of these than be president!"

For the next two days, an Army honor guard escorted the McKinneys through Washington and Arlington Cemetery.

Betty remembered that "the opportunity to meet the president of the United States was an honor *I'll* never forget. But the fact that General Eisenhower and Admiral Nimitz attended gave us all a special thrill, especially as the years went by and these men became even more famous."[6]

After their return to Sylvania, they were surprised by the local Merchants Association. They had raised $1,600 from a "grateful community" so J.R. could buy a farm.

Though a sizable sum in 1946, it unfortunately, and in spite of all good intentions, fell short of the amount needed to buy enough land for a farm.

But the money would be put to good use. J.R. had "always dreamed of owning a pickup truck," and now that he lived in the city, he would need transportation out to his favorite hunting and fishing areas. He announced he also planned to do "a little job hunting."

He purchased a used truck and deposited the balance of the money into a Sylvania bank, opening his first savings account. According to Betty, he managed the account himself.

Several months later he invested in a shotgun and a high-powered rifle for hunting. The old .22 single-shot rifle, which had helped provide food for the family for many years, was "retired" but not forgotten. Periodically, he cleaned and oiled it as he had before the war. J.R. owned many different firearms during his life, but the original Winchester remained his special treasure.

On February 8, 1946, Nattie McKinney wrote a letter to Ed Colwell's mother at J.R.'s request. Mrs. McKinney explained in the note that J.R. constantly expressed concern for his wounded friend. Mrs. Colwell's reply told of Ed's hospital stays and surgery. The two mothers began to correspond regularly by mail, Nattie signing her letters as most married women did at the time, with her married title, "Mrs. D.H. McKinney."

Nattie enclosed a number of newspaper clippings about J.R. so Mrs. Colwell could forward them on the Ed. In return, she received photos of Ed in his Army uniform.

As weeks drifted into months, Nattie related her concern for J.R.'s condition. "It seems," Nattie wrote, "he [J.R.] just can't bring himself to write any letters. He hasn't wrote a letter since he returned. I guess he can't be still long enough, he seems so nervous. Tell Edward he hasn't forgotten him and will write as soon as he can get himself together."[7]

That letter was written a few months after the White House ceremony. J.R. never did write a letter to Ed.

And in another letter, Nattie wrote, "J.R. is a quiet boy, always was, but even more so now. And he doesn't like what happened at all. He misses his buddies. He doesn't go anywhere. He is so yellow and keeps having attacks of malaria. I know he never feels good. He has talked a lot about Edward—more than he has anyone else. But it is so hard to get anything out of him about what happened that day."[8]

The sentimental side of Nattie was revealed in another letter, feelings shared by millions of other mothers in America in the 1940s. "It's funny how we feel about the boys that were in that fight with our sons, isn't it? But we do—I do, and I know you feel the same—all us mothers have been in the same boat through the war. I had four in at once!"

She signed that letter, "A friend—Mrs. D.H. McKinney of Sylvania, Ga."

Although Nattie extended an invitation for Ed to visit them in Sylvania, he never did.

There were no more news media interviews for many years, and that was just fine with J.R.

He worked as a part-time farmer about the county, and always found time to fish and hunt. But now he pursued it all as a hobby or sport rather than a necessity for survival. As before, he only killed (or caught) what his family could eat; then he was happy "just wandering in the woods."

He worked for a while at a local sawmill and developed a friendship with another quiet, honest man, Mr. Joe Evans, who remembered J.R. as a "peaceful man, a good man. He weren't no fast liver and he never bothered nobody around these parts."[9]

J.R.'s brothers eventually left home, married, and started their own families. Mr. McKinney passed away, never sharing a close friendship with J.R. The house was divided into two apartments, one for J.R. and a larger one for Betty and Nattie.

Soon after Mr. McKinney's passing, some "strangers" came to Sylvania from New York looking for "Sergeant John McKinney." They spread the word that they were thinking about producing a "motion picture on the life of Sergeant McKinney and needed to do a little scouting about the county."

Betty remembered the week the producers were in town, but could not recall their names. Other citizens of Sylvania also remembered the time J.R. was "almost in the movies."

"It was the only time in our lives," Betty said, "that J.R. and his brothers ever agreed on anything! They actually sat down together to discuss a project. Well, at least they agreed to *discuss* it, but J.R. just wasn't interested after the first meeting with the movie people."[10]

The producers filmed some local scenery for a day or two, then made arrangements to meet with the McKinneys the next morning at 9:00 A.M. At that time, Tink, who had been elected to serve as "agent" by the group, would discuss money and then instruct J.R. to sign contracts.

Everyone was present at 9:00 A.M. that special morning, everyone except J.R.

Agent Tink had to express an apology on behalf of J.R. It seemed Sergeant McKinney had had a "taste for red fin pike and went fishing."

The producers waited until late afternoon and then gave up.

J.R. did not return until after dark, carrying a string of fresh fish.

According to Betty, "J.R. was the only one relieved to learn the movie people had left town. His brothers were so disappointed and angry, they wouldn't speak to J.R. for days. But they knew how he was. He wasn't gonna change. He didn't want publicity and he didn't want to discuss the war. That was the only movie offer he almost got, and we never heard from those people again."[11]

When Nattie McKinney died, J.R., as could be expected, became more withdrawn, but he did continue to visit with relatives from time to time.

Only Betty understood the hurt he carried inside. "Mom" McKinney, J.R., and Betty had, after all, functioned as a unit and shared so much over the years. Except for the war years, they were always together, other than the times J.R. was wandering in the wilderness.

Betty had married and was raising her daughter, Sue, but she still found time to visit with J.R. and "let him talk out his hurt as much as he wanted to."

Twenty years after the war, J.R. was still not married and, according to relatives, never had a serious girlfriend. The wilderness remained his first love. He invested in a flat-bottomed boat that fit perfectly in the back of his pickup truck, and spent every free hour he could drifting about in the swamp, "fishing and thinking."

When his niece, Sue, started school, Betty had more time to join him for boat rides.

"Sometimes we fished, but more often we floated about," Betty said. "If J.R. wanted to talk, he talked. He mentioned God now and then and questioned why God saved him during the war. Then he might reveal some detail about that big battle, but what he said usually didn't make much sense; it was more like rambling memories. Maybe if I had been at that fight, I would have understood more of what was on his mind.

"Often he brought up the subject of guilt and he prayed that God would forgive him for killing so many people. He told me, 'I prayed during the fight that they would go away. We could all go home and live in peace. But it weren't gonna happen that-a-way.' Then he might cry a little, but I'd bring him back by talking about something funny that happened in our childhood. Next thing you know, we'd both be laughing."[12]

Apparently J.R.'s work at the sawmill was too confining. Though he enjoyed the relationship he had with the other employees (at a sawmill there is not much time to talk to one another), he needed freedom to drift about the county. For years, he moved from farm to farm, returning to the work and solitude he knew before the war.

Farm owners were proud to have him on the property and happy to get their money's worth from his labor. And J.R. was happy to find that his employers had invested in tractors. He enjoyed driving the equipment, and soon developed the skill to repair them.

The ever-restless J.R. heard from relatives in Florida that a new space center was under construction and the contractors needed laborers to work in the swamps. Many acres of lowlands had to be drained and cleared before the massive center could be completed. He stayed with those relatives and worked in the swamps for a year, earning more money during that time than he could "plowing fields for three years in Georgia."

But he longed to return to Screven County. Within fourteen months he was back on a tractor and close to the rivers and woods he loved.

In 1966, twenty years after the war ended, *Atlanta Magazine* decided to do an article on Georgia veterans who had received high awards for valor. Their interview with J.R. was his first since that flurry of attention in January 1946.

The magazine writers found J.R. on a tractor, working cornfields belonging to his cousin J.W. McKinney.

The photograph of J.R. they decided to publish revealed he had gained weight over the years, thanks to a return to his favorite foods. It also showed that he was still smoking cigarettes, a habit acquired during the war when they were distributed free as part of the GI's "rations."[13]

The writer recorded that, during the entire meeting, "Mr. McKinney's eyes never lost the terrible stare of sadness."

Jack Finch, one of J.R.'s hunting friends, was with him during the interview, and remembered one particular question asked about the battle at Dingalan Bay.

"Weren't you afraid?" The reporter studied J.R.'s wrinkled, suntanned face and waited for an answer.

J.R. stared off in another direction.

The reporter tried a different approach. "Didn't you have any fear?"

Still no answer. Perhaps J.R. was creating a dramatic, newsworthy answer. Or did he even hear the question?

The reporter pushed. "Is there anything that really scares you?"

Finally, McKinney turned to look the man in the eye.

"Scare me?" J.R. answered. "Yep. What scares me is to be a way out there in the field . . . all alone. Ain't no one near . . . ain't nothing there but me in an ocean of cotton. Then I reach in my pocket and realize . . . I done run out of bakke [tobacco]. Now, that can scare any man!"[14]

J.R. grinned as if satisfied with his teasing reply. The reporter stared, his face revealing no emotion.

Shortly after the *Atlanta Magazine* article appeared, J.R. developed an interest in country music. Betty had a "player" at the house, and he brought a few "hillbilly" records home.

"He never really started a collection," she said, "but he was very fond of Bill Monroe. Said he's the father of bluegrass. But he also liked Lester Flatt and Earl Scruggs and listened to "Blue Moon of Kentucky" over and over.

"As he got older, he went hunting less and had more time to watch television," Betty went on. "Baseball began to capture his attention, but he never played in a game after Army days, yet he enjoyed playing pitch and catch with relatives at family gatherings."

Although J.R. enjoyed target-practice with his guns, he never built a collection. Like the dogs he once owned, each firearm was good for "hunting something." So his "collection" was limited to only what he needed in the field. There was one exception. Years after the war, military weapons were released by the government to be sold to the public. These included the Army .45 automatic pistol, the semiautomatic carbine, and the M1 Garand rifle. J.R. purchased an M1, not for hunting, but "just to have an old friend close by," he told Jack Finch.

Mr. Finch recalled John McKinney's accuracy with a rifle "when he was way over fifty."

He related an incident that occurred one deer season. The two hunters agreed to separate and meet at a clearing a half a mile away. When Jack had reached the area, he spotted a large buck deer, fired, and the deer dropped, apparently killed instantly.

He approached the deer, set his rifle down against a log, drew his knife, and moved to the front of his "kill," admiring the animal's large set of antlers.

Suddenly, the deer leapt to his feet and sprang forward in an attempt to gore Jack with those antlers.

A shot rang out from somewhere in the distance. The deer, a red hole in the side of his head, fell at Jack's feet.

Jack looked around, his eyes searching the woods and distant hills. Then he saw J.R. walking toward him in another clearing three hundred yards away.

"I was a-watching you from over yonder," McKinney said as he reached his friend's side. "I've been stalking that deer for two seasons. I know he's smart and plenty tricky. When I seen you moving up in front of him, I think, 'Ole Jack might be in a heap of trouble,' so I put his head in my sights. When he jumped at you . . . bang! Now, he's yours. Don't ever get in front of something you shoot. Come up behind him first so he can't see you. Them Jap boys were good at playing dead; then they'd get you when you came close."

Jack Finch thanked J.R. for saving his life, and marveled at the fact that he had taken the shot at such a distance without the help of a telescopic sight. J.R.'s rifle was a 30:06 with "open iron sights."

"Shucks, I don't need no telescope to shoot, least not as long as my eyes stay good," J.R. remarked.

Then J.R. pulled out his Red Man chewing tobacco and offered Jack "a chew."

"You been smoking heavy since you come home from the war a long time ago. You gonna take up chewing?" Jack Finch asked.

"Yep," replied J.R. "I seen on the television that cigarettes might hurt my health. Betty been trying to get me to quit anyway."[15]

Betty's memories of her brother were quite vivid and often emotional. She understood his "hurts" and his loneliness and talked about his patience. "He was never in a hurry," she said, "and his wanderings took him into places in the woods and swamp that only he knows. He never took me to all his private places.

"But he also enjoyed drifting around the county, visiting briefly different stores in Sylvania. People would tell me that J.R. often appeared out of nowhere and after chitchatting a little, would be gone. They said they seldom heard his footsteps, but there he was. He talked about the old days and the hard times with some folks. The same was true about family gatherings. He loved to visit with cousins and such. He would eat, of course. J.R. never missed a chance for food. Then while people was talking, we'd look around—no J.R.! He just seemed to disappear.

"In the days following the war, people walked up to shake his hand and thank him for what he done for our country. But J.R. wouldn't talk about the war or even answer questions on the subject. He'd say, 'Thank you,' and that's it.

"Me and him come out of a store one day and a lady walked right up to J.R. and said, 'The Good Lord sure worked a miracle for you in that battle, J.R.!' And J.R. smiled and answered, 'Yep, seems like, don't it?' "[16]

Betty's marriage did not work out and eventually ended in divorce, but her daughter, Sue, had grown to be a beautiful, intelligent young woman. She caught the eye of a Georgia State Trooper who was also serving his country as a member of the Army National Guard. They married and Sue became Mrs. Danny Lynn Derriso.

These changes were to affect J.R. in a positive way. First, his closest friend, sister Betty, was more available to accompany him fishing at nearby rivers.

Next, J.R. gained a new friend and hunting companion—Danny Lynn. Soon, the two men were off to the fields target shooting and hunting whatever the season would permit.

"It seems God brought Lynn into J.R.'s life at the right time," Betty said. "The two of them hit it off in a wonderful way. Lynn admired and respected J.R., and the feeling was certainly mutual. To J.R., Lynn was the kind of American 'we need more of,' he would say. J.R. enjoyed being with Lynn more than his own brothers."[17]

Officer Derriso put it another way. "It takes a warrior to know another warrior."

True, Danny Lynn never experienced a battle like the one J.R. endured, few people ever have, but as a trooper he had his share of "close calls" and blood spilling.

During those hunting trips around Sylvania, he came to know and understand some of J.R.'s deep feelings.

"Over there near Cannon Lake, Uncle J.R. and I would sit on knee roots of those huge cypress trees," Mr. Derriso reported. "You know, those big roots sticking up from the water. It was very peaceful there, and I quickly learned that J.R. sometimes just wanted to sit and look off into space like he had sank into a deep daydream. He never revealed all of the thoughts, but often would snap out of his trance and make a little comment as if it was only an impulse. He would start off, 'Them Jap boys were brave. I never hated them. They were just doing their duty like me. Their leaders sent 'em at us, knowing we were gonna shoot 'em all.' Then he would return to the safety of his daydream. I think his whole life after the war was spent trying to analyze what happened during the big battle and why he was allowed to survive."[18]

Mr. Derriso believed sincerely, and all reports substantiate, that the tragedy for John McKinney was the fact that he could not enjoy a normal life. The memory of the battle haunted him constantly.

Danny Lynn and Betty concurred that J.R. carried deep emotional scars that no one could see. Mostly, it was from the guilt, the memory of killing so many people in order to survive.[19]

One can only guess that these factors may have contributed to the fact that he never married. Of course, his shyness made it difficult to court. But J.R. had said that he did not feel he needed "a girl." He had his wilderness, the freedom to hunt and fish and to wander when and where he chose. Later in life, he had his friends, Betty and Danny Lynn, as well as an assortment of cousins, nephews, and nieces to visit if he felt the need to do so. And he did cherish his time alone with his thoughts.

J.R.'s grandnephew, Dent (Danny Lynn's son), was very fond of his uncle J.R., and remembered one morning looking out the living room window and "to my surprise, there was Uncle J.R. sitting under a tree using his pocketknife to shave the plastic skin off of copper wire he had found at the city dump. I had no idea he was in the yard. When he was done, he just sat there and stared into space for the longest time. I guess that was his meditation time. Then he picked up the wire and was gone. I found out later he had sold the wire to a local scrap dealer."[20]

Like so many "old-timers" who remembered hard times, J.R. could not stand to see good things like copper wire go to waste. It wasn't that he needed the money. His Medal of Honor pension was by then more than $400 per month, and he had received good pay working as a farmhand.

J.R.'s standard of living would not have drained any budget in Sylvania, where the cost to survive was considerably less than other parts of the country.

On a warm Friday afternoon, May 12, 1995, fifty years and one day after his battle at Dingalan Bay, John McKinney, accompanied by Betty, grandnephew Dent, his mother, Sue Derriso, and Danny Lynn, attended a very special gathering at the edge of Sylvania.

There a color guard from Fort Stewart, two Army generals, a number of political dignitaries, representatives of the news media, and a crowd of citizens were waiting.

J.R. was presented a plaque from the State of Georgia in appreciation for his bravery and devotion to country. A United States flag that had flown over the Screven County War Memorial was also given to the aging hero.

One of the generals pinned a Bronze Star beside the other two on J.R.'s jacket. This award was for bravery in combat during a 1944 battle on New Guinea. The general apologized. The Army regretted that J.R. had had to wait so long for the medal.

Then the main purpose for the ceremony. Early in 1995, the Georgia Legislature unanimously passed a resolution designating Highway 21, which runs through Screven County and on to Savannah, the "Sergeant John R. McKinney Medal of Honor Highway."

The people of the State of Georgia and Sylvania had not forgotten what J.R. once did for his country.

A few months later J.R. again had to dress in coat and tie. This time Danny Lynn and Dent escorted the reluctant hero to Tennessee to attend the Thirty-third Infantry Division Association's fiftieth anniversary reunion.

The year 1995 turned into a busy year for one who had successfully avoided notoriety and public ceremonies for five decades.

By then, J.R.'s health had begun to fail. His days of wandering the pig paths in the Georgia wilderness were about over, and he even needed assistance loading the boat into his pickup truck.

But J.R. was never one to give up easily. Being a practical man, he started his first and only enterprise. In a one-level clapboard building with a rusty metal roof located at the corner of Industrial and Westchester Roads, he opened "The Bait and Tackle Shop," selling a variety of live bait to sportsmen like himself.

The bulk of his inventory was composed of minnows, crickets, meal worms, and the popular red wiggler worm. He raised all the live inventory on site, and, of course, now had an unlimited supply of bait for his own fishing. But those excursions were becoming less frequent each month.

One day in late summer in 1996, J.R. gathered some of his inventory along with his favorite rod and drove Betty to the other side of Sylvania.

The truck bounced along a sandy dirt trail until they arrived at one of his favorite spots. There the two struggled to get the boat into the muddy Ogeechee River, admitting to each other that age had drained their strength.

They drifted for an hour under big, dark tree limbs, their green leaves granting shade from the bright morning sun.

J.R. did not seem interested in fishing that day.

"Like so many times," said Betty, "he only wanted to drift and think. Yet, somehow, I felt things were different. I wanted to tell him something exciting, but he was peaceful with his thoughts and I knew I shouldn't interrupt him, so I waited.

"Finally, he looked at me from the other end of that old leaky boat and smiled. It was now okay to speak without bothering him.

" 'You know we're being watched,' I said to him.

" 'Yep,' he responded, already aware of what I was gonna say.

" 'We are always seeing unusual things in this here swamp.'

" 'Yep,' he repeated.

" 'Well, a big cat was lying on a tree limb back yonder a few minutes ago and watching us!'

" 'Yep,' he said. 'He's moved to another tree just now.' Then J.R. pointed to a hickory at the water's edge in front of us.

"Then I saw him. I didn't even know he had moved, but of course

J.R. did. He was a big, fuzzy bobcat, the biggest I'd ever seen. His ears were pointing right at us. His eyes never closed or blinked. For the longest time, he just stared at us, so curious, I guess.

"Then I said to J.R., 'He's watching like he *knows* you! How come he don't scat like most do?'

"J.R. chuckled. He paused a moment, then said something strange, 'His grandfather and me was friends. He's come to say good-bye.'

"I got a funny chill when J.R. said that. It was a hot summer day, but I felt cold. I tried not to cry, but it weren't no use. Then I knew. It was his way of telling me. We weren't never gonna go on a boat ride together again."[21]

POSTSCRIPT

J.R. McKinney had not been feeling well and, for the first time in his life (including his combat days), had begun to complain of fatigue and pains.

A local doctor prescribed some pills, which helped, but during the early morning of April 4, 1997, J.R. reported to his sister that his discomfort had increased significantly.

Betty immediately drove him to the Sylvania hospital. The staff there decided he needed a complete examination, which would require more than an overnight stay. Cost considered, it was believed that J.R. would be better served at the large VA Medical Center in Augusta, an hour away.

Around 11:00 P.M., an ambulance carried J.R. to Augusta, and Betty returned to her apartment.

At 3:00 A.M., she received a phone call from the VA Hospital. The nurse advised that a preliminary exam revealed there was nothing wrong with J.R. They wanted to do additional testing, but they were terribly short of beds. It was suggested that Betty take her brother home until space became available.

Betty phoned her son-in-law, Danny Lynn Derriso, who drove her to Augusta. They arrived at the VA Hospital at dawn and were directed to a hallway, where they found J.R. lying unconscious on a gurney.

Danny Lynn took his hand and squeezed it. "Uncle J.R., it's Lynn. Miss Betty is here with me. Can we get you anything?"

J.R. did not answer, but returned the squeeze.

Danny Lynn stayed, holding his friend's hand, from dawn until 3:00 P.M., when J.R.'s hand went limp.

The Phantom Warrior died Saturday, April 5, 1997, at 3:00 P.M. He was seventy-six.

The official cause of death was listed as "congenital heart failure."

The United States Army moved quickly and provided an honor guard for John McKinney. By direction of the Secretary of Army, he would be buried with full military honors.

Six soldiers from Fort Stewart Army Base carried the flag-draped casket through the old Double Heads Baptist Church Cemetery where seven riflemen stood at attention. On a command, they fired a volley three times—a twenty-one-gun salute to honor a national hero.

Later, members of the honor guard listened intently to the reading of the Army's official citation, which accompanied Sergeant John R. McKinney's Congressional Medal of Honor, the same words heard by President Harry Truman, General Dwight D. Eisenhower, and Admiral Chester W. Nimitz at the White House that January so long ago.

CITATION

Sergeant John Randolf McKinney

Rank and organization: Sergeant (then Private), U.S. Army, Company A, 123d Infantry, 33d Infantry Division. Place and date: Tayabas Province, Luzon, Philippine Islands, 11 May 1945. Entered service at: Woodcliff, Ga. Birth: Woodcliff, Ga. G.O. No.: 14, 4 February 1946. Citation: He fought with extreme gallantry to defend the outpost which had been established near Dingalan Bay. Just before daybreak approximately 100 Japanese stealthily attacked the perimeter defense, concentrating on a light machinegun position manned by 3 Americans. Having completed a long tour of duty at this gun, Pvt. McKinney was resting a few paces away when an enemy soldier dealt him a glancing blow on the head with a saber. Although dazed by the stroke, he seized his rifle, bludgeoned his attacker, and then shot another assailant who was charging him. Meanwhile, 1 of his comrades at the machinegun had been wounded and his other companion withdrew carrying the injured man to safety. Alone, Pvt. McKinney was confronted by 10 infantrymen who had captured the machinegun with the evident intent of reversing it to fire into the perimeter. Leaping into the emplacement, he shot 7 of them at pointblank range and killed 3 more with his rifle butt. In the melee the machinegun was rendered inoperative, leaving him only his rifle with which to meet the advancing Japanese, who hurled grenades and directed knee mortar shells into the perimeter. He warily changed position, secured more ammunition, and reloading repeatedly, cut down waves of the fanatical enemy with devastating fire or clubbed them to death in hand-to-hand combat. When assistance arrived, he had thwarted the assault and was in complete control of the area. Thirty-eight dead Japanese around the machinegun and 2 more at the side of a mortar 45 yards distant was the amazing toll he had exacted single-handedly. By his indomitable spirit, extraordinary fighting ability, and unwavering courage in the face of tremendous odds, Pvt. McKinney saved his company from possible annihilation and set an example of unsurpassed intrepidity.

EPILOGUE

In the general telling of American military history, the numbers involved in the Umiray outpost battle were small. The struggle was not for vast territory. The outcome provided no significant change in the overall course of conflict on Luzon, where American blood was spilled in copious amounts and the enemy was killed in staggering numbers.

On May 11, 1945, two groups of warriors, neither with artillery nor aircraft support, locked in a ferocious fight at close quarters.

The Japanese had numerical superiority and the element of surprise. Many soldiers were well-trained combat veterans. All were disciplined and determined, but most were hungry and exhausted. A victory at the outpost would have provided them with food and medical supplies they desperately needed.

They could have avoided the outpost by moving through the hills and mountains on their journey north. Was it hunger or stubborn arrogance that made them decide to attack the Americans? Or was it simply the fact that the outpost was there, occupied by their enemy? None survived to answer these questions.

The American defenders of the garrison at Umiray were few, thirty-eight at the most (counting Lieutenant Max Ladin's men) plus the guerrillas. All were well fed, morale was normal for any group of GIs dug in at a remote post, and they had sufficient weapons and ammunition to repel an enemy infantry unit. Every man at the outpost had months of combat experience. They knew what to expect and how to fight their enemy.

The shock of the sudden attack and the fact that a few Japanese penetrated the perimeter sent most of the Filipino guerrillas into panic and, thus, the defense was disrupted.

But the Japanese encountered something they did not expect. The fighting spirit and bravery of individual American soldiers.

John R. McKinney stood his ground, fought back, and helped turn possible defeat into victory. For that courageous action, he received the Congressional Medal of Honor, the highest award for bravery.

What saved John McKinney during the battle at the Umiray River outpost?

Most of the details of the battle and the events leading up to it are known. Can those facts be assembled to draw a logical conclusion?

McKinney was a superior marksman before the Army trained him. But his skills were more than simply having the ability to fire a rifle in a controlled environment such as a firing range. To that must be added the gift of patience, instinct, and the art of stalking and hunting in different lighting and weather conditions. Much of this he learned from the animals in his Georgia swamps as a young boy. Both he and the animals hunted and killed for survival.

Indeed, that is what he did during the battle—kill to survive.

The Army added new ways to kill and survive, emphasizing hand-to-hand combat and what to expect from the enemy.

The persistent Japanese use of the bayonet, often favoring an attack with that blade rather than firing their rifles, may have resulted in the deaths of a few of their soldiers as they attacked McKinney. But when they did shoot, even at close range, they missed.

Were scores of experienced Japanese infantrymen poor marksmen? Were they all too weak from hunger to hold a rifle steady? Not likely. Statistically, at least one bullet out of hundreds fired should have struck him during those thirty-five minutes.

And then there are the exploding hand grenades and mortar shells. To walk away from one blast, perhaps, is believable, but surviving three or four?

The Imperial soldier had the reputation of being the most aggressive, well-trained bayonet fighter during World War II, yet none even cut McKinney.

Can *luck* be considered? Perhaps. Someone survives an airliner crash and walks away while others die on impact. Four golfers are struck by lightning during a rainstorm; three die and one survives with no lasting injuries.

One moment of luck, but avoiding death moment after moment, minute after minute, for thirty-five minutes, is one for theologians to debate, not military historians.

Weapons, training, weather, fighting spirit, experience, instinct, marksmanship, valor, and luck, all are factors to consider. But even these do not give us an acceptable explanation.

John McKinney was a warrior, but was he a *phantom*? If one was facing a horrible-looking creature in a battle, and that thing was killing your friends but their bullets and yours did not stop him, you might think he was a phantom.

McKinney may have been a mysterious man, but he remained what he really wanted to be, a simple country boy trying to survive.

What saved McKinney during the battle? Scientific explanations thrown aside, it remains up to each individual to decide what they want to believe.

Perhaps 150 yards from where McKinney fought his lone battle, Second Lieutenant Edwin F. Voss reorganized the guerrillas and led them in a fierce counterattack. They killed all the Japanese in their sector. For his bravery Lieutenant Voss was presented the Silver Star Award.

A few yards away, Sergeant Leroy Nix stayed with his mortars, directing fire until his position was overrun by charging Japanese. He quickly organized and led his men in a counterattack, which drove the enemy from his section. For his bravery, Sergeant Nix was presented the Silver Star Award.

Close by, Staff Sergeant Neal A. Cowin risked his life to repair communication lines and directed his troops while standing near the enemy. For his "aggressive leadership," Sergeant Cowin was presented the Silver Star Award and later promoted to second lieutenant.

In the center of the outpost, Technical Sergeant Victor J. Wendling saved Lieutenant Ladin's life and killed Japanese soldiers while protecting his officer from those who had penetrated the perimeter. For his bravery, Sergeant Wendling was presented the Silver Star Award.

Five awards for courage were received by men who survived a battle lasting thirty-five minutes on an open, sandy beach, 150 yards long.

Some have speculated that the two-hundred-man Japanese force encountered by the Alamo Scouts may have regrouped and formed the nucleus of the unit that attacked the outpost on May 11. Would such a force have remained in the area for weeks? Unlikely, but possible. No records were uncovered to substantiate this.

In early June 1945, Major Robert Connolly was assigned to lead another Task Force, also bearing his name. They advanced along the west coast of Luzon linking up with the guerrilla army of Colonel Russell Volckmann. Harry Ice and John McKinney were not on that mission.

After the war, Robert Connolly left the Army and became commandant of cadets at Peekskill Military Academy. For a while his good friend Harry Ice served as assistant commandant.

Shortly after the Dingalan Bay assignment, Major Connolly and Captain Ice recommended First Lieutenant John F. Reardon for the Silver Star Award for his courage demonstrated during his intelligence-gathering patrols prior to boarding the B25's ill-fated flight.

Lieutenant Reardon's widow, Barbara, received the award posthumously on October 12, 1945.

The Army kept their promise to First Lieutenant Max Ladin. After he returned from Dingalan Bay, they granted the request for emergency leave so he could visit his ailing mother. But it was too late. He arrived home the day after she died.

Dr. Yoshio Nishima and his team lost the race to produce an atomic bomb before the United States, but he continued research for peacetime Japan. In 1946, Dr. Nishima was awarded the Order of Culture by the Emperor of Japan. Nishima worked in the field of cosmic rays and particle acceleration development.

Shortly after Japan's surrender the U.S. Army found five cyclotrons, part of the Japanese A-bomb project. The equipment was smashed and, on August 15, 1945, dumped into Tokyo Harbor.

The human-guided Baca suicide rocket did fly, and sank an American ship during the battle for Okinawa. Several ships were damaged by Bacas, but none of the other jet or rocket fighters, though advanced in technology, actually flew combat missions.

The outspoken Sixth Ranger captain who valued the lives of his men, Leo V. Strausbaugh, remained in the Army, retiring with the rank of colonel.

A few articles have appeared in the media over the years about the battle of Umiray outpost.

One claimed that the Japanese hid in nipa (grass) huts on the beach and waited until dawn to attack. Not true, there were no huts on the beach.

Typical of World War II propaganda, designed to inflame anger toward the enemy, another article claimed the Japanese soldiers "bayoneted a few babes in the huts before the attack." Although records indicate that the Imperial soldiers bayoneted infants during their occupation of the Philippines, there were no huts and no babies near the outpost. Children were bayoneted in the Umiray village, but that was a mile from the outpost.

Connolly Task Force patrols captured and questioned Japanese soldiers prior to May 11. None were officers. Someone may have revealed that Imperial troops were "massing" and planned to attack the outpost, but in the author's opinion, Japanese enlisted men would not have been privileged to the attack plan, especially the exact date and time.

The men I interviewed stated they had "no warning" of an attack coming at dawn on May 10 or May 11.

Lieutenant Ladin confirmed they'd received routine radio messages advising the outpost to stay alert, but that was all. As Max Ladin put it, "If we knew the Japanese planned to attack that morning, would I be sleeping in the open with a helmet over my face?"

Contrary to published reports, the surviving members of the Umiray outpost state that Major Connolly and Captain Ice never visited their base before May 11. The "bunkers" at the outpost had no logs or sandbags to strengthen their defense; only sand and dirt piled up for protection.

When I traveled in Luzon, the Sierra Madre Mountains near Dingalan Bay still supported lush, green forests. But logging operations have removed large sections of vegetation. The Philippine government finally stepped in to control the logging and establish programs of conservation.

But in some areas around the bay, mud slides destroyed or buried sections of the beach.

There are resorts at the bay now where people from all over the world (including Japan) come to swim, fish, and water-ski in the beautiful waters once sacred to the Dumagats.

Nothing remains at the Umiray River outpost area to remind anyone of that battle on the sandbar long ago. Even the name of the province has changed from Tayabas to Aurora.

Do Aswangs and the Dwende really exist? John McKinney didn't believe in them, but the majority of Filipinos then and many today still hold on to the superstitions.

I questioned an older Filipino about the Dwende. (It was 2006 in the States, not the Philippines.) His strong answer in Tagalog was, *"Hindi brio ito!"* Then he followed up in English: "It is not a joke, sir! But where I come from, the Dwende does not live in a tree. They live under little dirt mounds. You must walk around that place, so you do not disturb them!"

In mid-January 1946, John McKinney was no longer in Japan, but some of the men of his 123rd Regiment still patrolled sectors around Takarazuka.

On January 20, patrols were called in to base. At 11:59 P.M. the regiment was relieved of occupation duty. By January 28, men who had not accumulated enough "points" to return to the States were transferred to other units. The 123rd Infantry Regiment had ceased to exist.

The Golden Cross Thirty-third Infantry Division was officially "inactivated" on February 5, 1946. As it was when they departed in secret for the Pacific, there were no parades or handsome ceremonies to honor the men who had served their country so gallantly.

Shortly before John McKinney left Japan, a news reporter for AP cornered Captain Harry Ice. Word had circulated that McKinney was to receive the Congressional Medal of Honor from President Truman. Armed Forces Radio and military and civilian media raced for the best "inside" story.

"Did McKinney save the entire unit?" the reporter asked Captain Ice.

"Yes," Ice replied. "If the Japs had advanced ten more yards before McKinney went into action, it would have been just too bad for them all!"

"Tell us about Private McKinney, Captain. What sort of man is he?"

"*Sergeant* McKinney," Ice countered. "He's been promoted to sergeant."

Captain Ice paused, perhaps to let his announcement sink in, or maybe he searched for words to describe a rifleman no one really knew very well.

"It's hard to tell you much about Sergeant McKinney," Ice finally answered. "He's one of those boys who has always done his job."

There are no previous books on the life of John R. McKinney. He left no personal papers or diary, according to his sister, Betty, who remained close to him until his death.

I never met J.R. He had passed away shortly before I connected his name to the battle at Dingalan Bay. He was a man of quality I would have liked to know, not so much because of his war record but for his uniqueness.

In some ways I related to J.R. I grew up in the South a few years behind his generation, and I fished and hunted in wilderness country similar to Screven County, Georgia.

A treasure of detailed information and feelings were generously shared with me by his family, wartime buddies, and hunting pals so I could tell his story. I walked the pig paths through the woods and swamps J.R. once traveled, and visited the hot, humid, insect-infested sandbar where he fought to save the lives of his friends.

The likes of John R. McKinney are fading from existence in America just like the mountain men of an earlier time. Those who know how to support their family from the wilderness are few. Indeed, in many areas of the country, even the wilderness is gradually disappearing. But it is reassuring to know that in an hour of need, America has and still produces brave, unselfish warriors who are willing to sacrifice for what our country believes right and decent.

ACKNOWLEDGMENTS

Human memory is fragile, often incomplete, and subject to suggestion. The mind is not a video recorder. It does not record accurately and play everything back on demand.

One might think that details of a battle would be etched into a soldier's memory forever. Watching friends die, listening to screams of pain, bullets snapping past, and the concussion of exploding shells are memories never forgotten completely. But to survive and continue a somewhat normal life, the brain blocks, rearranges, and often hides images and feelings.

New recollections, replacing the original, cover the more painful memories.

The need to remember things a certain way sometimes leads one to report details incorrectly. Time isn't the only factor obscuring memories. Stress and danger play a part from the beginning.

Regardless of good intentions, people often remember a particular incident differently. Oddly, I have discovered the same is not always true when one recalls conversation. Two former warriors may differ on who fired a machine gun during an enemy attack, but they often agree on just who said what and how it was said.

The people of Screven County, Georgia, proved their reputation of being some of the most polite, hospitable souls in America. They provided the valuable information about "J.R." McKinney's prewar and postwar days. Many had stories to tell about their hero. But John

McKinney himself, though polite and friendly, was at the same time quiet and elusive. To many he remained as much of a phantom in Screven County as he was to the Japanese soldiers trying to kill him on May 11, 1945.

Some county residents, including relatives, report that J.R. would suddenly appear at church, a store, or a gathering. Then, it seemed, he vanished. No one saw or heard him leave.

All the farmers knew John McKinney. He was welcomed to hunt any time on any farm. And the streams and rivers all belonged to him when it came to fishing. The workers of the land knew more about J.R.'s skills as a woodsman than thay did about his war record.

Many I interviewed said, "J.R. was a good man! He would always stop and say 'Howdy' and then seem to disappear."

The people knew him and liked him and respected him, but they did not know his thoughts and true feelings. Fortunately, there were a few who really *knew* John R. McKinney.

Betty McKinney Pitts shared her childhood memories of growing up with her "favorite" brother, J.R. They lived together before the war, experiencing the poverty and hard work of a sharecropper's family in that cabin with no electricity. They fished and hunted and shared secrets together until the war. Then, when J.R. returned, he lived with his family. When their parents were gone, brother and sister had apartments in the same building in Sylvania, Georgia.

Ms. Pitts was an elegant, proud lady with an extraordinarily colorful memory sprinkled with calmness and controlled emotion.

We spent many hours on the telephone over three years during which she shared her memories of her brother. I was especially interested in J.R.'s *feelings*. What sort of man was he? These were things no one else could relate, information so important in my construction of J.R.'s personality profile.

When I visited Sylvania, Georgia, Ms. Pitts, her daughter, Sue, and Sue's husband, Danny Lynn Derriso, were very generous with their time and hospitality. We had spent hours on the phone for so many years, it was truly like visiting relatives or, perhaps better still, close friends.

Emotions often were heavy as Ms. Pitts recalled certain events.

One which will always haunt me is her description of J.R. the day the wagon wheel ran over a quail nest and his efforts to reconstruct the nest. We were at the spot where it occurred, and I felt as if I had been there with them as Mrs. McKinney convinced her son to join the family for dinner.

Sadly, Betty McKinney Pitts passed away as I completed my manuscript.

When Betty's daughter, Sue, married Danny Lynn Derriso, J.R. received a new friend and a very special one at that.

Danny Lynn had served his country both in the National Guard and as a Georgia State Trooper. He was just what the aging war hero needed.

As Danny Lynn once put it, "It takes a warrior to recognize and understand a warrior." And so the two soon became hunting and fishing buddies.

Mr. Derriso is a powerful, large, but gentle man with strong religious convictions. And his friendship with J.R. developed into an extremely close one over the years; not only because of family ties, but because of the quality of two individuals with mutual interests.

Even though John McKinney was a very private sort of man, he felt comfortable from time to time confiding in Danny Lynn.

"Sometimes we would sit on a log during hunting and let the dogs run on ahead of us," Mr. Derriso told me. "Then, sometimes Uncle J.R.'s face would freeze and he seemed to be staring at something far away. Then, after a while, he would make a short statement, remembering the war. 'I felt real bad for them Jap boys being a-wasted in stupid attacks. They must of known they were all gonna die.'" Such was one comment.

The entire Derriso family made me very comfortable during my visit to Screven County. Their kindness and interest in my project is certainly appreciated. We ate together and went to church together and traveled the old road around J.R.'s birthplace. And I learned more about John McKinney the man.

I carry the little New Testament Bible given to me by Danny Lynn in my briefcase every day. And yes, my friend, I read it.

After four years of researching the story of John McKinney, my notes, articles, interviews, archives, after-action reports, photographs, and maps fill drawers of file cabinets. So please forgive me if I accidentally missed crediting someone who assisted me in my research. The omission is certainly not intentional.

Special thanks to former members of the 123rd Infantry Regiment who shared their personal photographs, collections of news clippings, notes, diaries, and memories, many often painful and sad.

A few of those who knew and served with John McKinney and spent hours with me on the telephone relating experiences are: Gene A. Maziarz, Donald W. Murphy, Gerry Rampy, Gerry Nutt, Raymond H. Timmer, Dr. Sol Rocke.

Also my gratitude to Bill Endicott, editor (and author) of the Thirty-third Infantry Division Newsletter; Henry Van Westrop, the Thirty-third Division's historical photographer, who provided some of his fascinating photos; Master Sergeant Ed Hines, USMC (Retired), for his work on maps and related graphics; and my typist, Ms. Linda L. Heimerman, who had the marvelous ability to understand my scratched-over pages of notes I called "chapters" and my Southern dialect on tapes.

In 2004 I traveled to Houston, Texas, to interview Max Ladin, who, at age eighty-nine, was the only living officer who fought at the Umiray River outpost. Max no longer had the helmet that saved him from that first sword blow, but he did have the sword.

We spent the day discussing the battle from his perspective, viewing old photographs, military and personal records. As luck would have it, Max had carried a small camera with him to the outpost. The photos he permitted me to use may be, as faded as they are, the only (ground-level) ones in existence giving us some record of the results of that terrible battle.

The hospitality of Max and his family made my learning experience and visit there most pleasant.

Within a year, both Mrs. Ladin and Max Ladin had passed away. I am grateful to their daughter, Michelle Ladin Blackburn, and the Ladin family for continuing to provide valuable records for my work.

The knowledge of the Alamo Scout history of my friend, author Lance Q. Zedrick, was very helpful. I strongly recommend his book, *Silent Warriors of World War II—The Alamo Scouts Behind Japanese Lines,* to all who are interested in "Special Operations" and the history of those brave Americans.

Colonel Sanford H. Winston was ordered (some say, "requested") by Major General P.W. Clarkson, the Thirty-third Division commander, to compile a World War II history of their unit. Colonel Winston's extensive work, entitled *The Golden Cross: A History of the 33rd Infantry Division,* served as an encyclopedia for my book. Sanford Winston accomplished what many would have considered an impossible mission, but the results are informative, exciting to read, and a very valuable contribution to U.S. military history.

Stan W. Carlson's *Regimented History—123rd Infantry* provided me with basic information on each soldier who fought with John McKinney.

I owe sincere gratitude to my literary agent, Agnes Birnbaum of Bleecker Street and Associates of New York City, who was blessed with patience, understanding, and marketing (as well as editorial) intelligence. So often I would seek her guidance and beg forgiveness for my delays. "I have found some new fantastic data I must analyze and maybe include," I would explain. And her reply: "Don't worry, I'm right here, I'm not going anywhere!" Thank you for being "there."

And finally my wife, Chieko Takeuchi, who grew up in Japan during the American bombing raids and later "occupation." Long before we met, she became a recording star in Japan, had her own radio show, and with the stage name of "Chiaki Keiko" went on to dominate the top ten charts for five straight years. Producers arranged performances in America, and later Chiaki stayed in the U.S. as a performer.

Her knowledge of Japan's culture and history provided accurate color for some of my descriptions. But her greatest contribution was her gift of listening and understanding the feelings of those involved— both Japanese and American. Thank you for keeping my ship on course and assuring me that it would make it through all the storms in my life.

Alamo Scouts Contributors

Frank Fox
Sergeant Major Galen Kittleson
  (deceased)
Colonel Bob Sumner (deceased)

6th Rangers Contributors

Roy Potts
Robert Prince
James Robbins
Colonel Leo Strausbaugh

Guerrilla Warriors (Luzon) Contributors

Colonel Bernard Anderson
  (deceased)
Major Robert Lapham
  (deceased)
Major Juan Pajota (deceased)
Luis Taruc
Josefa Hilado Torre, R.N.

Japanese Culture and History
Contributors

Chiaki Keiko (Chieko Takeuchi
  Johnson)
Professor Hitoshi Miyake
Wally Morishige
Kunio Yahiro

Other Contributors

Atlanta Chamber of Commerce
Atlanta Historical Society
*The Atlanta Journal-
  Constitution*
Atlanta Public Library

Augusta Chronicle
The Department of the Air Force,
  Historical Research Agency
Department of History, Georgia
Dixon, Illinois, Fire Department
Franklin D. Roosevelt Presidential
  Library, Hyde Park, New York
Georgia Department of Industry,
  Trade, and Tourism
Georgia Historical Society
Illinois State Museum of Military
  History
Live Oak Public Library,
  Savannah, Georgia
Many citizens of Screven County,
  Georgia
Sylvania, Georgia, Chamber of
  Commerce
Sylvania, Georgia, Visitors Center
Sylvania Telephone News
33rd Infantry Division Newsletter
The United States National
  Archives

Tom and Lynda Avery
G. L. Bergen
Jaffre Boston
Charles Burow
Charles Duncan
Gerry Edenfield
Ms. Nellie Edenfield
Jack Finch
Tom Frates
Jesse Frazer

George Leoni
William Mallory
Mr. and Mrs. William McKinney
Nolen Miller
Harold and Joann Parker
Alan Pohl
Colonel Andy Pribnow
Lieutenant Colonel Ted
  Pribnow
Paul Rusnak

General Frank Sackton
Donald Scott
Donald L. Singer, National
  Archives
Bennie Villamin
Clair Wagner
John Weatherwax
Marion Williams
Morton Wolfson
Colonel Chan Wysor

NOTES

Chapter 1

1 33rd Infantry Division Newsletter, Vol. 10, No. 4, Dec. 1995.
2 *The Golden Cross,* pp. 186–187.
3 *The Golden Cross,* pp. 313–317.
4 33rd Infantry Division Newsletter, Vol. 1, No. 3, June 1986.
5 Danny Lynn Derriso, John McKinney's nephew and hunting companion, furnished most of the information for the Nashville trip during a series of interviews. Lynn later retired from the Georgia State Police.
6 Interview, Danny Lynn Derriso.
7 Ibid.
8 John McKinney had discussed his feelings regarding "moving about" or changing positions with his sister, Betty. Interview with Betty Pitts.
9 John McKinney often referred to the animals in the swamp as "my friends," crediting much of his "backwoods" knowledge to them. Interview, Betty Pitts.
10 Pig path—a trail through underbrush or through the woods, created by wild pigs traveling along the same path, over and over. Story of this particular hunt related in interviews with Betty Pitts and Jack Finch, a hunting companion of J.R.'s.
11 Jenk had a reputation of repeating "ghost" stories he heard from county African American farmers. J.R. told his sister Betty that he never believed in ghosts. Still, he said, "When one is in the dark swamp and thinks about those stories, it can give you the creeps!"
12 J.R. reported to Betty that he had the feeling more than once that he was the "hunted."
13 Interview with Betty Pitts. There were many bobcats in the area when J.R. was young. They were seldom seen by farmers. But J.R. told his sister he credited the cats with introducing him to the importance of patience as much as his father had emphasized it for fishing.
14 Interview with Betty Pitts and Danny Lynn Derriso. J.R. learned to identify the sounds made by animals in the woods and he understood the meaning of a few of them.
15 Interview, Betty Pitts. From time to time, many years later J.R. questioned if changing positions played a significant part in his battle on May 11, 1945.

Chapter 2

1 Interview, Betty Pitts.
2 Ibid.
3 Fifteenth Census of the U.S., 1930, District 1653, Screven County, Georgia. sheet No. 34, roll 3841, book 1, page 198.
4 Interview, Betty Pitts.
5 Ibid.
6 In later years, some of J.R.'s hunting friends who noticed the scar thought it resulted from a war injury. Actually, the scar was from his pneumonia surgery.
7 Interview, Betty Pitts.
8 Interview, Betty Pitts and Danny Lynn Derriso.
9 Interview, Danny Lynn Derriso.
10 Interview, Betty Pitts.
11 Opinions expressed by a number of family friends in and around Sylvania, Georgia—author's note.
12 Interview, Betty Pitts.
13 Interview, Harold Parker, Jr.
14 Ibid.
15 Interview, Betty Pitts, and Harold Parker, Jr.
16 Interview, Danny Lynn Derriso.
17 Interview, Betty Pitts.
18 Ibid.
19 Ibid.
20 Ibid.

Chapter 3

1 Banzai, literally, ten thousand years. A cheer used to wish one long life and good luck. During World War II the Japanese used this cheer as a shout of encouragement and reassurance when charging American positions; thus, the GI labeled the attacks "banzai charges."
2 Forbes Monagham, *Under the Red Sun,* p. 124.
3 Hiroo Onoda, *No Surrender,* p. 60.
4 Interview, Kunio Yahiro, former Imperial Navy pilot.
5 Cook & Cook, *Japan at War,* pp. 40–46.
6 Robert Lapham and Bernard Norling, *Lapham's Raiders,* p. 9.
7 Ray C. Hunt and Bernard Norling, *Behind Japanese Lines,* p. 29.
8 Author's interviews: Juan Pajota, Major, USA; Josefa Hilado Torre, First Lieutenant U.S. Army Nurse.
9 Ray C. Hunt and Bernard Norling, *Behind Japanese Lines,* p. 29. The "religion" explanation was mostly advanced by Catholic priests living in Japan prior to the war. It only scratches the surface of a very complex subject. Japanese Christians in Japan during World War II were about 2 or 3 percent of the population. In 1995, perhaps they were 5 percent. It is the observation of the author that some Japanese Christians exhibit the same shifts in mood during a single conversation.

With the very tight cultural restrictions in Japan, such behavior is not well accepted. The "flip-flop" shifts in mood still continue. But it would not be fair nor accurate to generalize and say that "all" Japanese behave with this trait, any more than it is to say that all Americans are talkative and love to fight with little provocation; some do, some do not.

10 Hiroo Onoda, *No Surrender,* p. 161.

11 Ibid.

12 Bushido, literally, "the way of the warrior," a code and way of life developed for a class of warriors known as samurai between the ninth and twelfth centuries, A.D. These men were similar to medieval knights of Europe, serving a lord and assisting in maintaining order in the country while always preparing to be the first line of defense against outside aggressors. Amongst many things, Bushido placed emphasis on obedience, service, self-sacrifice, loyalty, and honor.

13 James Bradley, *Flyboy,* p. 40.

14 *Tonto,* literally, "short sword," usually a handmade knife about six to twelve inches long with one edge sharpened, similar in size (but not shape) to American hunting knives.

15 "Japanese soldiers function with group mentality. The men are almost helpless when their leaders are killed." *War Reconn,* report of Captain Andy Pribnow, S3, 98th Field Artillery Battalion and Captain, W.C. Porter, asst., S3, Headquarters, First Corps, U.S. 6th Army, dated March 31, 1943.

16 Cook and Cook, *Japan at War,* pp. 145–167.

17 Robert Lapham and Bernard Norling, *Lapham's Raiders,* pg. 217; Hiroo Onoda, *No Surrender,* p. 69.

Chapter 4

1 Interview, Betty Pitts.

2 Interviews, Betty Pitts and Danny Lynn Derriso.

3 Interview, Betty Pitts.

4 Betty Pitts retained a vivid memory of the quail nest incident. Sixty-two years later she and the author visited the exact location and she related the entire story in emotional detail.

5 Interview, Betty Pitts.

6 Speech, Franklin D. Roosevelt Presidential Library, Hyde Park, N.Y. "I Can Hear It Now" by Edward R. Murrow and Fred W. Friendly. "Actual voice of Roosevelt" (recorded, 78 RPM), Columbia Records, 1948.

7 Interview, Betty Pitts.

8 Fireside Chat #140, Franklin D. Roosevelt Presidential Library, Hyde Park, NY.

9 Ibid.

10 Interview, Betty Pitts, who believed J.R.'s shyness and lack of social awareness prevented him from developing a serious relationship with a girl. More on this subject in future chapters.

Chapter 5

1 Most American guerrillas promoted themselves to a higher rank not so much to impress the Filipinos, but also to serve notice on the Imperial Army that American officers were still

leading Filipinos. General MacArthur later acknowledged and honored each rank, concluding that those men had not only endured extreme hardships, but were successful in commanding combat units large enough to be worthy of the rank. Robert Lapham and Bernard Norling, *Lapham's Raiders,* p. 217.

2 Ibid.
3 Interview, Juan Pajota.
4 Robert Lapham and Bernard Norling, *Lapham's Raiders,* p. 219.
5 Ibid.
6 Luis Taruc, *He Who Rides the Tiger,* p. 18.
7 Interview, Luis Taruc.
8 Interview, Robert Lapham.
9 Interview, Bernard Anderson.
10 Interview, Juan Pajota and Robert Lapham.
11 Robert Lapham and Bernard Norling, *Lapham's Raiders.* Also, interview, Robert Lapham.
12 Interview, Juan Pajota.

Chapter 6

1 Interview, Betty Pitts.
2 Nattie McKinney related this to Betty Pitts near the end of the war. Interview, Betty Pitts.
3 Ibid.
4 Uncle Russ, the moonshiner. Not his real name, and the true name of the location of the still was "Nigger Island." Russ discussed his visit with J.R. a year or two into the war with Nattie McKinney and Betty Pitts. Interview, Betty Pitts.
5 Interview, Betty Pitts.

Chapter 7

1 *The Golden Cross.* Considerable information for this chapter can be found in this historical report of Captain Sanford H. Winston. Captain Winston was ordered by Major General P.W. Clarkson in 1948 to assemble the data for this book, which remains the most complete record available of the Thirty-third Division in World War II.
2 Ibid., p. 17.
3 *History of the 123rd Infantry Regiment,* p. 28.
4 U.S. Archives, Washington, D.C.
5 Interview, Betty Pitts.
6 Robert Wilcox, *Japan's Secret War.*
7 Ibid.

Chapter 8

1 Interview, Betty McKinney Pitts.
2 *The Golden Cross,* p. 19.
3 Interview, Betty Pitts.
4 Ibid.

5 *The Golden Cross*, p. 20.

6 Interview, Gerry Rampy who overheard the Johnson and McKinney conversation.

7 Robert Lapham and Bernard Norling, *Lapham's Raiders*, p. 41.

8 *The Golden Cross*, p. 21.

9 The details of the party were conveyed to author during an interview with Gene Maziarz.

10 *The Golden Cross*, p. 36.

Chapter 9

1 *The West Point Atlas of American Wars*, Vol. II, p. 139.

2 *The Golden Cross*, p. 41.

3 Interview, Betty Pitts.

4 *The Flying Dinosaur* was so named for the appearance of the silhouette of the island of New Guinea on a map. Some believed that outline resembled a dinosaur with its head at the north and its tail pointing south.

5 *History of the 123rd Regiment*, p. 78. Interview, Betty Pitts, who also reported that after the war John showed no interest in baseball until later in life when, through the marvels of television, he could watch a game once more she said that "JR before the war, never had the time to play anyway. He might watch part of a game at a school or churchyard, then return to his chores or be off fishing and hunting."

6 *The Golden Cross*, p. 51.

7 Interview, Dr. Sol Rocke and Gene Maziarz.

8 Interview, Dr. Sol Rocke.

9 Interview, Gene Maziarz.

10 Interview, Gerry Rampy.

11 Interview, Dr. Sol Rocke.

12 Interview, Eugene Maziarz.

13 Interview, Bob Colwell.

14 A Company, 123rd Infantry morning report, August 28, 1944, National Archives Data provided courtesy of Colonel Ray H. Timmer.

Chapter 10

1 *The Golden Cross*, pp. 51–67.

2 *History of the 123rd Infantry*, p. 210.

3 Bazooka, a portable shoulder weapon for firing armor-piercing 2.36-inch rockets. Gained its name from its resemblance to the crude musical horn of the same name used by a radio comedian at the time, Bob Burns.

4 Historical records—Headquarters 123rd Regimental Combat Team, APO 323, 1 Sept 44–27 Jan 45, #735017, p. 1. Declassified from "Secret," 1996.

5 *The Golden Cross*, p. 54.

6 The most complete history of the Alamo Scouts is provided by historian Lance Q. Zedric in his book *Silent Warriors of World War II*.

7 *The Golden Cross*, p. 58.

8 Interview, Betty Pitts. According to his sister, J.R. spoke little about his experiences in New

Guinea, but did describe one firefight in which he noted Ed Colwell performing in combat one night "like an experienced rifleman."

9 The complete story of Lieutenant Durant's ill-fated mission can be found in *The Golden Cross*, p. 65.

Chapter 11

1 Letters to author from Colonel Leo Strausbaugh. Both Strausbaugh and Simons became colonels before retiring from the Army. "Bull" Simons is a legend to those familiar with military Special Operations. He led an attack force behind enemy lines in Vietnam in an attempt to rescue American POWs held at Son Tay, and was later involved in military rescue missions in the Middle East. Captain James Fisher, M.D., was killed by metal fragments from a Japanese mortar round during the Ranger raid on POW Camp Cabanatuan, Luzon, on the night of January 30, 1945. (Colonel Strausbaugh emphasized in a letter to the author about the lighthouse battle: "Bull was not cursing me; that was his vocabulary!")

2 *West Point Atlas of American Wars*, Vol. II, pp. 146–150.

3 Ibid.

4 *The Golden Cross*, pgs. 68–80.

5 Ibid., p. 70.

6 *West Point Atlas of American Wars*, Vol. II, pp. 146–150.

7 Letters to author from Professor Hitoshi Miyaki.

8 U.S. Air Force Museum, Wright Patterson Air Force Base, Ohio. *Japanese Aircraft of the Pacific*, Naval Institute Press, 1979, Carlos Iodon.

Chapter 12

1 For a detailed, accurate accounting of the Rangers' Cabanatuan Raid, see *Hour of Redemption* by author.

2 Robert Lapham and Bernard Norling, *Lapham's Raiders*, pp. 207–217.

3 Ibid.

4 *The Golden Cross*, p. 119.

5 Ibid., p. 123.

6 Interviews with Gene Maziarz and Gerry Rampy. A "spent" round (or bullet) is one that has lost its full velocity and impact because of the distance it traveled, or because it struck something en route, or because the explosive charge propelling it was insufficient.

7 Napalm, gelled petroleum used to make fire bombs.

8 *123rd Infantry Historical Report—Luzon Campaign*. Originally classified "Secret." Declassified and released in the National Archives, 1947.

9 Ibid.

10 Interview, Gerald Nutt.

Chapter 13

1 Interview, Gene Maziarz.

2 Interview, Sol Rocke.

3   *The Golden Cross,* p. 151.

4   Interview, Betty Pitts.

5   *The Golden Cross,* p. 152.

6   *123rd Infantry Historical Report,* National Archives, 1947.

7   *The Golden Cross,* pp. 159–160.

8   *Japan's Secret War* and notes by historian Robert Wilcox.

Chapter 14

1   Interview (and letters from) Lance Q. Zedric, author of *Silent Warriors of World War II—The Alamo Scouts Behind Japanese Lines.* According to Mr. Zedric, there were so many missions assigned the Scouts in the Philippines between February and August 1945 that some reports simply became "missing." Being an excellent military researcher, Lance has, by employing his own unique technique, uncovered most of those misfiled reports. Fortunately, he located the Umiray River report in time for this book. There are historical documents reporting the fact that Alamo Scouts were active in the Dingalan Bay area in April-May 1945, but not one identified the team until Lance Zedric worked his magic.

2   National Archives, "Alamo Scouts Training Center—Report of Umiray River Dingalan Bay Mission, April 23, to May 10." Furnished to author by Lance Zedric. Most of the data regarding Scout activities at Dingalan is from this report.

3   "United Nippons"—although Sergeant Farrow's report does not elaborate or identify the nationality of those men, it is the author's conclusion that they most likely were Taiwanese (Formosans) or Koreans. Both countries were under Japanese domination at the time and furnished men to serve as soldiers or workers. Many young women from Formosa and Korea were forced to serve as "comfort women" or "sex slaves" for the Imperial Army.

4   Some historical reports state that the sawmill (actually two mills very close together) was operated by I Corps. No one "operated" the mill in April-May 1945. Anderson's guerrillas simply moved in after the Japanese workers fled. Contrary to other reports, the mill had no strategic value until the American task force arrived, turning the area into their headquarters and command center.

5   *The Golden Cross,* p. 284.

6   Ibid.

7   Ibid. As stated, the sawmill had no strategic value to the Americans. The Filipino guerrillas called it a "valuable installation" in hopes I Corps would pay more attention to their request for American support. The mills, of course, would become important after the war during the rebuilding of the country.

8   Interview, Betty Pitts.

9   Interview, Chiaki Keiko, music historian and Japanese recording star of the 1950s and 1960s.

Chapter 15

1   Interrogation Reports—I Corps, May–June 1945, National Archives. Survivors reported that Masayuki was uncharacteristically nervous during his confrontation with the geisha. We can only guess about his personal relationship, if any, with the girl.

2 Chiyo was not her real name.

3 *"Western-style dress ... undergarments." Golden Cross,* pp. 297–298. 123rd Infantry Historical Report—National Archives; 136th Infantry Division, May–June 1945; "After Action Report"—National Archives.

4 Description of Colonel Muto offered by Japanese POWs—U.S. Archives, Provost Marshal Report, I Corps, National Archives.

5 *Tonto,* hand-made knife with straight blade, one edge sharpened, blunt tip, usually 6–12 inches long.

6 Interrogation Reports—I Corps Intelligence Section; also, Provost Marshal Reports, I Corps, National Archives.

Chapter 16

1 Interview, Max Ladin.

2 Interview, Donald Murphy, then Second Lieutenant, 136th Infantry.

3 123rd Infantry After-Action Report, National Archives.

4 Interview, Roy Potts.

5 Interview, Colonel Leo Strausbaugh.

6 Interview, James Robbins.

7 Interview, Gene Maziarz.

8 Ibid.

9 Interview, Max Ladin—also, "Qualification Record—U.S. Army WD-AGO Form 100, July 1, 1945—1st Lieutenant Max Ladin, Infantry.

10 Interview, Betty Pitts.

11 Interview, Max Ladin.

12 History of Operations, 136th Infantry, Februay 11–June 30, 1945, National Archives.

13 *The Golden Cross,* p. 291.

Chapter 17

1 Interview, Gene Maziarz.

2 Ibid. The ambush story was shared with author by Gene Maziarz.

3 The flag is often called a *hinomaru yoseguki.* The accepted meaning is "Rising Sun flag-gathered writings." A small (usually about two feet by three feet) flag carried by most Imperial soldiers as an inspiration and for good luck. Often signed by friends and family in black ink, offering words of encouragement ("fight hard," "be brave," etc.).

4 Interview, Gene Maziarz. Flag translation by Chiaki Keiko Johnson.

5 *The Golden Cross,* p. 289.

6 Ibid., p. 292.

7 Ibid., p. 291.

8 Interviews, Colonel Leo Strausbaugh, and letters from the colonel regarding the confrontation with Major Connolly over the Dingalan assignment.

9 All information regarding the B25 Lieutenant Reardon boarded was provided by The Department of the Air Force Historical Research Agency, Maxwell Air Force Base, Alabama.

10 *The Golden Cross,* p. 289. "Headquarters, I Corps, General Order 231, October 12, 1945—Sect 1."

Chapter 18

1 Bolo, a narrow, single-edge blade with a slight curve, usually eighteen to twenty-four inches long, similar to a machete. The handle is made of wood or caribou horn. Used as a harvest tool or weapon.

2 Juan Pajota, hero of the Cabu Bridge battle during the Ranger raid on POW Camp Cabanatuan, became military governor of Nueva Ecija Province and later a college professor in the Philippines. Pajota came to the States and lived with the author for a year. Pajota often shared his Aswang stories and had a "little black book" that contained the "magic words" to be chanted over a bolo before "one does battle with an Aswang." In 1976 he permitted the author to see the "book."

3 Alamo Scout Report of Umiray River-Dingalan Bay mission, May 10, 45—National Archives.

4 *Japan's Secret War* by Robert Wilcox, and *Hirohito, Behind the Myth* by Edward Behr.

5 POW Interrogation Reports, 6th U.S. Army, Luzon 1945, National Archives.

6 After Action Report, 123rd Infantry, May–July 1945, National Archives.

7 *The Augusta Chronicle,* Sunday, January 13, 1946, p. 18, part 2.

8 Allied Geographical Terrain Handbook, Luzon, 1945, National Archives.

9 Connolly Task Force After Action Report, Luzon, April–May 1945, National Archives.

10 POW Interrogation Reports, 6th U.S. Army, Luzon, 1945.

11 The adulteration of the Filipino word *bondoc* (mountain) became a part of American slang (*boondocks*).

12 Interview, Gerry Rampy.

13 Ibid.

14 Ibid.

Chapter 19

1 Interview, Betty Pitts. McKinney told his sister, Ms. Betty Pitts, after the war that the Dwende story gave him "a few chuckles." According to Ms. Pitts, McKinney respected people's superstitions having encountered a variety of them in rural Georgia from "both white and black folks."

2 The "new sun" often referred to as "rising sun," thus the expression "land of the rising sun."

3 Interview, Jack Fench. Years after the war, McKinney, admiring the bobcat's natural instincts, often related his experiences with the cat to his hunting pals.

4 The Defense Agency War History Department, Army Units in the Pacific, Book One, Tokyo, Japan. Imperial Army strategy usually called for encircling attacks before a massive assault on the center of enemy defenses. But at this outpost, with a river on one side and the bay on the other, the tactics were impossible. Therefore, according to Japanese military thinking at the time, the whole weight of the unit must be launched to attack at one point, usually at the center.

Interview, Juan Pajota, Major, U.S. Army. "You can eventually expect the entire Jap unit to come right down the alley, as you Americans say."

5   *Lapham's Raiders,* p. 192, and interview, Major Robert Lapham. "Japanese military lead-ers often displayed narrow-minded mentality in planning assaults, even when they must have known they had no chance of success. They assumed what they wanted to assume, their plan was perfect so no alternatives were necessary."

6   Literally means "high-above-the-head style," a form used by ancient Japanese swordsmen. The weapon is pointed upward, perpendicular to the ground.

7   Interview, Max Ladin. Sergeant Morii Fukutaro was identified by his personal flag, which, on May 11th, he carried under his shirt. Recovered after the battle, the flag is now in the possession of Max Ladin, former first lieutenant, United States Army. Writings on the flag read, in part, "Presented to Morii Fukutaro with a prayer to try to fight hard."

8   Ibid. Sergeant Yamashita was identified by his personal *inkan* and a cloth ID tag inside his uniform. Both are in possession of Max Ladin, who also has the sword that Yoshi tried to decapitate him with.

9   Technical Sergeant Victor Wendling received the Silver Star for saving Lieutenant Max Ladin's life and killing all five members of Sergeant Yoshi's squad with his M1 rifle.

10 BAR, Browning automatic rifle.

11 Interview, Jack Finch. McKinney told his hunting friend Jack Finch that the first sight of Japanese troops charging made him feel "like something was crawling just under my skin."

12 Interview, Betty Pitts. McKinney told his sister Betty that he didn't expect to survive the first charge.

13 Ibid. Sensations as explained to his sister Betty.

14 *Chicago Daily News,* May 21, 1945. McKinney mentioned this to war correspondent Ger-ald R. Thorp, and two days later, the paper ran Thorp's report describing McKinney as an American hero and labeled him as "The Georgia Cyclone."

15 Banzai (literally, ten thousand years), used by Japanese during World War II as a salute, victory cheer, and often a battle cry. GIs called suicide-type attacks "banzai" charges due to the shouting of the word by enemy troops. Used in modern times as a greeting or salute to wish someone or one's self good luck and long life.

Chapter 20

1   John McKinney, in various media interviews, referred to the spear as a "long pole," never comprehending just how critical the moment might have been if the spearman had used a different movement and jabbed with the sharpened point.

2   Interview, Gene Mariarz.

3   Interview, Betty Pitts. McKinney once told his sister that for a moment during the battle he questioned if "God didn't want me dead."

4   This chapter was assembled from a variety of sources, including interviews by the author with survivors of the battle, news articles written about John McKinney days after the battle, U.S. Army Archives, and interviews with Betty Pitts, McKinney's sister, with whom he confided some memories of the battle.

Chapter 21

1 *The Chicago Daily News,* June 1, 1945, war correspondent Gerald Thorp reports, "Sylvanian Private Bags 36 Japs in One Cyclone Combat Mission."

2 After Action Report—the Connolly Task Force—123rd Infantry Regiment, declassified August 1945. National Archives.

3 *Mabaroshi*—literally means *phantom* or *apparition.* Red Barrette remembered the *roshi* sound, but did not catch the first part of the word. Ed Colwell insisted the word shouted was *mabaooshi.* At the time of the interview for the 123rd Regiment After Action Report, the correct translation of the word mattered little. It was considered only a shout.

4 Part of Sergeant Johnson's official report, requoted in many newspapers and magazine accounts. Also, *The Golden Cross,* p. 294.

5 John McKinney often repeated his praise for Red Barrette, and his statement was printed in several newspaper accounts later.

6 Interview, Max Ladin.

7 *The Golden Cross,* p. 294.

8 After Action Report—the Connolly Task Force—123rd Infantry Regiment, declassified August 1945. National Archives.

9 *The Golden Cross,* p. 294.

10 Interview, Robert Colwell.

11 *The Golden Cross,* p. 297.

12 Interview, Gerry Rampy.

13 Interview, Jesse Frazee

14 Interview, Gerry Nutt.

15 Ibid.

Chapter 22

1 Interview, Donald Murphy.

2 *The Golden Cross,* p. 297.

3 *The Golden Cross,* p. 298. After Action Report, 123rd Infantry Regiment, declassified, National Archives. After Action Report, 136th Infantry Regiment, declassified, National Archives.

4 Interview, Donald Murphy.

5 *The Golden Cross,* p. 298.

6 Ibid., p. 298.

7 Copies of telegrams and letters furnished to author by Ed Colwell's brother, Bob. It is with the kind permission of the Colwell family that these documents can be quoted and discussed.

8 *The Golden Cross,* p. 299.

9 National Archives documents related to John McKinney dated May 12, 1945, June 27, 1945, July 17, 1945, and August 16, 1945.

10 *The Golden Cross,* p. 317.

11 Interview, Henry Van Westrop.

12 Letter to Nattie McKinney discussed with author during interview with Betty Pitts.

Chapter 23

1 Interview, Henry Van Westrop.
2 Documents pertaining to Sergeant John McKinney's award—Congressional Medal of Honor. National Archives.
3 *The Golden Cross,* p. 367.
4 123rd Infantry Historical Report—Honshu, Japan, August 15–November 30, 1945, declassified. National Archives.
5 Interview, Betty Pitts.
6 123rd Infantry Historical Report, August 15–November 30, 1945, declassified. National Archives.
7 Company A, 123rd Infantry Regiment Morning Report dated December 6, 1945 and December 7, 1945. National Archives.

Chapter 24

1 Interview, Betty Pitts.
2 *Augusta Chronicle,* January 15, 1946.
3 *Chicago Daily News,* January 20, 1946.
4 *Atlanta Journal,* January 16, 1946.
5 Associated Press, *Atlanta Journal,* January 17, 1946.
6 Interview, Betty Pitts.
7 Nattie McKinney's letters to Mrs. Colwell shared with author by Bob Colwell, Edward's brother.
8 Ibid.
9 Interview, Joe Evans.
10 Interview, Betty Pitts.
11 Ibid.
12 Ibid.
13 Ibid.
14 Interview, Jack Finch. Also, "Georgia's Forgotten Heroes," *Atlanta Magazine,* March 1966.
15 Interview, Jack Finch.
16 Interview, Betty Pitts.
17 Ibid.
18 Interview, Danny Lynn Derriso.
19 Ibid.
20 Interview, Dent Derriso.
21 Interview, Betty Pitts.

BIBLIOGRAPHY

Books

Agoncillo, Teodoro A. *The Fateful Years: Japan's Adventures in the Philippines.* Quazon City, Philippines: Garcia, 1965.

Behr, Ed. *Hirohito—Behind the Myth.* New York: Villard Co., 1989.

Black, Robert. *Rangers in World War II.* New York: Ballantine Books, 1992.

Bradley, James. *Flyboys.* Boston: Little Brown and Co., 2003.

Carlson, Stan. *A Pictorial History of the 123rd Infantry Regiment.* Minneapolis: Stan Carlson, Publishing, 1946.

Cook, Haruko Taya, and Theodore F. Cook. *Japan at War.* New York: New Press, 1972.

Esposito, General Vincent J. *The West Point Atlas of American Wars.* New York: Praeger Publishing, 1978.

Golden Cross, A History of the 33rd Infantry Division—Historical Committee. Nashville, Tenn.: Battery Press, 2000. (Originally published 1948.)

Hartendorp, A.V.H. *The Japanese Occupation of the Philippines.* Manila: Bookmark, 1967.

Hieb, Lt. Col. Harley F. *Heart of Iron.* Lodi, CA: Pacifica Publishing, 1987.

Hunt, Ray C., and Bernard Norling. *Behind Japanese Lines.* Lexington, KY: University Press of Kentucky, 1986.

Johnson, Forrest Bryant. *Hour of Redemption—The Ranger Raid on Cabanatuan.* New York: Warner Books, 2002; New York: Manor Books, 1979.

Krueger, General Walter. *From Down Under to Nippon.* Washington, D.C.: Combat Forces Press, 1953.

Lapham, Robert, and Bernard Norling. *Lapham's Raiders.* Lexington, KY: University Press of Kentucky, 1996.

MacArthur, General Douglas. *Reminiscence.* New York: McGraw-Hill, 1964.

Manchester, William. *American Caeser: Douglas MacArthur 1880–1964.* Boston: Little Brown and Company, 1978.

Monagham, Forbes J. *Under the Red Sun.* New York: McMillan, 1946.

Murphy, Lieutenant Audie. *To Hell and Back.* New York: Henry Holt and Company, 1949.

Nakata, Tadao, and Thomas B. Nekon. *Imperial Japanese Army and Navy Uniforms and Equipment.* Virginia: Ironside International Publishers, Inc., 1973.

Onoda, Lieutenant Hiroo. *No Surrender, My Thirty-Year War.* Annapolis, MD: Naval Institute Press, 1999.

Pajota, Major Juan. *We Kept the Torch Burning.* Manila: Manila Press, 1982.

Perry, John. *Sergeant York, His Life, Legend and Legacy.* Nashville, Tenn.: Broodman and Halman Publishers, 1997.

Smith, Robert Ross. *Triumph in the Philippines.* Washington, D.C.: U.S. Government Printing Office, 1963.

Taruc, Luis. *He Who Rides the Tiger.* New York: Praeger, 1967.

Toland, John. *The Rising Sun.* New York: Random House, 1970.

Wainwright, General Jonathan M. *General Wainwright's Story.* New York: Doubleday, 1946.

Watari, Gasei. *Philippine Expeditionary Force.* Tokyo, Japan: Group Information Publishing, 1943.

Wilcox, Robert. *Japan's Secret War.* New York: Marlowe Co., 1995.

Volckmann, Colonel R.W. *We Remained.* New York: W.W. Norton, 1954.

Zedric, Lance Q. *Silent Warriors—The Alamo Scouts Behind Japanese Lines.* Ventura, CA: Pathfinder Publishing, 1995.

Magazines

"Die Free: The Escape of a Bataan Battler." Leon Beck and Neal Matthews, San Diego Reader; April 23rd, 1992.

"General Hideki Tojo—Prison Diary." Sanae Sato, translation by General Hideo. Miki and Henry Symington. Hoseki Magazine, Japan, 1991.

"Georgia's Heroes." Atlanta Magazine, Atlanta: Chamber of Commerce of Atlanta, GA, 1966.

Pamplets, Manuscripts, and Military Reports

123rd Infantry Historical Report, Luzon Campaign, Feb 13th–June 30, 1945. Dept. of the Army, T/AG Office, The Pentagon, Washington, D.C. (Declassified)

136th Infantry Historical Report, Luzon Campaign, Feb. 6th–July 1, 1945. Dept. of the Army, T/AG Office, The Pentagon, Washington, D.C. (Declassified)

Allied Geographical Section, Southwest Pacific Area. "Terrain Handbook #34, Sept. 1944. Philippine Series." National Archives, Washington D.C.

"Japanese Ground and Air Forces." Military Intelligence Service, War Department, 1942, National Archives, Washington, D.C.

Japanese Studies in World War II, 14th Army Area Operations Chief of Military History, United States Army, Washington, D.C.

"The 6th Rangers—Narrative of the 6th Ranger Battalion." Jan. 2, 1945–Jul. 1, 1945. U.S. Government, National Archives, Washington, D.C.

"They Were First—The True Story of the Alamo Scouts." Lt. Louis Hockstrasser. National Archives, Washington, D.C.

War History #6, Defense Training Institute, The Japanese Defense Agency. War History Department, Tokyo, Japan.

"War Reconnaissance Reports—Headquarters, 6th United States Army." 1945. National Archives, Washington, D.C.

Printed News Media Accounts

The Atlanta Journal, "Japs and Squirrels Die. Medal of Honor and Farm to Reward Screven Hero." Davenport Steward, Wed. Evening, Jan. 19th, 1946.

The Augusta Chronicle, "Just Shot Few Little Japs, All He Did, Says Sylvanian." Tues., Jan. 22, 1946, p. 1.

The Augusta Chronicle, "Sylvania Hero to Get Medal from Truman." Friday, Jan. 11, 1946, p. 1.

The Augusta Chronicle, "Two Georgians Receive Cherished Military Award." AP release, Washington, Jan. 23, 1946.

The Chicago Daily News, "Sylvania Private Bags 36 Japs in One Cyclone Combat Mission." Gerald R. Thorp, War Correspondent, June 1, 1945.

The Dinosaur, (123rd Infantry Regiment Newsletter) Vol. V #29, May 22, 1945.

INDEX

Page numbers in *italic* indicate maps.